Lived Experience and Co-Production in Philosophy and Mental Health

ROYAL INSTITUTE OF PHILOSOPHY SUPPLEMENT: 94

EDITED BY

Anna Bergqvist,
David Crepaz-Keay and
Alana Wilde

CAMBRIDGE
UNIVERSITY PRESS

T0373803

PUBLISHED BY THE PRESS SYNDICATE OF THE UNIVERSITY OF CAMBRIDGE
The Pitt Building, Trumpington Street, Cambridge, CB2 1RP,
United Kingdom

CAMBRIDGE UNIVERSITY PRESS
Shaftesbury Road, Cambridge CB2 8EA, United Kingdom
32 Avenue of the Americas, New York, NY 10013–2473, USA
477 Williamstown Road, Port Melbourne, VIC 3207, Australia
C/Orense, 4, planta 13, 28020 Madrid, Spain
Lower Ground Floor, Nautica Building, The Water Club, Beach Road,
Granger Bay, 8005 Cape Town, South Africa

Printed and bound by CPI Group (UK) Ltd, Croydon, CR0 4YY
Typeset by Techset Composition Ltd, Salisbury, UK

A catalogue record for this book is available from the British Library

ISBN 9781009469043
ISSN 1358-2461

Contents

Notes on the Contributors

Panayiota Vassilopoulou (p.vassilopoulou@liverpool.ac.uk) is Reader in Philosophy at the University of Liverpool. She publishes in Neoplatonism and Aesthetics and has co-edited *Thought: A Philosophical History* (Routledge, 2021) and *Late Antique Epistemology: Other Ways to Truth* (Palgrave Macmillan, 2009). She has held numerous residencies with leading cultural and health institutions in the UK and abroad, pioneering a new model for practicing philosophy with non-academic publics.

Sofia Jeppsson (sofia.jeppsson@umu.se) is Associate Professor of Philosophy at Umeå University in northern Sweden. She started her career publishing on free will, moral responsibility, and applied ethics. In later years, she has increasingly focused on the philosophy of psychiatry and madness, an interest that grew out of her previous philosophical work as well as her own experience with psychosis. In her 2021 paper 'Psychosis and Intelligibility' in *Philosophy, Psychology, and Psychiatry* she shows that more psychosis phenomena than previously believed can be rendered at least somewhat intelligible. 'Exemption, Self-Exemption and Compassionate Self-Excuse', published in 2022 in the *International Mad Studies Journal* and soon to appear as a chapter in the *Bloomsbury Guide to the Philosophy of Disability*, discusses complicated questions of agency and moral responsibility in madness. 'Radical Psychotic Doubt and Epistemology', published in 2022 in *Philosophical Psychology*, uses madness to challenge certain common epistemological arguments and assumptions.

Sam Fellowes (m.fellowes1@lancaster.ac.uk) is an autistic individual who did his PhD at Lancaster University in Philosophy of Psychiatry and his Masters at Leeds University in History and Philosophy of Science. He has written on the metaphysical and epistemological status of psychiatric diagnoses. He has aimed to increase the scientific status of psychiatric diagnoses by portraying them as idealised models that abstract away from particular individuals but then guide, building more specific models of particular individuals. He has more recently become interested in the role of experts-by-experience in psychiatric research, seeking to explore how it relates to idealisations and theory-laden observations.

doi:10.1017/S1358246123000280   © The Royal Institute of Philosophy and the contributors 2023
Royal Institute of Philosophy Supplement **94** 2023

Notes on the Contributors

Zsuzsanna Chappell (zsuzsanna.chappell@gmail.com) is currently an independent scholar specialising in the fields of philosophy of psychiatry, moral, and social philosophy. She is especially interested in ethical problems associated with mental health, and issues related to the diversity in our mental experiences. She received her PhD from the London School of Economics and held academic positions at the London School of Economics and the University of Manchester. Her previous research is in the area of political philosophy and democratic theory. She is the author of *Deliberative Democracy: A Critical Introduction* (Palgrave Macmillan, 2012).

Lucienne Spencer (l.spencer@bham.ac.uk) is a postdoctoral researcher for the Wellcome Trust funded project 'Renewing Phenomenological Psychopathology' at the Institute of Mental Health, University of Birmingham. She completed her SWW-DTP funded PhD in Philosophy at the University of Bristol in 2021 under Prof. Havi Carel. Her research primarily focuses on phenomenology, epistemic injustice, and the philosophy of psychiatry. She is also a member of the executive committee for the Society for Women in Philosophy, UK. Her website is https://luciennespencer.com/.

Ian James Kidd (ian.kidd@nottingham.ac.uk) teaches and researches philosophy at the University of Nottingham. His research interests include topics in epistemology, philosophy of illness and psychiatry, and phenomenology. His website is www.ianjameskidd.weebly.com.

Alana Wilde (ALANA.WILDE@stu.mmu.ac.uk) is a NWCDTP funded PhD candidate at Manchester Metropolitan University, supervised by Dr Anna Bergqvist and Dr David Crepaz-Keay (Mental Health Foundation). Her thesis argues that the exclusion of experts by experience in mental health research projects is a form of epistemic oppression. She primarily works in the philosophy of psychiatry and mental health space, but has research interests also in social epistemology, philosophy of disability, and feminist philosophy.

Edward Harcourt (edward.harcourt@philosophy.ox.ac.uk) is Professor of Philosophy at the University of Oxford and a Fellow of Keble College. He recently completed a four-year secondment to the UKRI Arts and Humanities Research Council as Director of Research, Strategy and Innovation. In addition to his role in the Philosophy Faculty, he is Professor of Philosophy in Oxford's

Department of Psychiatry where he leads on Patient and Public Involvement for the Oxford Health Biomedical Research Centre. His research interests lie on the boundaries between ethics and the philosophy of mind, and include neo-Aristotelianism and child development, ethical dimensions of psychoanalysis and psychotherapy, the moral emotions, love and the virtues, and Nietzsche's ethics; the philosophy of mental health and mental illness; literature and philosophy; and Wittgenstein.

David Crepaz-Keay (dcrepaz-keay@mentalhealth.org.uk) is Head of Research and Applied Learning at the Mental Health Foundation, where he is responsible for developing and delivering research in England and contributing to UK wide and international research. He is a Fellow of the Royal Society for Public Health and of the Institute for Mental Health. David has extensive personal experience of using mental health services and has used this experience to inform his academic research. He was a founding member of the National Survivor User Network (NSUN), a leading organisation led by people with direct experience of mental health service use. He also co-chairs the International Society for Psychiatric Genetics' Ethics, Policy and Public Position committee and has written widely on mental health and public mental health.

Anna Bergqvist (a.bergqvist@mmu.ac.uk) is Reader in Philosophy at Manchester Metropolitan University and Theory Network lead for the Values-Based Theory Network at St Catherine's Collaborating Centre for Values-Based Practice at the University of Oxford. She is also Senior Editor of the journal *Philosophy, Psychiatry and Psychology*. She specializes in metaethics (especially moral perception and moral psychology) and philosophy of psychiatry and mind with a focus on moral particularism, self-ownership, and relational moral agency. She is editor of *Evaluative Perception* (Oxford University Press, 2018) and *Philosophy and Museums: Essays on the Philosophy of Museums* (Cambridge University Press, 2016), and presently prepares as lead editor *The Handbook Oxford of Philosophy and Public Mental Health* (under contract with Oxford University Press). Bergqvist serves as Secretary of the World Psychiatric Association (WPA) Section for Philosophy & Humanities in Psychiatry and is an Executive Committee Member of the Royal College of Psychiatry Special Interest Group in Philosophy. She is also Centre Fellow at the Centre for Ethics as Study in Human Values at the University of Pardubice and External Research Fellow at VID Specialized University in Oslo.

Notes on the Contributors

Mohammed Abouelleil Rashed (mohammed.rashed@kcl.ac.uk) is a philosopher and psychiatrist with interests in the philosophy of madness, culture, and mental health. His recent research examined social identity and the philosophy and politics of recognition in the context of Mad Pride and Mad-positive activism. He is the author of *Madness and the Demand for Recognition* (Oxford University Press, 2019).

K.W.M. (Bill) Fulford (kwmf@kwmfulford.com) is a Fellow of St Catherine's College and Member of the Philosophy Faculty, University of Oxford; Emeritus Professor of Philosophy and Mental Health, University of Warwick; and Founder Director of the Collaborating Centre for Values-Based Practice, St Catherine's College, Oxford (valuesbasedpractice.org). His previous posts include Honorary Consultant Psychiatrist, University of Oxford, and Special Adviser for Values-Based Practice in the UK Department of Health, London. He is Founding Editor and Chair of the Advisory Board of *Philosophy, Psychiatry, & Psychology* (*PPP*). He has published widely on philosophical and ethical aspects of mental health, including *Moral Theory and Medical Practice*, *The Oxford Textbook of Philosophy and Psychiatry*, *The Oxford Handbook of Philosophy and Psychiatry* and *Essential Values-Based Practice*. He edits the Cambridge University Press book series on Values-Based Medicine. He was awarded the 2022 Margrit Egnér Foundation Award and the 2023 Aristotle Gold Medal.

Ashok Handa (ashok.handa@nds.ox.ac.uk) is Professor of Vascular Surgery at Oxford University and Honorary Consultant Vascular Surgeon at the John Radcliffe Hospital in Oxford. He has been the Director for Surgical Education for Oxford University since 2001. He is Director of the Collaborating Centre for Values-Based Practice in Health and Social Care based at St Catherine's College, Oxford, and responsible for leading on education and research for the centre. He is Fellow in Clinical Medicine and Tutor for Graduates at St Catherine's College, responsible for 450 graduates across all disciplines. He has over 200 publications in vascular surgery, surgical education, patient safety, and many on the topic of values-based practice, shared decision-making, and consent. He is the Principle Investigator of the OxAAA and OxPVD studies in vascular surgery.

Introduction: What is the Role of Lived Experience in Research?

ANNA BERGQVIST, DAVID CREPAZ-KEAY AND ALANA WILDE

Experts by Experience in the context of mental health are those who have personal experience of using, or of caring for someone who uses, health, mental health, and social care services. How do people with lived experience of mental illness contribute to scientific knowledge and personal growth? This volume comprises three distinct philosophical perspectives focused on specific theoretical and practical challenges for theorising about *expertise by experience* in the philosophy of mental health research: the idea of subjectivity in 'lived experience' and the issue of scientific validation, the prospects of shared meaning-making, and the problem of injustice in 'co-production', and the philosophical role of values in navigating difference and value disagreement in psychiatry.

The philosophical concepts of 'expertise by experience', that is, expertise based on one's personal experience of some condition, and 'participatory research' are rapidly expanding areas of interdisciplinary research. Both concepts are increasingly present in medicine and mental health, and link academics, clinical practitioners, charitable foundations, and policy makers to develop an inclusive and efficient approach to mental health in the service of patient empowerment and agency. Towards the end of the twentieth century, it became increasingly clear that the scientific empiricism of modern medicine, although necessary, was not sufficient as a basis for delivering clinical care that best served the patient. The first indication of the centrality of patient values and the notion of *expertise by experience* as essential components of adequate mental health research, in reaction to the technical professionalism of medical science (and what we may think of as the contrastive concept of *expertise by medical training*), was the development of medical ethics with its promotion of patient autonomy. However, as noted by Bergqvist's contribution to this volume below, while autonomy-driven approaches went some way to reinstate the importance of the person in medical science, medical ethics itself has developed into a new form of increasingly professionalised medical science rather than offering mechanisms for empowering patients. (See also Fulford and Bergqvist, in press.)

doi:10.1017/S1358246123000292   © The Royal Institute of Philosophy and the contributors 2023
Royal Institute of Philosophy Supplement **94** 2023   1

Anna Bergqvist, David Crepaz-Keay and Alana Wilde

It was against this background that in the early years of the twenty-first century, concepts like person-centred care, co-production, and shared decision-making made their appearance in medicine and related areas of clinical practice (Fulford and Bergqvist, in press). These concepts were each concerned, in different ways, with restoring the patient to centre stage in health care. Salient examples in psychiatry that centre on the individual historical person and their ecological context are found in associated models of recovery and person-centred management. Such models are geared towards the restoration of well-being and re-engagement in major social, vocational, and family roles (Maj *et al.*, 2020).

Philosophical methodologies are well positioned to address the gaps in our theoretical understanding of concepts of *quality of life* and *shared decision-making*, both of which are key to the development of an inclusive and efficient approach to participatory mental health as the gold standard for good practice. This is particularly true regarding the role of patients as experts, as real contributors of knowledge in the establishment of health literature bases, especially in areas of what is sometimes described as severe and enduring mental illness ('SMI'). Other emergent research areas in the adjacent cognate field of public mental health include how we might best improve the mental health of our populations, and how we consider incidence and prevalence of both mental illness and poor well-being. Potential tensions between mental health advocacy and public health campaigning may include the impact upon admission rates and levels of stigma if public mental health approaches were designed with the intention of reducing prevalence of mental illness rather than identifying what, if any, levels of well-being amongst populations necessitate a cohesive approach to mental health. This is especially pertinent given existing philosophical disagreement in relation to diagnosis and diagnostic precision.

How we understand our own experiences, and what insights those experiences give us into the generalisable nature of some phenomenon or other are much discussed topics in epistemology alongside the social dimension of knowledge (where the latter concerns social injustice and positionality in our knowledge-gathering capacities). Epistemological arguments have been given which indicate that lived experience, that is, first-person, direct acquaintance, with some phenomena or other provides an unrivalled insight into some specific quality of that experience. This is sometimes, though not always, associated with standpoint epistemologies (e.g., Harding, 2004; Medina, 2013), whereby one's experiential horizon and socio-historical situatedness guides what one can know. Put in simple terms, if you are not personally acquainted with some phenomena, the standpoint theorist would argue, your knowledge of that phenomena should not have parity of importance when compared to lived experience. Even those who disagree with standpoint theory seem to agree that there is a role – an important one – for insight derived from lived experience. When it comes to scientific research itself, notably that which focuses on the role of first-person testimony, this is no exception.

Researchers in the helping professions such as clinical psychology and psychiatry, for example, are increasingly asked to think about the role of participatory research with people with lived experience of mental illness in designing and delivering salient empirical studies and research projects. The consensus, whether driven by desires for equal participation, or for broadly applicable research findings, is that lived experience ought to have a role in how we conceive of knowledge. The same holds true for research into mental (ill) health. Mental health is itself a contested and complex concept. Often, individuals who have lived experience of mental ill health can be considered less reliable as knowers and as agents in interpersonal settings, as irrational, or as otherwise lacking in some important virtue required to be considered an authority. This is often indicated as being in large part because of historic and enduring stigma associated with mental ill health and its association with criminality, dangerousness, and untruthfulness. Those with a diagnosis, or who are presumed to have a psychiatric disorder or condition, often are marginalised. Even without such presumptions, the role for knowledge derived from lived experience is unclear. Testimony, narratives, and anecdotes are not viewed, in many instances, as being of the same calibre as scientific testing, which is supported by repeatability, hypothesis, and quite often, large-scale trialling of pharmacological, technological or community-based intervention. This raises the question of whether knowledge derived from lived experience *should* be valued as equal to that gained via traditional scientific methodologies. Impartiality and objectivity are called into question when we attempt to generalise from our own experience. And psychiatric or psychological disorders are somewhat unique in that they affect one's experiential states. When one's own psychological systems are in some way affected by a mental illness, can that individual appraise those experiences as if an impartial bystander?

While there are many research development reports on what in the United Kingdom is known as Patient and Public Involvement (PPI)[1]

---

[1] Other cognate terms to that of 'PPI' and 'EbE' (that are *not* equivalent in meaning) found in the literature surrounding shared decision-making

Anna Bergqvist, David Crepaz-Keay and Alana Wilde

and Expertise by Experience in mental health research this volume is unique in the ways that it both highlights the relationship between conventional areas in philosophy, psychiatry, and mental health research, and further crosses conventional boundaries in philosophy (such as social epistemology, moral philosophy, and philosophy of science) in order to understand the ethical and scientific significance of lived experience in the philosophy of psychiatry and mental health. New understandings of the role for and of lived experience in philosophical discourse, clinical practice, and more traditional mental health research, as discussed in this volume, are varied and lively. The essays contained in this collection engage with lived experience at a range of levels of the research process and propose a variety of novel views. First, by focussing on the scientific impact of patients as stakeholder experts, Experts by Experience (sometimes abbreviated 'EbE'), rather than on individual vulnerability to mental ill health and responsiveness to categorical diagnostic measures and treatment involving predictive biomarkers (as seen in the growing field of psychiatric genetics), it reframes the philosophical question of subjectivity in 'lived experience' in connection with the question of scientific validation. Second, by exposing the ways EbEs contribute as knowers in articulating values as theorists, advocates, and peer-support in meeting the complex challenges of knowledge transfer in helping people make better decisions, it targets the social dimension of knowledge and epistemic injustice in received models of 'co-production'. Third, by interrogating the diversity of factors that contribute to individual people's well-being, it addresses possible conflicts between different stakeholders arising from value pluralism and a multiplicity of perspectives that often frame the use of psychopathological concepts, which often play a role in determining aspects of quality of life in mental health contexts. Below, we briefly discuss each philosophical thematic research area in turn.

Voicing Lived Experience as Scientific Knowledge

The first section of this volume examines the moral and scientific value of lived experience as scientific knowledge. Research methodologies, and present debates over 'expertise by experience', and funder

---

include 'experience-based co-design' (EBCD), 'service-user engagement', 'participatory research', 'action research', 'user-led research', 'survivor-led research' – to name but a few.

recommendations (such as that of the Wellcome Trust)[2] about the very concept of mental health research as research with 'lived experience experts', agree that there is an important role for individual testimony in research. But, given the contentious way in which lived experience is viewed, particularly in terms of its (lack of) scientific status as validated evidence, inclusion of those with lived experience in research into mental health requires a careful approach to mediating different, and sometimes opposing, values. Mental ill health is linked in important ways to one's social positionality, and relative degrees of privilege and belonging to a particular community create inextricable links with values and accepted understandings of important concepts. What does it mean to be 'ill'? How ought society treat those with a psychiatric diagnosis? What is the legitimacy of psychiatry as a discipline of medicine in the philosophy of science in relation to other social movements such as mental health 'survivor' activism (Rashed, 2019) and what Peter Sedgwick (1982) calls psycho politics? How an individual engages with such questions, and the view they ultimately take, will depend on such values. These guide decisions individuals make, or preferences that an individual may have, when making judgements or decisions about their own care. The role of lived experience in such participatory research approaches in clinical psychology and psychiatry is not a substitute for but is complementary to 'traditional science'. Perhaps, others argue (Tekin, 2011, 2019), self-understanding as guided by social positionality requires that lived experience be used in ways which may not be considered science *proper*, but which nonetheless allow shared understanding and knowledge advancement to take place. Might phenomenological tools, or accounts of aesthetic value, allow us to further our understanding of psychiatry and psychiatric diagnosis?

There are many, of course, who contest the very notion of psychiatric diagnosis whilst simultaneously recognising that support for those in distress is, in almost all cases, dependent upon such diagnoses. Making room for different, and competing, understandings of how our social notions of normal psychological function, illness,

[2]   The Wellcome Trust identifies mental health as one of its three key research funding priorities and further defines the very concept of 'mental health research' in co-productive and participatory terms. As they express their position: 'We are committed to the meaningful involvement of lived experience experts in the direction and decision making of the mental health team; the projects and research that we fund; and in the field of mental health science'. See: https://wellcome.org/what-we-do/mental-health.

5

and dependency may affect the weight assigned to one's testimony is argued, by some, to be a necessity in making room for lived experience. Power dynamics, historic institutionalisation of those considered deviant from the accepted norm, and institutional arrangements, including those prevalent in higher education and research culture, privilege voices considered expert. The notion of lived experience as qualifying one as an expert based on experience (EbE) is an attempted redress of such historic inequities. As the essays in part I illustrate, although the concept of *expertise by experience* has been introduced into the literature and also clinical practice, it has so far done little to allay the philosophical concerns regarding the asymmetry and disparity of weight assigned to knowledge credentials offered by those with traditional expertise in comparison with the voices from individuals with lived experience.

Co-Producing Meaning

Person-centred medicine seeks to mediate such differences in knowledge credentials, stakeholder voice, and power by creating space for lived experience and individual value preferences in what is known as 'shared-decision making'. Genuine involvement of those with lived experience of mental health concerns, particularly regarding mental ill health prevention, mental health and well-being promotion, and collaborative treatment design, raises a whole host of questions about the prospects of shared decision-making and co-production that are both theoretically and practically important. In addition to the doubts regarding credibility of individuals with lived experience – as noted above – *how* EbEs ought to be included in discussions, in planning, and in implementation of public mental health approaches, is a contentious topic. Research has indicated that thus far, even well-intentioned researchers exclude the views of EbEs in producing summary reports and policies, raising the question: if the narratives of those with lived experience are ignored, how are we to truly consider any approach to mental health to be 'co-produced'?

Related and relevant further questions include: what might the impact be upon individuals of being considered at risk of being mentally ill? Are there positive duties that bear on clinicians and those implementing mental health as a public health approach to empower patients? What is the moral significance of the first-person perspective? And how do epistemic violence and social injustices impede or impact upon our sense of self in living with a mental health condition? Given recent focus upon public campaigns promoting discussion of mental ill health, additional questions focus upon access to mental health support services resulting from health promotion campaigns. Should peer support services be viewed as sub-clinical and less effective? Who is responsible for ensuring population mental health? How should the 'othering' of EbEs in research design be countered in order to achieve a genuinely collaborative public mental health strategy?

Navigating Values and Difference

What guides the design of a participatory mental health approach, and indeed the inclusion of those with lived experience in mental health care design and treatment methodologies, is dependent upon mediation of differing values. Mental ill health is commonly cited as being largely caused by social factors, and accordingly, individuals and differing social community groups prioritise different values and goals dependent upon their experience. Values-based medicine and related person-centred approaches to health care purport to offer ways of competing values being accommodated, and several practical guides exist, offering support for clinicians adopting a person-centred approach. However, clinicians and those with lived-experience disagree often, leading to debates around values and how best to proceed with preventative and recovery-focused interventions. For instance, how should public mental health accommodate the positive experience reported by many with the lived experience of a severe and enduring mental illness (SMI) of their symptoms? Philosophers have contributed to the debates surrounding the 'Mad Activism' movement, and these and related areas are addressed by several authors in this volume below.

The volume's experience-led philosophical focus, incorporating a co-production approach, considers the communal, shared aspects of identity and experiences beyond recording patient values from a culturally neutral, single management perspective. Special attention is placed on the role of contested concepts and on alternative interpretative approaches based on value pluralism and diverse storied experiences to understand the mechanisms by which shared decision-making can play a transformative role in creating healthier societies. For example, how can peer support assets to build the capacity for self-management support societal well-being? What is the role of intersectional (for instance as articulated by the black feminist Patricia Hill Collins, 1990), contextualised experiences and needs of persons with lived experience including their self-identified social networks, such as family?

Other important questions concern what is permissible to value. How do differing cultural attitudes and approaches to psychopathology and spirituality differ in their perspectives on the goals of mental health prevention? Should narratives which report a positive experience of symptoms be dismissed in light of credibility doubts regarding the mental health of speakers? Finally, how should we think about value shifts, particularly in mental health, where certain illnesses have been proven to distort individual beliefs and desires?

Future Practices

Going forward, there is much scope for research in philosophy of psychiatry and medicine to shape future education, training, and procedures in medical colleges nationally. This potential lies not only in the ability to recommend best practices, and to highlight the ethical risks of co-produced approaches to mental health care, and to public mental health, but also in terms of maximisation of public benefit. However, currently, measures of efficacy of public mental health approaches and of treatment interventions are based largely on quality-of-life assessments, on cost-benefit analyses, and on minimisation of disability and related financial costs. Such evaluative practices are commonplace in public health more generally. However, they raise substantive questions about future recommendations. How might we ensure equality in participatory mental health approaches, for instance, when disparities in mental ill health are so often resultant from existent societal, racial injustices? Is it possible to standardise quality of life assessments relative to mental ill health? Relatedly, what if anything, do such assessments tell us about the efficacy of public mental health strategies?

Part of the theoretical complexity concerns value pluralism and different health priorities between different stakeholder experts (including EbEs and carers, psychiatrists, policy makers, regulators, economic beneficiaries, academics, *etc.*) of a given mental health intervention. Different groups prioritise different metrics of value measurement and often *disagree* about which measure is the most important and why. Philosophy, conversely, has an exceptionally well-established literature relating to contested ways of measuring mental health and well-being. Philosophical scrutiny of *quality of life* and *shared decision-making* in received methodologies in

8

measuring mental health, including Stewart-Brown's Warwick-Edinburgh scale (discussed extensively in Bhugra *et al.*, 2018, *Oxford Textbook of Public Mental Health*) and other 'self-assessment' techniques, reveals the theoretical significance of the complexities in measuring what is, to many, a subjective 'felt' concept. Such analysis includes discussions surrounding fallibility in personal evaluations, i.e., phenomenological experiences of mental health – both poor and robust.

Part One of this volume focuses on the scientific value of 'expertise by experience' by engaging with issues of art, self-description, as well the role of, and barriers to, lived experience as an important dimension of knowledge. The papers in this section examine, in various ways, tensions, opportunities, and analogies that are useful in understanding how lived experience can be voiced in ways which could be termed 'science'.

Panayiota Vassilopoulou's essay, 'Art and the Lived Experience of Pain' is the first paper which picks up on this issue. Arguing that art, particularly works which publicly share the lived experience of pain, can contribute to public mental health and holistic approaches to care, Vassilopoulou's discussion of the role of aesthetic experience in understanding and communicating about pain – even that which is not felt physically – highlights the interplay between the private and the public, the personal and the universal. Vassilopoulou emphasises the potential of art to create communal spaces for reflection, much in the same way as scientific research allows the advancement of common understanding.

The next essay by Sofia Jeppsson, 'A Wide Enough Range of "Test Environments" For Psychiatric Disabilities', focuses upon the barriers and issues requiring redress such that we can gain an understanding of the impact of social and environmental factors on individuals' likelihood or predisposition of experiencing psychiatric disability. Using schizophrenia as an example, Jeppsson considers a range of socio-ecological test environments which emphasise that addressing disclosure rates and stigmatisation alone would likely be insufficient to engender an environment whereby all neurodivergent identities were able to openly embrace their ways of being without backlash. Picking up on key social issues, including racism, poverty, and academic job precarity, Jeppsson calls for a range of societal improvements that go beyond anti-stigma campaigns and increases in funding to lessen the impact of broader socio-political factors which heighten the propensity of poor mental health.

Sam Fellowes continues the discussion of the role of socio-political factors in affecting self- and scientific understanding with the essay,

Anna Bergqvist, David Crepaz-Keay and Alana Wilde

'Self-Diagnosis in Psychiatry and the Distribution of Social Resources'. Fellowes discusses the ways in which recognised and scientifically validated psychiatric and neurodevelopmental diagnoses, despite concerns regarding nosological legitimacy, affect what 'social resources' individuals are deemed entitled to or else deserving of. Whilst advocating for some of the potential benefits of self-diagnosis, Fellowes emphasises the need for further research focusing on the outcomes for those who self-diagnose, and for an assessment of which social resources unofficial or self-ascribed diagnosis permits an individual to access, have, or take part in. As Fellowes' essay illustrates, lived experience is in many contexts taken as a supplement to, and not a substitute for, 'science'. The challenge, as research into the philosophy of psychiatry has shown, is that psychiatry has been repeatedly challenged itself as being science *proper*.

The section concludes with Zsuzsanna Chappell's essay, 'In Defence of the Concept of Mental Illness'. Written from a lived experience perspective, Chappell argues that we should not abandon the term 'mental illness' because it is a useful way of understanding a type of human experience, in so far as the term (i) is apt or accurate, (ii) a useful hermeneutical resource for interpreting and communicating experience, and (iii) can be a good way for at least some of us to establish a liveable personal identity within contemporary Western social and political culture. Chappell's counterargument in favour of the concept of mental illness also responds to salient psycho political objections to the notion of self-identifying as 'mentally ill' on the grounds that it is important that we continue to accept that mental illness experiences do exist and must be named in order to treat people justly or morally. Such identity recognition is part and parcel of what it is to 'treat persons as persons' (Spelman, 1978), especially as a lack of recognition of their suffering is very threatening to those who suffer (Wilkinson, 2005). Chappell calls for better clarity in distinguishing the concept of 'illness' from both of 'disease' and 'sickness', arguing that there is a phenomenon that we experience as illness-like that is usefully described as illness-like within our culture and that there are people who can benefit from identifying, either personally or socially, as someone having or living with mental illness. As Chappell's essay illustrates, through an illness identity it is possible to make a claim on others for a positive caring relationship.

Part Two of this volume addresses the topic of lived experience and its role in research practice by looking at co-production. Viewed as a gold standard of participatory research by many, co-production is framed as a desirable and well-received research methodology.

Lucienne Spencer and Ian James Kidd's jointly written essay, '"The Hermeneutic Problem of Psychiatry" and the Co-Production of Meaning in Psychiatric Healthcare' discusses how meaningful communication between patients and clinicians in clinical settings is affected by both contingent factors and by features intrinsic to psychiatric or mental ill health problems themselves. Spencer and Kidd draw out the ways in which power dynamics and institutional barriers can affect meaningful communications, as well as note the inherent features of many episodes of mental ill health – the ways in which individual self-expression and understanding can go awry. Analysing a range of methods by which clinicians might incorporate phenomenological tools to make sense of what patients are experiencing might, Spencer and Kidd argue, improve meaning-making by empowering patients. Addressing contingent features of clinical interactions such as power, marginalisation of minoritized individuals, and institutional barriers, the authors claim, is key to improve understanding and treatment of those with mental ill health impairments.

Issues relating to co-production, however, are not present solely at the level of individual interactions. Alana Wilde, in her essay, 'Co-Production and Structural Oppression in Public Mental Health', focuses on analysis of epistemic injustice in co-production as a kind of systemic oppression, diverging from the common consensus that injustices arise at the level of interactions themselves. Drawing on the framework of epistemic oppression, the paper highlights the tensions at play, such as the dismissal of EbE knowledge as 'expert' and the way in which research paradigms perpetuate exclusionary practices. Wilde emphasises the need for fundamental revisions in our epistemological systems to allow a role and to make room for the valuing and inclusion of knowledge of EbEs. Wilde's analysis underscores the challenges in overcoming entrenched norms and calls for a shift towards more equitable research practices.

The challenges of injustice in co-production sets the scene for Edward Harcourt and David Crepaz-Keay's essay, 'Co-Production is Good, but Other Things are Good Too'. This essay critically engages with the complex dynamics at play in participatory research that have contributed to co-production becoming a much-discussed and much-used methodology in academic psychiatry and mental health research. By drawing on a range of illustrative case studies, the authors show that there are proven and effective means of delivering positive change in mental health care, treatment, and service-design which, though not befitting of the label 'co-production', have nevertheless had success and demonstrated the role and benefit of progressive, innovative means of revolutionising existent processes. As do many of the chapters within this volume, Harcourt and Crepaz-Keay keenly engage with both methodological and empirical questions about the merit of solely focusing upon equalisation of power in research.

Part Three of this volume picks up on themes that Harcourt and Crepaz-Keay touch upon, namely the role of values in navigating difference and disagreement in psychiatry. Anna Bergqvist's 'Shared Decision-Making and Relational Moral Agency: On Seeing the Person Behind the "Expert by Experience" in Mental Health Research' explores the role assigned to lived experience, in terms of both moral and scientific value, arguing for a relational approach which considers patient perspective equal to, as opposed to lesser than, clinical narratives. Bergqvist argues that shared decision-making promotes a dynamic partnership, balancing patient self-knowledge with clinical expertise, ultimately arguing that a holistic understanding of the personal self which encompasses agency, history, perspective, and identity is required. Supporting the assimilation of lived experience and personal accounts into mental health research as an equally valuable source of knowledge, Bergqvist argues, would allow the integration of such narratives into clinical practice.

Mohammed Abouelleil Rashed's essay, 'Mad Pride and the Creation of Culture' takes this notion of novel contributions that lived experience provides, highlighting the ways in which Mad Pride activism looks to add conceptual understandings of experiential states to our shared narratives which are non-pathologizing. This, Rashed claims, is akin to creating a new culture of madness.

Through a range of poignant examples, Rashed shows how the re-visioning and revaluing dimension of madness as a form of cultural identity recognition requires transformations in the basic concepts constitutive of current mental health narratives. Drawing on the concept of the self, and the phenomena of thought insertion to illustrate this claim, Rashed gives new means of understanding how lived experience might work to shift our shared understandings of what madness *is* and how we ought to understand it societally.

The central role of individuals and the psychiatric significance of the personal self (Sadler, 2007) in health care is what motivated the appearance of a new resource for tackling contested values, called values-based practice (Fulford *et al.*, 2012). This practical resource for shared decision-making is the focus of K.W.M. (Bill) Fulford and Ashok Handa's chapter, 'Values-Based Practice: A Theory-

Practice Dynamic for Navigating Values and Difference in Health Care'. Values-based practice is a process-driven rather than an outcome-driven methodology that works in partnership with evidence-based practice in 'linking science with people' (Fulford *et al.*, 2012). The authors argue that the central difference between the two modalities, evidence-based practice and values-based practice, is found in the corresponding methodological process element. Where evidence-based practice relies on meta-analyses of the results of high-quality clinical trials to inform a consensual model of decision-making, values-based practice builds on learnable clinical skills and other process elements to inform an open-ended and ongoing *dissensual* model of decision-making, rather than seeking to overcome value-conflicts in reaching consensus based on the stakeholder dynamic and treatment circumstances presented by the health care situation in question.

References

Dinesh Bhugra, Kamaldeep Bhui, Samuel Yeung Shan Wong, and Stephen E. Gilman, *The Oxford Handbook of Public Mental Health* (Oxford: Oxford University Press, 2018).

Patricia Hill Collins, *Black Feminist Thought: Knowledge, Consciousness, and the Politics of Empowerment* (London: Routledge, 1990).

Sandra Harding, *The Feminist Standpoint Theory Reader: Intellectual and Political Controversies* (New York: Routledge, 2004).

K.W.M. (Bill) Fulford, Ed Peile, and Heidi Carrol, *Essential Values-Based Practice: Clinical Stories Linking Science with People* (Cambridge: Cambridge University Press, 2012).

K.W.M. (Bill) Fulford and Anna Bergqvist, 'The Curatorial Turn in Aesthetics as a Resource for the Contested Values at the Heart of Person-Centred Clinical Care', in Helena Fox, Kathleen Galvin, Michael Musalek, Martin Poltrum and Yuriko Saito (eds.), *The Oxford Handbook of Mental Health and Contemporary Western Aesthetics* (Oxford: Oxford University Press, in press).

Mario Maj *et al.*, 'The Clinical Characterization of the Adult Patient with Depression Aimed at Personalization of Management', *World Psychiatry* 19:3 (2020), 267–93.

José Medina, *The Epistemology of Resistance: Gender and Racial Oppression, Epistemic Injustice, and the Social Imagination* (Oxford: Oxford University Press, 2013).

Mohammed Abouelleil Rashed, *Madness and the Demand for Recognition: A Philosophical Inquiry into Identity and Mental Health Activism* (Oxford: Oxford University Press, 2019).

Anna Bergqvist, David Crepaz-Keay and Alana Wilde

John Z. Sadler, 'The Psychiatric Significance of the Personal Self', *Psychiatry*, 70:2 (2007), 113–29.

Peter Sedgwick, *Psychopolitics: Laing, Foucault, Goffman, Szasz, and the Future of Mass Psychiatry* (London: Pluto Press, 1982).

Elizabeth V. Spelman, 'On Treating Persons as Persons', *Ethics*, 88:2 (1978), 150–61.

Şerife Tekin, 'Self-Concepts through the Diagnostic Looking-Glass: Narratives and Mental Disorder', *Philosophical Psychology*, 24:3 (2011), 357–80.

Şerife Tekin, 'The Missing Self in Scientific Psychiatry', *Synthese*, 196:6 (2019), 2197–215.

Iain Wilkinson, *Suffering: A Sociological Introduction* (Cambridge: Polity Press, 2005).

Art and the Lived Experience of Pain

PANAYIOTA VASSILOPOULOU

Abstract

Mental health has become a key concern within social discourse in recent years, and with it, the discussion about the lived experience of pain. In dealing with this experience there has been a shift away from merely relying on medical care towards more holistic approaches involving community support, public awareness, and social change. However, little if any attention has been paid in this context to the contribution of aesthetic experience engendered by art that expresses and publicly shares with others the lived experience of pain. With reference to *Phantom Limb*, an art exhibition curated by Euan Grey and held at the Victoria Galleries and Museum Liverpool in 2016, I argue that aesthetic experience plays a crucial role in making sense of pain and suffering, thus breaking new ground in the appreciation of the significance of art for public mental health and holistic approaches towards patients.

1. Introduction

Mental health has become a key concern within social discourse in recent years, and with it, the discussion about the lived experience of pain. In dealing with this experience there has been a shift away from merely relying on medical care towards more holistic approaches involving community support, public awareness, and social change. Here I make a case for one underappreciated resource for public mental health and holistic approaches to care, namely the aesthetic experience engendered by art that expresses and publicly shares with others the lived experience of pain.

While art has been increasingly recognised as an effective means of expression and communication of lived experience in the context of art therapy, its value is associated almost exclusively with its benefits as a form of treatment for the patient. Art produced in this context is rarely, if at all, valued for its artistic or aesthetic merits and their impact on the patient or the audiences that may encounter it. Aesthetic experience, I will claim, plays a crucial role in allowing us to make sense of the lived experience of pain or suffering embodied in art, precisely because aesthetic experience – at least on one understanding of the concept, which I will be defending – brings the totality of the lived experience of pain to the fore while creating the

doi:10.1017/S135824612300022X © The Author(s), 2023. Published by Cambridge University Press on behalf of The Royal Institute of Philosophy reflective space necessary for this to be effectively communicated to others.

I make my case on the basis of a close engagement with *Phantom Limb*, an exhibition curated by Euan Grey and held at the Victoria Galleries and Museum Liverpool, as part of the Liverpool Biennial 2016 Fringe, July–October 2016. The exhibition comprised works by eight artists in different media – including photographs, drawings, comics, sculpture, film, and sound – that centre around pain in all its manifestations: as physical or mental illness and suffering, as loss of one's limbs or sense of body and self, as mental anguish at the prospect of one's own death, or as mourning for the death of those close to us. But the exhibition also addresses the ways in which we deal with pain; the ways, so to speak, in which we domesticate pain in our life: treatment, recovery, memory. I will be discussing three of the works presented in this exhibition: Hannah Wilke's *Intra-Venus Series, No. 6* (1992), Nancy Andrews' *On a Phantom Limb* (2009), and Tabitha Moses' *The Go Between* (2016, specifically commissioned for this exhibition) in order to demonstrate how such works afford the gallery audiences with an experience very different to our ordinary ways of experiencing and learning about the world, namely aesthetic experience. My argument is that aesthetic experience plays a crucial yet overlooked role in making sense of pain and suffering, thus breaking new ground in the appreciation of the significance of art for public mental health and holistic approaches towards patients.

2. Pain

Pain is undoubtedly a very complex phenomenon, a fact reflected in the philosophical and medical debates concerning its nature and definition. Central to this complexity is that the experience of pain has clearly two aspects. On the one hand, given the analogy between pain and perception, one may claim that pain is a form of perceptual awareness, a sensory-discriminative state with its appropriate representational content, or more broadly, intentional object. In this sense, the claim 'I have a pain in my hand', like the claim 'I have an apple in my hand', reports an objective state of affairs. This state can be plausibly construed as some disturbance or damage localised in a specific part of my body, as registered through the activity of appropriate neurons, and represented in my perceptual experience as having a certain quality and intensity. On the other hand, there is a phenomenal quality of pain, a negative affective or evaluative (and eventually behavioural) component in the overall experience ('it hurts') that goes beyond the representational content of the perceptual experience and resembles more an act of introspection than an act of perception, since it does not seem to be about anything outside the experience itself.[1]

The various positions articulated in the philosophical debate on the nature of pain can be considered as responses to this duality, trying to combine these two aspects in various ways or to prioritise one over the other. However, this is not an easy task to the extent that the perceptive and the phenomenal aspects of pain can also exist independently and are thus not necessarily connected. There are well-known conditions in which the appropriate representational content is there, but the painfulness of pain is missing (pain asymbolia or various forms of analgesia), as well as conditions in which the painfulness of pain is there, but in the absence of the bodily damage that could be represented by the appropriate perceptual experience (phantom limb syndrome). Uniquely, pain is a form of perception for which no hallucination or delusion is possible, and this is reflected in the definition offered by the *International Association for the Study of Pain*, according to which pain is defined in an objectivist manner as 'unpleasant sensory and emotional experience associated with, or resembling that associated with, actual or potential tissue damage', but under the subjectivist qualification that, '[p]ain and nociception are different phenomena. Pain cannot be inferred solely from activity in sensory neurons. [...] A person's report of an experience as pain should be respected'.[2]

For the purposes of the present discussion, I shall adopt a broad and subjectivist understanding of pain, where the emphasis is on the 'painfulness' of pain and not on its specific perceptual or causal aspect. While by no means intended as an assessment of the debate presented above, I believe that this approach is particularly helpful for elucidating the lived experience of pain and our ways of dealing with it. The importance of drawing clear distinctions between different aspects or components of the experience of pain, as well as, say, between physical and psychological pain, or between pain and other forms of physical or mental unpleasantness or suffering, is evident. However, any significant lived experience of pain does not

---

[1] For an initial orientation and further references see Corns (2017, pp. 19–69), Hardcastle (1999), Corns (2020), Schleifer (2014), and Jung (2016).

[2] The definition can be found on the IASP website, https://www.iasp-pain.org/resources/terminology/?navItemNumber=576#Pain.

merely contain distinct episodes of physical pain (of the kind, say, that we may experience after a minor accident or before a visit to the dentist), but is shaped by all kinds of physical, mental, or even social conditions. To understand, for example, how a terminally ill person may try to deal – through art or otherwise – with an experience of persistent pain, while in fearsome anticipation of the future and mourning recollection of the past, in a situation of physical incapacitation and social isolation, we need an expansive definition of pain, in which 'the boundaries of the word "pain" are characteristically blurred by connotations of suffering and trauma' (Fernandez, 2010, p. xiii).[3]

The various aspects of the subjective nature of the experience of pain have been frequently noted in the philosophical reflection on pain. At the core of this subjective understanding of pain lies the claim, expressed here in Hannah Arendt's words, that 'only pain is completely independent of any [external] object, that only one who is in pain really senses nothing but himself' (Arendt, 1958, pp. 309–10).[4] A first implication of the lack of an external intentional object in the experience of pain is the radical isolation of the subject of pain. If the pain is intense enough, its experience absorbs the subject

---

[3]   From a theoretical point of view, there are two separate sets of issues here. The first continues the debate on the nature of pain in order to examine the validity of distinctions between different putative kinds of pain (e.g., physical vs psychic or psychogenic pain) or between pain and other unpleasant sensations or affective mental states (see Biro, 2014; Sullivan, 2017). The second concerns more broadly the relation between a philosophically or scientifically constructed concept of pain and the corresponding common-sense or folk-psychological notions. Rejecting our ordinary understanding of pain (with all its fuzziness, metaphorical associations, ambiguity, or even incoherence) in favour of a philosophically sophisticated scientific theory of pain does not contribute directly to dealing with or making sense of our lived experience of pain. For a strong defence of the claim that we must abandon our ordinary talk about pain, and the definition of IASP, see Hardcastle (1999, pp. 145–62); for a defence of the mental-social aspects of pain experience captured in our ordinary ways of talking about it see Derbyshire (2016).

[4]   This claim provides the starting point of Elaine Scarry's well-known work *The Body in Pain*: '[P]hysical pain is exceptional in the whole fabric of psychic, somatic, and perceptual states for being the only one that has no object. Though the capacity to experience physical pain is as primal a fact about the human being as is the capacity to hear, to touch, to desire, to fear, to hunger, it differs from these events, and from every other bodily and psychic event, by not having an object in the external world', (Scarry, 1985, p. 161).

as the body is thrown back upon itself. When one withdraws into oneself, the normal function of one's senses is disrupted and so the subject loses touch with the reality of the external world. At the same time, one establishes an intentional relation with oneself in a state of negative and dissociative affection, sensing oneself in opposition to oneself.[5] A second implication is that this experience is radically private, since there is no obvious way to objectify it in order to express and communicate it publicly through linguistic or material signs: 'the experience of great bodily pain, is at the same time the most private and least communicable of all. [...] it [is] perhaps the only experience which we are unable to transform into a shape fit for public appearance' (Arendt, 1958, pp. 50–1; see also Scarry, 1985, p. 162). In fact, one could go even further and claim that, in its radical lack of an intentional object that could guide the process of signifying, 'physical pain does not simply resist language but actively destroys it, bringing about an immediate reversion to a state anterior to language, to the sounds and cries a human being makes before language is learned' (Scarry, 1985, p. 4).

I have already noted above the unusual status of pain as a form of perception for which no hallucination or delusion is possible. This paradox can now be intensified by noticing that, given the objectless nature of the experience of pain, 'for the person in pain, so incontestably and unnegotiably present is it that "having pain" may come to be thought of as the most vibrant example of what it is to "have certainty," while for the other person it is so elusive that "hearing about pain" may exist as the primary model of what it is "to have doubt"' (Scarry, 1985, p. 4).[6] Bridging the gap between private certainty and public doubt cannot be easily accomplished, but is imperative in both directions: the person in pain cannot make sense of their experience without making it public in some way, while the person who is not experiencing this pain cannot remain deaf to the disclosure of a fundamental aspect of human existence. It is thus necessary to come up with ways to 'reverse the de-objectifying work of pain by forcing pain itself into avenues of objectification' (Scarry, 1985,

---

[5] 'Nothing, by the same token, rejects one more radically from the world than exclusive concentration upon the body's life, a concentration forced upon man in slavery or in the extremity of unbearable pain' (Arendt, 1958, p. 113).

[6] Cp. 'Pain is the only inner sense found by introspection which can rival in independence from experienced objects the self-evident certainty of logical and arithmetical reasoning' (Arendt, 1958, p. 310).

p. 6). In what follows, the task is precisely to examine how works of art of a certain kind can help us achieve this aim.

3. Art

Creating works of art is one of the most prominent ways to transform experiences, thoughts, or feelings 'into a shape fit for public appearance' (Arendt, 1958, p. 51). The nature of pain entails, of course, that, in a variety of ways, pain is not a particularly appropriate subject for aesthetic or artistic representation, especially if we identify the objective of our engagement with art as a kind of pleasure or delight. Nevertheless, there are many fictional representations of pain in art and literature, shaped by purely artistic exigencies and creative aims against the background of diverse lived experiences of pain that each one of us (and, presumably, the relevant artists) inevitably accumulates through life.[7] Sophocles' *Philoctetes* and the statue of Laocoon and his sons, are classical examples where the depiction of the experience of pain is the primary aim of the work.[8] However, artistically informed explorations of pain need not be purely fictional. There are also documentary or quasi-documentary representations of human pain or suffering, ranging across the entire spectrum from journalism to 'high' art, usually associated with political or social agendas against injustice, oppression, or exploitation.[9] What brings these two different ways of dealing with pain through art together is their 'third-person' perspective: typically, neither the artist nor the audience claim a 'first-person' experience of the pain

---

[7] For a broad survey of the Western tradition of works of art dealing with pain, see Spivey (2001). For the visual arts, see Di Bella and Elkins (2013) and Biernoff (2021). For a brief overview of the relevant literature, see also Mintz (2013).

[8] In this respect, Lessing's discussion of the Laocoon group and Sophocles' *Philoctetes* is still instructive. Lessing accepts that the artistic depiction of pain is legitimate within the 'wider boundaries of art'. However, he argues for strategies of artistic presentation that would objectify more effectively (even if indirectly) the experience of pain, associate it with other more easily communicable aspects of experience, and keep it within bounds that would sustain the audience's engagement with it, which are different in the visual and literary arts (Lessing, 1985, pp. 61–75).

[9] Works of this kind provide the focus for Sontag (2003). For the issues they raise, see also Grønstad and Gustafsson (2012). One could include here documentary representations of pain in various kinds of medical literature, see Rees (2014) and Bourke (2019).

or suffering depicted: the pain is that of 'others'. The 'first-person' experience of pain is however crucial in the way art is used to deal with pain in health care practice, as evidenced in various forms of art therapy.[10] What typically happens in art therapy is that under the guidance of the therapist patients are involved in art-making and in reflecting on both the process and the artistic objects they produce, in order to deal with their own pain or suffering. The artistic or aesthetic project is thus fully subordinated to the therapeutic aim and the purpose of art is to transform directly in some desired way the immediate lived experience of pain, to heal those who participate in the therapeutic practice.

However, there is a third possibility, which is what I am interested in pursuing here, namely works of art, which may or may not have been produced in the context of therapeutic practice, but are published or presented in a gallery space, i.e., they become candidates for public aesthetic or artistic appreciation. Such works, rather than being fictional representations of pain, act as (autobiographical) records of a specific lived experience of pain or suffering that their creators had, either in dealing with their own pain or with the pain of individuals close to them.[11] This direct access to lived experience largely determines the response of the audience. It also generates the main question: what is the significance and the distinctive contribution of these works and their aesthetic appreciation to dealing with the lived experience of pain?

Much of the art included in *Phantom Limb* is precisely about articulating what pain was for those that experienced it, what it was to be in pain *for them*, and in that sense, it seems to go beyond an understanding of aesthetic experience as a form of universal pleasure generated by a beautiful representation. This is, then, a case in

[10] For a useful overview of diverse approaches to art therapy, see Gussak and Rosal, (2016, pp. 7–131). For a discussion of the effectiveness of art therapy in dealing with chronic pain, see Hamel (2021, pp. 41–5).

[11] The earliest example of such works is perhaps the *Sacred Tales* of Ailios Aristeides, written c.175 CE, which 'recount the *minutiae* of their author's pained existence throughout his extended illness and recovery' (King, 2018, p. 130). An intense modern example are the notes written by Alphonse Daudet between 1887 and 1897 recording his lived experience of the sufferings caused by neurosyphilis, published posthumously (Daudet, 2002). Daudet intended to write a novel based on these notes, but this project was never realised. Ofri (2010) discusses several contemporary poets who recorded personal experiences of pain and illness in their works. Harris (2003) highlights the proximity of literary expression and therapeutic practice in this context.

which art goes against the reticence associated with experiences of pain in many social contexts and directly attempts to make public that pain which is so private that 'it cannot assume any appearance at all' (Arendt, 1958, p. 51). So, what is it that we are presented with?

Hannah Wilke's Intra-Venus Series, No. 6 *(1992)*

Hannah Wilke's performalist nude bust-length self-portrait (taken by her husband Donald Goddard), *Intra-Venus Series, No. 6* (1992), is an imposing 'larger than life' 120.7 x 181.6 cm chromogenic print, documenting the artist's battle with lymphoma, which led to her death in 1993. The artist is looking directly at the viewer; her thinning hair, presumably from chemotherapy, is gathered in threads draping gently over her piercing red watery eyes. This image is part of an extensive series of photographic and watercolour self-portraits, which were not intended to be a private documentation of her illness, but rather were 'conceived for public display, to be shared with others' (Crippa and Rogers, 2018, p. 68). As the title suggests, in its allusion to the goddess of love and beauty and its reference to a detached enumeration associated with formalist works (both points may be ironic, but could also be taken quite seriously), the portrait as part of the larger project makes a strong claim to engage with this illness, the ways in which the illness manifests itself externally in the appearance of the patient/artist as an objectification of internally felt pain, as a work of art. This affirmation of art, Wilke's resolve to respond to her condition with the creation of a work of art, becomes more evident in the context of her overall work. The portrait continues the engagement of the artist with her own body and self-image, a theme that unifies Wilke's artistic production along recognizably artistic aims within the context of performance and feminist art, i.e., using 'her body as material to be used for underlining personal and cultural statements' (Tierney, 1996, p. 49), or 'in order to propose, chastise, play with or make fun of particular ways of being and engaging with reality' (Crippa and Rogers, 2018, p. 67). Indeed, the 'seamlessness' with which this image fits into Wilke's body of work (Perchuk, 1994, p. 94; cp. Wacks, 1999, p. 106), as well as the fact that the powerful impact of *Intra-Venus Series* necessitated a retroactive assessment of the whole 'of Wilke's art and legacy' (Jones, 2003, §2, §18) clearly indicate the artistic achievement of these portrayals of pain and illness.

Considered as a portrait of a person suffering, the work is in a sense quite traditional. Although it clearly presents the condition and effects of suffering in a very stark or realistic way, it captures a moment of relative repose in which the subject can compose herself, presumably in between states of intense and debilitating pain. As a result, we are captivated by this image in ways that point to different, or even opposite, directions, and that sustain all kinds of ambiguity. This is clearly a person ravaged by illness and pain, but also surprisingly beautiful despite the circumstances; this is a person suffering a terrible misfortune, but also managing to retain her dignity, and even project a sense of defiance or disdain for her condition that appears to be characterised by equal amounts of resignation, resilience, and anger. This ambiguity is related to the interplay between the 'internal' and the 'external', or the 'real' and the 'apparent', established by the work. According to Amelia Jones, this and other works by Wilke,

> stubbornly resists the notion that representations reveal some latent knowledge about who and what the subject actually is. The subject is known only through her appearance – via the image or in the "flesh" – and yet this appearance is infinitely variable. The portrait's subject calls out to us, but each of us receives it in our own particular way. (Jones, 2003, §6)

From one point of view, this could mean that the work – perhaps necessarily given its aesthetic constitution as a (visual) semblance – cannot capture and communicate what pain 'really is' for the person in pain, but it can merely present to us the 'appearance' of pain, what *it looks like* to be in a state of pain as opposed to what *it is to be* in a state of pain. From another perspective, this point may be taken to mean that there is nothing to be known or to be valued behind this appearance, that the accomplishment of the artist is to project an appearance of the subject that will eliminate the need for or appeal to some latent knowledge about what this subject 'really is' or how she 'really feels'.

And, of course, in this context, it is of crucial importance that we are dealing with a self-portrait. The portrait is staring directly at the viewer, at each one of us, capturing our attention. In this connection, the defiance of Wilke's gaze may not be directed solely against her condition, but also against any viewer who may consider illness and pain – and a mature female body ravaged by them – as matters that should be kept private. However, as with every self-portrait, the image presented here could be considered also as a reflective image, the object that the artist herself as subject sees when looking in a mirror. This reflective interplay that places the female body depicted in the work under the gaze of the artist can be appreciated as an important aspect of the kind of feminist artistic project sustained by Wilke throughout her entire oeuvre. In this particular case, however, the reflective duplication, the artist looking at her suffering self, becomes particularly poignant. Given the negative affection with which the self takes itself as the internal object in pain, Wilke's highest achievement may be the self-love that informs the gaze of the artist to which the portrayed person responds. This self-love is an important factor in putting the viewers in the same position as the artist. They are invited to look at the work as if looking at themselves in a mirror, entertaining the possibility that this pain could also be theirs. This is clearly not an image that we would strive to identify with, and yet it is not an image that we can dismiss either: averting our eyes from it would involve rejecting one's own self, if found in the same situation, that of suffering and being in pain.

Thus, Wilke's self-portrait functions as a public placeholder for our private experiences of pain by effecting a shift in the interpretation of 'being in pain'. At a first level, the work objectifies, makes it appear in public, *the state* of being in pain by selecting and presenting appropriate visible attributes of the experience of pain. At a second level, however, it reveals the existential predicament of the subject, the *being*, not only the artist, but any being who finds oneself in pain and looks at oneself as if in a mirror: 'is this me?'.[12] The oscillation between our attraction to the work and our aversion from it correspond to the artist's oscillation between recognizing and not recognizing herself in the artistic projection of herself and parallels the biological and psychological function of pain which could be equally protective and destructive. If intense pain alienates us from ourselves and from others, then perhaps what Hannah Wilke saw when she looked at her self-portrait looking back at her, and what we see when we look at its mixture of resilience and resignation is how precarious the project of holding ourselves and everything else together really is.

Nancy Andrews' On a Phantom Limb *(2009)*

Nowhere is this fragmentation and strained relationship with oneself and others more evident than in Nancy Andrews's film *On a Phantom Limb* (2009), from which the exhibition derives its title. Andrews was

---

[12] For the distinction between being in pain=being in a state of pain, where 'being' is taken as a verb and being in pain=an entity in pain, where 'being' is taken as a noun, see Jung (2016, pp. 27–8).

diagnosed with Marfan Syndrome, a genetic disorder affecting her heart and aorta. She underwent surgery for replacing a part of the aorta in her 20s, followed by multiple surgeries for a dissected aorta about a decade later. Although the surgery, as she writes, restored her to 'normal functioning', she suffered Intensive Care Unit delirium and Post Traumatic Stress Disorder, conditions that point to the blurred boundary between physical and mental pain.[13]

This 35-minute film – written and directed by Andrews, with music by John Cooper – incorporates footage from Andrews' surgery as well drawings she created during her illness and recovery to present the story of a surgically created creature returning to life after having experienced death and purgatory. For Andrews, art as an activity served in a broadly therapeutic context as 'a way to understand her experience and connect to others', be it sufferers of similar conditions who may hereby find solidarity, or medical professionals and the public, who may become more aware of such conditions. But her art as an object, situated now in an art gallery, has more far-reaching aspirations. In her own words, it is an invitation extended to the viewer 'to enter the in-between, fluid, unstable, fluctuating space [that she inhabited]. [...] Reality, I think, is less stable that we like to believe'. This world, the world of the artwork, is marked by antithetical narratives: 'reconstruction of the body vs. deconstruction of the self; mutilation vs. repair; delirium vs. heightened awareness of existential truths'.

Andrews' work can thus be considered as an artistic reflection both on the diverse ways in which the identity of the self, one's capacity to recognise oneself or one's own body, is seriously compromised in conditions of severe pain, and on the therapeutic practices that may assist someone to restore one's own relation with oneself. As I suggested earlier, this destruction of the self under intense pain starts paradoxically with a maximal affirmation of subjectivity: 'pain individualizes the self to that extent where nothing else exists but the victim's bare self, ipseity' (George, 2016, p. 59). However, this immediate and self-contained awareness of the self is experienced as a form of thorough self-alienation – in pain nothing matters but me, but at the same time I am set against myself – while, at the same time, the emergence of the 'bare self' is made possible by the destruction of all the complex bodily and psychological structures and relations that sustain and give meaning to ordinary subjective experience

---

[13] Relevant information and quoted passages in this and the next few paragraphs come from Andrews' blog: https://artandscienceofdelirium. wordpress.com/2012/09/15/an-invitation/, accessed 3 June 2023.

(e.g., the spatio-temporal structure of the experience of myself and the world, the affective connections to other human beings).

A first example of such pain-induced disruptions of subjectivity explored in Andrews' work is precisely the phantom limb experience. 'Phantom limb' denotes a usually painful perception of a missing, amputated limb as being still present, fully attached to the body and thus still existent as part of the human being.[14] While absent in a third-person perspective, the limb is still present in a first-person perspective. In this situation, there is a tension between the physical reality that underlies and supports the existence of the self and the way in which the 'I' is conscious of this reality, of its body and its various parts. The experience undermines one's capacity to recognise adequately oneself in a double sense. On the one hand, it amounts to a false impression of one's own bodily integrity; on the other, it rests on a state of negative affection: the part of the body that is absent becomes present through pain.

In Andrews' case, parts of the amputated aorta were replaced, as is also rather common with many amputees who are provided with various sorts of prosthetics. The drawings thus depict herself as a mechanical, surgically re-constructed being, part-woman and part-bird. The paradox of Theseus' ship comes to mind here: if all the parts of an object, a ship, are replaced, is the object fundamentally the same, identical to itself? However, in the case of phantom limb experiences associated with these prosthetics, the main issue is not the identity of a material object ('Is my body the same after all its parts have been replaced?'), but rather the re-imaging or re-experiencing of the whole self – of which the body is, so to speak, a part – under a new mixture of familiarity and strangeness experienced primarily through pain. In Andrews' work, in contrast to Wilke's *Intra-Venus Series*, pain is not associated with the prospect of imminent death. Andrews' project is to continue living with/after pain, or, in other words, to move beyond an artistic depiction of the state of pain in order to recover or construct, in terms of her lived experience, a new sense of herself that would allow her to understand her experience and to re-establish a working relation with other human beings or the world at large.

[14] For a useful and concise survey of the issue of phantom limb pain, see Richardson (2010). Merleau-Ponty's discussion of phantom limb, in the context of an elucidation of the way one's experience of one's living body is localised, forcefully makes the point that understanding this experience requires the combination of a physiological and psychological approach (Merleau-Ponty, 2005, pp. 87–92).

In the art I have discussed so far, artistic activity as a form of work on lived experience can be associated clearly with the therapeutic or cathartic effects that it has on their artists. This is, of course, a widely recognized instrumental value of art within the context of medical humanities, especially in art therapy.[15] Accordingly, the artworks produced through this kind of creative activity can be seen as records of the ways in which individuals deal with their own pain. In other words, if we consider these works as exemplary repositories of some kind of knowledge, what they can teach us primarily is how to deal with our own experience of pain by artistically representing it. But what about the ways of dealing with the pain of other people, especially since, when we view works like the ones created by Wilke or Andrews as gallery visitors, we are *de facto* observers of (records of) the pain of other people? Approached by the exhibition curators, Tabitha Moses responded to this question through her work *The Go Between* (2016).

Tabitha Moses' The Go Between *(2016)*

The work is an installation piece continuously evolving. Gallery visitors are encouraged to share their experiences of pain by writing on cards provided by the artist and posting them on a noticeboard. In this way, gallery audiences are invited to assume an active role by telling their story, and thus fostering a community. But what makes this process different to, say, sharing an account of their lived experience on an online forum, is that the artist then responds to the stories by creating votive offerings. Moses uses different materials and techniques to produce these offerings, which she pins to a stuffed fabric body that lies on a plinth at the centre of the room. In this sense, the artist responds to the audience's experience, while each member of the audience responds to the votive offerings that respond to other members of the audience; the task of the artist is precisely to create the space in which these responses are possible. Herself deeply moved by this process, the artist wonders if 'like leaving a votive object in a chapel, the person might take comfort in taking action, getting it off their chest, telling the universe. Is that a form of healing in itself?'[16] Judging from the overwhelming response of gallery visitors to her call, this seems to be the case.

---

[15] For a collection of essays exploring the therapeutic potential of various forms of art, see Bates *et al.* (2014).

[16] See https://thevotivesproject.org/2016/09/25/go-between/, accessed 22 June 2023.

Catharsis in the context of art is a homeopathic process that works 'by administering, repeating, imitating, and symbolizing' the relevant reality in a way that affects 'the entire human being' (Meinhold, 2016, p. 96). The re-experience and re-enactment of painful experiences leads to the discharge of the participants' emotions, which, for Aristotle, refers particularly to pity, 'a powerful emotion associated with undeserved suffering […] akin to the shared or public lamentation which is part of life in small and closely knit communities', and fear: 'we fear for them [the characters] the things they fear for themselves' (Lucas, 1980, p. 273–4).

But beyond its immediate personal effects in terms of discharge of emotions, this act of secular intercession, as it were, transforms the gallery space into a communal place for meditation and reflection, and art becomes the channel or the mediator, connecting but at the same time separating participants. The dimensions of the central figure in Moses' installation, the white cloth – reminiscent of a shroud – which dresses it, and the placement of the votive offerings of 'affected parts' of the sufferers on corresponding parts of it, point to the creation, or rather co-creation of a public domain, a shared world, in the form of a body that, by being no one's in particular, is everyone's. Hannah Arendt defines the 'public' as,

> the world itself, in so far as it is common to all of us and distinguished from our privately owned place in it […]. This world is related, rather, to the human artifact, the fabrication of human hands […]. To live together in the world means essentially that a world of things is between those who have it in common, as a table is located between those who sit around it. (Arendt, 1958, p. 52)

In its formal simplicity and performative complexity, in installing a representation of the human body in pain as the central artifact at the core of the public world of the gallery, Moses' work captures concisely the essential aspects of art's contribution to dealing with the experience of pain.

4. Aesthetic Experience

In the previous section, I identified several ways in which the particular artworks discussed contribute to our dealing with the lived experience of pain. This contribution, whether from the point of view of the individual, the artist/sufferer, or the audience who engages with the work, is both cognitive and practical, descriptive and transformative.

These works capture and elucidate aspects of our experience of pain, but also articulate active responses to this experience. They try to make sense of the experience of pain by exploring the self-transformations initiated and suffered because of pain. But the leading question of my discussion remains and requires a more systematic elucidation: what is the specificity and significance of art and aesthetic appreciation in this context?

The issue can be broken down in a series of related questions. First, building on a question raised by Ian Williams (Williams, 2011, p. 361), 'is art made as therapy still art?', we may ask: does it make sense to show such works in a public space, consider them as art, and enjoy them aesthetically? Second, could the fact that a work of art is created on the basis of a specific lived experience contribute something special to its artistic or aesthetic value? And finally, assuming the broad cognitive and practical interest underlying our desire to make sense of our experience of pain and respond to it, how and what does art allow us to learn about pain or suffering that would be difficult to learn in other ways?

In response to the first question, neither every artistic product of therapeutic activity or practice will necessarily be a publicly appreciable work of art, nor does the fact that a work was initially conceived or realised in a therapeutic context prevent it from being art and become a candidate for public appreciation, especially if its creator already has relevant qualifications or experience as an artist. In this sense, it seems that the issue cannot be decided as a matter of principle but should be evaluated on a case-by-case basis. What is clear as a matter of principle is that the criteria of appreciation of the work are different in the two contexts, and one should be careful in applying them appropriately in order to avoid misapprehending the significance of the work, which could be either therapeutic or aesthetic, or both.

The response to the second question seems more complex. Generally, artistic activity is considered as a matter of the imaginative and reflective (re)creation of experience, while the work of art is granted relative autonomy from the circumstances of its creation, such as the conditions or the immediate intention of the artist. So, in that sense, it could be argued that the aesthetic value of the work would be the same regardless of the particular circumstances of its creation. However, from the perspective of the artists, that these works are records of an intense and immediate lived experience, aiming directly to make sense of and respond to this experience, presumably sets them apart from works just conceived in an ordinary manner against the background of the overall experience or empathetic imagination of the artist. Moreover, it is undoubtedly the case that the audience's appreciation of and response to the works in the *Phantom Limb* exhibition were crucially shaped by their authenticity as vouched for by the actual, specific experience behind them – which, more generally, is also the case with much performance and feminist art. What is worthy of special admiration in the work of Hannah Wilke, for example, may not be that she managed through her art to make sense of pain in a novel or insightful way (she may have done this, but other artists not necessarily having this experience may do so too), but rather that she managed to do so in her condition, hindered, so to speak, instead of being assisted by the immediacy of her experience. In this sense, the special appeal or significance of this kind of art may be that it stands as a testament to the human ability to make sense of any lived experience and respond to it in an admirable way, however horrible and however horribly it affects us.

The final question touches upon a broader issue that has been discussed extensively in aesthetic literature, starting from Aristotle's *Poetics*, namely the so-called paradox of tragedy or paradox of negative emotions: we seek out and value works of art that depict distressing or horrifying situations which we would normally avoid in real life in order to spare ourselves from the negative emotions generated by the experience.[17] One way of dealing with this paradox is the position developed by the early Nietzsche under the influence of Schopenhauer. In the *Birth of Tragedy*, Nietzsche asserted that suffering is a fundamental and inevitable element of human existence and attributed to art the task to help us deal with it in the most effective way. The superiority of art in this respect is not, of course, practical in the ordinary sense: art is not in competition with medicine for providing more effective pain relief treatments. Rather, according to Nietzsche, the cognitive superiority of art is grounded on the refusal to evade the inevitability of suffering in human life – metaphysically grounded in the philosophy of Schopenhauer but also supported through empirical evidence – by articulating a prospect of a human life free of pain. Its practical superiority rests on its capacity to present that insight in a way that does not affect negatively the will of human beings to live. Depending on how strong one takes Nietzsche's claims to be, art can either provide some kind of justification for suffering, i.e., show how it contributes to the value of human existence, or, more modestly, help us discover or construct the significance and meaning of our experience of suffering in a

[17] For a useful recent survey of the issue, with further references both to the historical and contemporary literature, see Levinson (2014).

way that enhances the capacity of the subject to pursue their funda-mental interests.[18]

It may be argued that the suffering of a patient undergoing chemo-therapy or heart surgery in a present-day hospital is quite different, say, from the tragic pain of Prometheus or Philoctetes. In this sense, the *Phantom Limb* exhibition is a difficult case, if not for the substance of Nietzsche's views, at least for his excessive rhetoric. I propose an alternative yet so far underappreciated way of approaching this issue, arguing that the specific contribution of these works lies in affording us the possibility of dealing with the reality of pain or suf-fering through aesthetic experience.

The notion of aesthetic experience can be traced back to the begin-ning of modern aesthetics, especially to Kant's work, but it also informs the work of many contemporary philosophers of aesthetics. The fundamental idea behind it is that our encounter with certain objects – whether natural or human-made – leads to a special kind of experience different from any other form of experience arising from our cognitive and practical engagement with the world. Further and beyond this generally agreed understanding, everything that pertains to aesthetic experience – the way in which it can be cap-tured and described, the way in which it informs our response to works of art, its function in explaining the task and value of art, its very existence as a distinct kind of experience – has been a matter of extensive debate in the philosophical literature.[19]

The particulars of these debates shall not concern us here, but two points of orientation will be helpful. First, the traditionally prevalent understanding of aesthetic experience is a rather narrow one, both

[18] Nietzsche's actual position was far more complex than this brief sche-matic overview allows and was developed significantly throughout his career. For a nuanced discussion, see the collection of essays in Came (2014). It may be helpful to associate Nietzsche's claim on the inevitability of suffering with his own lived experience of pain as reported in a letter written in 1888: 'Around 1876 my health grew worse. [...] There were ex-tremely painful and obstinate headaches which exhausted all my strength. They increased over long years, to reach a climax at which pain was habitual, so that any given year contained for me two hundred days of pain', (Nietzsche, 1996, p. 293). Nietzsche's intimacy with pain and the import-ance he attributed to his experience of it, is well attested in his published works (see in particular Nietzsche, 2001, pp. 6–7, 60–1, 177, 179, 181–2).

[19] Kant (2000). For a broad and concise survey, see Matravers (2012). For a reconstruction of older debates and a defence of a revised notion of aes-thetic experience, see Shusterman (1997). For a detailed discussion of more recent developments and further references, see Carroll (2002 and 2012).

regarding its content and its overall aim. The content is limited to the appreciation of variously defined formal properties of the object – the unity, complexity, or variety of a composition, or its expressive purposiveness, i.e., the optimal relation of its form to the content it signifies. The aim of aesthetic experience is taken to be reflective pleasure, made possible by the temporary exclusion of any personal, cognitive, ethical, or socio-political interests. Second, given this narrow understanding of aesthetic experience, it is not surprising that its relevance for illuminating our complex responses to contemporary works of art motivated by all kinds of agendas that both exceed the traditional pursuit of beauty and undermine a conception of art as an autonomous social activity, have been increasingly questioned from the early 1960s, which, in the 1990s, even led to the identification of aesthetic experience as 'the central blunder of modern aesthetics' and to a 'reasoned account of its demise' (Shusterman, 1997, p. 29).

On both these counts, invoking the notion of aesthetic experience in the context of the theme and the provenance of works like the ones presented at the *Phantom Limb* exhibition would seem even less helpful than employing a 'heroic' Nietzschean framework, to the point of being inappropriate or disrespectful. Clearly these are not works particularly suited to a primarily formal appreciation, while their artistic motivations and objectives, as well as the audience's response, evidently go against the appreciation of art for art's sake associated with an aesthetic understanding of art.

However, adopting a broader account of aesthetic experience, a trend evident in the recent revival of theoretical interest in the notion of aesthetic experience, may provide a more promising point of reference for determining the specificity and significance of art in the context of dealing with pain. Perhaps the broadest of these accounts has been articulated by Alan Goldman in a series of publications.[20] According to Goldman, our response to a work of art must focus on 'the interaction of formal, expressive, and representational aspects of the works appreciated' (Goldman, 2013, p. 329). Aesthetic experience, as the subjective counterpart of this interaction, includes 'cognitive, imaginative, and emotional engagement with artworks, along with perceptual grasp of their formal structures' (Goldman, 2013, pp. 326–7). Moreover, to the extent that the work develops moral or political themes in a way that is relevant to our overall appreciation of it, 'prompting engagement with a work on a moral level' and thus, for example, gaining moral insight or

[20]   See Goldman (2013 and 2020).

knowledge, can also 'be an integral and inseparable aspect of our full experience of or engagement with the work' (Goldman, 2013, p. 331). In this broad sense, then, aesthetic experience cannot be radically distinguished or separated from the interests or capacities (theoretical, practical, and affective) that inform both our experience in general and our engagement with art in the context of our life. Rather, we should try to understand aesthetic experience in a fully inclusive way: the conditions of the reception of a work of art allow for 'the simultaneous and harmonious interaction and engagement of all these mental capacities' (Goldman, 2013, p. 329). In other words, what the experience of the work of art affords us is a reflective mental space in which all our interests, despite their relative priorities and antinomical tensions that inform and fracture our ordinary life experience, are allowed full and free simultaneous expression. In the case of works like the ones discussed here, these will include our interest to know the worst and hope for the best; our desire to do the right thing, but safeguard our happiness; our curiosity for the life of others and our respect for their privacy; our urge to sympathy and our concern for our self-preservation; our 'unsocial sociability', to use a Kantian phrase, that motivates equally both our pursuit of self-interest or relief for being spared some suffering and our capacity for empathy or longing for community.

It is important to note however, that inhabiting this reflective space is not the result of one's choice, but points to a certain passivity that characterises aesthetic experience: 'one must be captured or "grabbed" by an artwork in order to have an aesthetic experience of it, and one cannot normally successfully will to be so fully engaged' (Goldman, 2013, p. 330). One may thus consider aesthetic experience as the experience of losing oneself in the unfamiliar territory of an artwork, while at the same time recovering a new and reflective sense of oneself through a 'fully active' engagement of 'all mental faculties operating in concert' (Goldman, 2013, p. 330) with the content of the artwork in terms of the interests expressed or captured in the work itself.

So, how can works of art like the ones included in *Phantom Limb* help their creators and their audience make sense of pain? The first step, which is made by the artist, is the effective realisation that one cannot make sense of one's pain through art as *one's own* pain. This claim can be understood in two senses. First, whether we say that *her* pain is inherently private and hence cannot be publicly communicated, or that *her* pain, like any other specific experience, cannot be captured in its full particularity, the fact is that by creating the work, a public material sign highly motivated through an indefinite and opaque mixture of conventional generality and significant particularity, the artist effectively gives up *her* pain in its ineffability or particularity. At the same time, the artist gives up *her* pain as an immediate and legitimate object of her cognitive and practical interests, renounces, that is, the project of communicating her experience of pain in the way one may try to communicate it in the context of a medical interview or an ordinary testimonial record. We may think of this as the contribution, or even the sacrifice, of the artist: she gives up the specifics of *her* pain in order to build a common world around the semblance of her pain, which can invite multiple interpretations and meanings.

The accomplishment of the artist is to create a significant object motivated enough as to capture the attention of the spectator, making thus possible the aesthetic engagement with the work. The distinctive mark of this intense engagement, the absorption in the world created by the artwork, is precisely the inclusive and 'lingering' nature of aesthetic experience. When one reads, for instance, an article on pain in an academic journal, there is clearly a cognitive interest; there may also be corresponding practical interests (e.g., how to use this knowledge to alleviate the pain of patients) of a moral or self-interested nature (to help others or to become a famous doctor). However, the way in which the relevant motivations, intentions, or circumstances inform the experience precludes the exploration of innumerable other interests and issues that would be present during the appreciation of a work of art dealing with pain. For example, a doctor listening to a patient giving an account of their pain need not reflect on the simultaneous resilience and fragility of beauty in the defiant gaze of the patient in the way suggested by Wilke's self-portraits. At the same time, in our normal engagement with reality on the basis of our interests, we do not typically 'linger' on our experiences, exploring carefully the various aspects of their contents, not only because, as in this case, they may be painful, but also because we need to refocus our attention on the ways we can deal cognitively or practically with the demands of this experience (e.g., the doctor listening to a patient's account of their pain may be, justifiably or even necessarily, already thinking of the relative merits of different medications). The affective component of the aesthetic experience is especially important in this respect. Depending on the circumstances of any actual encounter with an experience of pain – for example, whether it is my pain, or the pain of someone I love or I feel indifferent about, or whether this is a pain pointing to the prospect of recovery or of death – one's affective response will be correspondingly determined, both in quality and quantity, by the immediate exigencies of the situation. The aesthetic experience makes possible the communication of these affective states to people who are not facing the same circumstances. And it is the inclusivity of the aesthetic experience that grounds the specific contribution of art in this context because it makes possible the kind of global orientation towards an experience that we usually seek when we try to make sense of the lived experience of pain.

Art of the kind I have been discussing succeeds in attracting us, absorbing us in a peculiar interplay between the private and the public, the personal and the universal, the familiar and the strange. It is this interplay that holds together the world opened up by the artwork – the world, to recall Arendt, which acts as the in-between that simultaneously unites and separates those that have it in common. In artistic creation, the artist renounces the privacy or ownership of her pain by creating a public semblance of it potentially owned by everybody, an accomplishment much more difficult, and thus rightfully praised, if wrested directly from an actual lived experience of pain. In aesthetic experience, the receptive counterpart of artistic creation, the 'being' in pain, deeply rooted in the human condition, is experienced as if the being in question were each one of us, something made possible precisely because the pain is not ours in the ordinary sense. While in art therapy art is undoubtedly valued as an alternative treatment for patients, here we see the potential for art to play a more central role in the holistic approaches to public mental health needed to meet the increasingly more complex and urgent socio-political challenges we are now facing. And this is because, as I have been arguing, the aesthetic experience of art uniquely allows the bringing to the fore of all different aspects of one's lived experience at once and their effective communication to others. If one of the goals of new approaches to public mental health is indeed to treat mental health in a holistic way, to make sense of the lived experience and see the patient more as a person, then the aesthetic experience through art that expresses and communicates publicly the lived experience of pain may provide a new model for reaching this goal.[21]

[21] I am indebted to the editors of this volume and to the organizers and participants of the Royal Institute of Philosophy Public Festival 2022 'Philosophy of Psychiatry and Lived Experience: New Models of Mental Health' for their insightful comments and suggestions. I would also like to thank Professor Amelia Jones for helping me access her work and my colleague Dr Vid Simoniti for his valuable feedback on previous versions of this chapter.

References

Nancy Andrews, 'What This Blog is All About', available online at https://artandscienceofdelirium.wordpress.com/2012/09/15/an-invitation/.

Hannah Arendt, *The Human Condition* (Chicago and London: University of Chicago Press, 1958).

Victoria Bates, Alan Bleakley, and Sam Goodman (eds.), *Medicine, Health and the Arts: Approaches to the Medical Humanities* (New York and Abingdon: Routledge, 2014).

Suzannah Biernoff, 'Picturing Pain', in Deborah Padfield and Joanna M. Zakrzewska, (eds.), *Encountering Pain: Hearing, Seeing, Speaking* (London: UCL Press, 2021), 190–213.

David Biro, 'Psychological Pain: Metaphor or Reality?', in Rob Boddice (ed.), *Pain and Emotion in Modern History* (New York: Palgrave Macmillan, 2014), 53–65.

Joanna Bourke, 'Visualising Pain: A History of Representations of Suffering in Medical Texts', in Berenike Jung and Stella Bruzzi (eds.), *Beyond the Rhetoric of Pain* (New York and Abingdon: Routledge, 2019), 11–34.

Noël Carroll, 'Aesthetic Experience Revisited', *British Journal of Aesthetics*, 42:2 (2002), 145–68.

Noël Carroll, 'Recent Approaches to Aesthetic Experience', *The Journal of Aesthetics and Art Criticism*, 70:2 (2012), 165–77.

Daniel Came (ed.), *Nietzsche on Art and Life* (Oxford: Oxford University Press, 2014).

Jennifer Corns (ed.), *The Routledge Handbook of Philosophy of Pain* (New York and Abingdon: Routledge, 2017).

Jennifer Corns, *The Complex Reality of Pain* (New York and Abingdon: Routledge, 2020).

Elena Crippa and Anna Backman Rogers, 'Interview: The Final Projects of Hannah Wilke and Jo Spence', in Boel Ulfsdotter and Anna Backman Rogers (eds.), *Female Authorship and the Documentary Image: Theory, Practice and Aesthetics* (Edinburgh: Edinburgh University Press, 2018), 66–71.

Alphonse Daudet, *In the Land of Pain* (New York: Knopf, 2002).

Stuart W.G. Derbyshire, 'Pain and the Dangers of Objectivity', in Simon van Rysewyk (ed.), *Meanings of Pain* (Cham, Switzerland: Springer, 2016), 23–36.

Maria Pia Di Bella and James Elkins (eds.), *Representations of Pain in Art and Visual Culture* (New York and London: Routledge, 2013).

Jane Fernandez (ed.), *Making Sense of Pain* (Oxford: Interdisciplinary Press, 2010).

Siby K. George, 'The Familiar Stranger: On the Loss of Self in Intense Bodily Pain', in Siby K. George and P.G. Jung (eds.), *Cultural Ontology of the Self in Pain* (Heidelberg and New York: Springer, 2016), 51–74.

Alan H. Goldman, 'The Broad View of Aesthetic Experience', *The Journal of Aesthetics and Art Criticism*, 71:4 (2013), 323–33.

Alan H. Goldman, 'What is Aesthetic Experience?', in Steven M. Cahn, Stephanie Ross, and Sandra Shapshay (eds.), *Aesthetics: A Comprehensive Anthology* (Hoboken and Chichester: Wiley Blackwell, 2020), 581–8.

Asbjørn Grønstad and Henrik Gustafsson (eds.), *Ethics and Images of Pain* (New York and London: Routledge, 2012).

David E. Gussak and Marcia L. Rosal (eds.), *The Wiley Handbook of Art Therapy* (Malden, MA and Oxford: Wiley, 2016).

Johanne Hamel, *Somatic Art Therapy: Alleviating Pain and Trauma through Art* (New York and Abingdon: Routledge, 2021).

Valerie Gray Hardcastle, *The Myth of Pain* (Cambridge, MA: MIT Press, 1999).

Judith Harris, *Signifying Pain: Constructing and Healing the Self through Writing* (Albany: State University of New York Press, 2003).

Amelia Jones, 'Everybody Dies... Even the Gorgeous: Resurrecting the Work of Hannah Wilke', *Marks* 4.01 (2003).

P.G. Jung, 'Ontology of Pain', in Siby K. George and P.G. Jung (eds.), *Cultural Ontology of the Self in Pain* (Heidelberg and New York: Springer, 2016), 25–50.

Immanuel Kant, *Critique of the Power of Judgment* (Cambridge: Cambridge University Press, 2000).

Daniel King, *Experiencing Pain in Imperial Greek Culture* (Oxford: Oxford University Press, 2018).

Gotthold Ephraim Lessing, 'Laocoon or on the Limits of Painting and Poetry', in H.B. Nisbet (ed.), *German Aesthetic and Literary Criticism* (Cambridge: Cambridge University Press, 1985), 58–134.

Jerrold Levinson (ed.), *Suffering Art Gladly: The Paradox of Negative Emotion in Art* (Basingstoke and New York: Palgrave Macmillan, 2014).

D.W. Lucas, *Aristotle: Poetics* (Oxford: Clarendon Press, 1980).

Derek Matravers, 'The Aesthetic Experience', in Anna Christina Ribeiro (ed.), *The Continuum Companion to Aesthetics* (London and New York: Continuum, 2012), 74–83.

Roman Meinhold, 'Pain and Catharsis in Art, Ritual and Therapy', in Siby K. George and P.G. Jung (eds.), *Cultural Ontology of the Self in Pain* (Heidelberg and New York: Springer, 2016), 93–109.

Panayiota Vassilopoulou

Maurice Merleau-Ponty, *Phenomenology of Perception* (London and New York: Routledge, 2005).

Susannah B. Mintz, *Hurt and Pain: Literature and the Suffering Body* (London and New York: Bloomsbury, 2013).

Tabitha Moses, *The Go Between*, (2016), https://thevotivesproject.org/2016/09/25/go-between/.

Friedrich Nietzsche, *Selected Letters* (Indianapolis and Cambridge: Hackett, 1996).

Friedrich Nietzsche, *The Gay Science* (Cambridge: Cambridge University Press, 2001).

Danielle Ofri, 'The Debilitated Muse: Poetry in the Face of Illness', *Journal of Medical Humanities*, 31 (2010), 303–17.

Andrew Perchuk, 'Hannah Wilke. Ronald Feldman Fine Arts', *Artforum*, 32:8 (1994), 93–4.

Danny Rees, 'Down in the Mouth: Faces of Pain', in Rob Boddice (ed.), *Pain and Emotion in Modern History* (New York: Palgrave Macmillan, 2014), 164–86.

Cliff Richardson, 'Phantom Limb Pain: Prevalence, Mechanisms and Associated Factors', in Craig Murray (ed.), *Amputation, Prosthesis Use, and Phantom Limb Pain: An Interdisciplinary Perspective* (New York: Springer, 2010), 137–56.

Elaine Scarry, *The Body in Pain: The Making and Unmaking of the World* (New York and Oxford: Oxford University Press, 1985).

Ronald Schleifer, *Pain and Suffering* (New York and Abingdon: Routledge, 2014).

Richard Shusterman, 'The End of Aesthetic Experience', *The Journal of Aesthetics and Art Criticism*, 55:1 (1997), 29–41.

Susan Sontag, *Regarding the Pain of Others* (New York: Picador, 2003).

Nigel Jonathan Spivey, *Enduring Creation: Art, Pain and Fortitude* (Berkeley and Los Angeles: University of California Press, 2001).

Mark D. Sullivan, 'Psychogenic Pain: Old and New', in Jennifer Corns (ed.), *The Routledge Handbook of Philosophy of Pain* (New York and Abingdon: Routledge, 2017), 165–74.

Hanne Tierney, 'Hannah Wilke: The Intra-Venus Photographs', *Performing Arts Journal*, 18:1 (1996), 44–9.

Debra Wacks, 'Naked Truths: Hannah Wilke in Copenhagen', *Art Journal*, 58:2 (1999), 104–6.

Ian Williams, 'Autography as Auto-Therapy: Psychic Pain and the Graphic Memoir', *Journal of Medical Humanities*, 32 (2011), 353–66.

A Wide-Enough Range of 'Test Environments' for Psychiatric Disabilities

SOFIA JEPPSSON

Abstract

The medical and social model of disability is discussed and debated among researchers, scholars, activists, and people in general. It is common to hold a mixed view and believe that some disabled people suffer more from social obstacles and others more from medical problems inherent in their bodies or minds. Rachel Cooper discusses possible 'test environments', making explicit an idea which likely plays an implicit part in many disability discussions. We place or imagine placing the disabled person in a range of different environments. If there is a relevant test environment in which they do fine, their problem was societal/external; if there is not, it was medical/internal. Cooper admits that deciding on the appropriate range of test environments is an ethical and political question. In this chapter, I argue that we often ought to widen our scope when discussing psychiatric disabilities.

1. Medical and Social Theories

It is common to distinguish between medical and social *models* of disability. According to the medical model, disabled people are limited by their impaired bodies or minds. Ideally, disability should be cured through medical interventions (Anomaly, Gyngell, and Savulescu 2020). The social model sees disability as a social construct; people are disabled by the barriers and attitudes that exist in society. We should remove these barriers and make society more inclusive to enable everyone to participate fully (Tremain, 2017; Chapman, 2020). However, a model cannot strictly speaking be true or false; insofar as scholars, researchers, and activists attempt to present a *true* account of what, in fact, mostly hinders disabled people from living fulfilling lives, or what mostly causes disabled people to suffer, it makes more sense to talk of social and medical *theories* (Wasserman and Aas, 2022).

One might think of these models or theories as endpoints on a spectrum. Many people, including disabled people themselves, have a mixed view which lies somewhere in between (e.g., Vedder, 2005; Shakespeare, 2006). Moreover, the social and the medical aren't the

doi:10.1017/S1358246123000206   © The Royal Institute of Philosophy and the contributors 2023 only games in town. One might speak of an analytical model, a relational model (Wilson, 2003), or even an economic model (Wolff, 2020, pp. 157–9). Still, much of the non-academic discussion focuses mostly on the medical, the social, and various intersections and mixes between the two, and this book chapter follows this example.

I believe there are important pro tanto reasons to accept disabled people's own explanations of their struggles and difficulties, whether they lean more towards the medical or social end of the spectrum. Only pro tanto, since it's clearly possible to be mistaken about one's own situation – as my own case, to be discussed later in this chapter, will show. Still, we need overriding reasons not to trust people's self-explanations; for this reason, and because 'psychiatrically disabled people' are such a big and diverse group, I will not argue that a social theory is true across the board.

I will, instead, argue for the weaker but nevertheless important claim that we tend to use a very narrow range of 'test environments' when considering whether someone's problems are mostly social or more medical in nature. If there's a tendency to overestimate the extent to which people's problems are medical, and underestimate the extent to which social factors make people struggle and suffer, any efforts to help psychiatrically disabled people and ease our burdens will be decidedly suboptimal.

2. The Concept of Test Environments

Rachel Cooper (2017) explicitly introduced the term 'test environment' in disability discourse, though I believe this concept often plays a role, at least implicitly, in many social-medical debates, whether it's given a name or not. Cooper argues that a person's condition might be considered an inherently neutral neurodivergence – rather than an inherently bad mental impairment – if there's 'some acceptable test environment' in which the person's problems would disappear.[1] She uses the analogy of a water kettle: a kettle with a three-pronged plug doesn't work in a two-holed socket, but that doesn't mean there's anything inherently wrong with it. If we use a

---

[1]   We should likely interpret this as a necessary rather than sufficient condition. Robert Chapman points out – personal conversation – that early-stage Alzheimer's might otherwise serve as a counterexample. In early stages, the person might do fine in an adjusted environment, but we still consider it an illness – perhaps because of its progressive nature, perhaps for other reasons, too.

suitable test – plug it into a three-holed socket – and it boils water under those conditions, it's fine. However, we can't say it's fine just because the water inside would boil if we hung it over an open fire – a kettle which only boils water under those conditions is still broken. So how radically changed may a 'test environment' be? Cooper doesn't say, but admits that it's at least partly an ethical and political issue. Still, much of Cooper's text is focused on criticizing Laing and Esterson's 1960's schizophrenia theory according to which it's a family problem rather than an individual disorder. They don't, she writes, show that there's any environment in which their interviewed schizophrenia patients function fine. Though she doesn't rule it out, she seems doubtful that any such unproblematic test environment can be produced for schizophrenia.

Alison Jost's (2009) critique of Mad Pride provides a good example of implicit use of the concept. Jost writes that a social model might provide an adequate framework for discussing many disabilities and disabled people's problems, but it won't work for mental illness. She writes: 'Most mental illnesses for most people are inherently negative [...]. No matter how destigmatized our society becomes, mental illnesses will always cause suffering'. She acknowledges that stigma can be a big problem for both physically and psychiatrically disabled people. Still, Jost argues, being psychiatrically disabled or mentally ill is, in addition to the stigma, *inherently* bad. But Awais Aftab and Mohammed Abouelleil Rashed (2021) criticize her claims – how do we determine when society is sufficiently destigmatized? What would such a society look like? Can we really be confident that mentally disordered people would still suffer then? In effect, Aftab and Rashed question whether Jost imagines a sufficiently wide range of test environments.

3. Popular Media Debates with a Narrow Range of Test Environments

Neurodiversity advocates often focus on quite small changes in the school environment or workplace. This isn't inherently problematic: many people only require fairly small changes to function well, and writers may naturally focus on what has helped them personally. It is also worth drawing attention to how many people might actually require fairly small adaptations, even if they initially seem quite disabled. Nevertheless, it's a problem if these often-discussed small workplace changes end up creating paradigms for which test environments we should use in thought experiments or actual experiments to see whether someone is mainly disabled by external circumstances or suffer from inherent, neurological impairments. For instance, some autistic advocates write about how they need a sufficiently calm office space and the opportunity to work from home a few days a week. It's disabling for them to demand that they come to the office each day and work in a glaring light with noise from other people (De Vries, 2021; Enright, 2021). These are also the kind of adjustments that can be demanded by disabled people in US workplaces under the American with Disabilities Act, the Disability Discrimination Act in the UK, and similar legislations in other countries. The adjustments are important to discuss and sufficient for some disabled people, but not for everyone.

An extremely narrow view on what environmental changes we might make to better accommodate disabled people in the workplace is presented by Nancy Doyle, the founder of *Genius Within*.[2] She writes that there's a new workplace threat to disabled people – computer algorithms used to assess employees' productivity (Doyle, 2022). She focuses on how such algorithms judge everyone *by the same standard*, regardless of which diagnoses they might have.

Now, perhaps one might ease the stress of disabled people in such computer-supervised workplaces a teeny bit if the algorithms somehow took disabilities into account. Maybe some psychiatrically disabled people would do quite well under those conditions. However, looking back on my own life and times when I was much more distressed than is presently the case, I would likely have cracked under the pressure of constant productivity supervision *regardless* of whether the algorithm was programmed to give me some slack due to disability. I'm sure I'm not the only psychiatrically disabled person for whom this would be the case – and who might therefore be seen as neurologically impaired rather than disabled by an inhospitable environment, if it were the case I worked in that kind of place. 'We fixed the algorithm, we made it take disabilities into account, and these people *still* suffered mental breakdowns? The problem must be in their brains, then. Nothing more to do'.

4. How Many People Become Impaired in Different Environments?

Cooper is not interested in what might cause a condition to arise in the first place; she explicitly focuses on whether an already disabled

---

[2]   Described, in her Forbes writer's profile, as 'a company specializing in neurodiversity and disability inclusion at work'.

person might do well in a different environment, or struggle in every relevant test environment. However, I will discuss *causes* in this section before returning to the issue of how different environments affect the already disabled.

There's a traditional version of the Social Model of Disability which distinguishes impairments from disabilities (Oliver, 1996, p. 22). On this view, *impairments* are (in one way or another *negative*) bodily or mental traits that are turned into *disabilities* when societal barriers of various kinds prevent impaired people from full participation in society. Philosophers who see themselves as adherents of some version of the Social Model debate to what extent it's feasible and desirable to draw a line between impairment and disability. On the one hand, talking about inherently negative impairments as something residing in people's bodies and/or minds might seem like a problematic concession to the medical model.[3] On the other hand, if we get rid of the 'impairment' concept, how do we explain that, e.g., the physical trait of having dark skin isn't a disability, even though it's stigmatized in many societies? Theories that deal in 'marginalized functioning' (Jenkins and Webster, 2021) or 'non-normative functioning' represent attempts to navigate this problem. Radical social model scholars may still struggle with how to reconcile the idea that, e.g., it's horrible if a company pollutes a poor area in a global south country so that more and more babies are born without limbs, with the idea that disability isn't some inherent tragedy. Eli Clare offers a nuanced and, well, *brilliant* discussion without arriving at any easy answers in his *Brilliant Imperfection: Grappling with Cure* (2017). I can't, in this chapter, dive deep into these tensions. I will, however, use the term 'impairment' in this section in its admittedly problematic traditional sense – though I will complicate the matter in later sections.

As long as people are willing to use the term 'impairment' in the first place, they will readily acknowledge that the external environment may cause impairments, and that there may be widespread problems in society that cause an unnecessarily high number of impaired people. Suppose, for instance, that some country has terrible traffic. Car crashes happen often, and many people drive cars that would be considered unacceptably unsafe in most other countries. Because of this, many people end up losing a leg or two or breaking their spines in car accidents, and subsequently use wheelchairs. An adherent of the medical model, who believes that we should ideally find

---

[3]   Shelley Tremain (2001, p. 632) writes: 'impairment has been disability all along'.

some way to, e.g., mend all the nerves in previously broken spines so that people can walk again rather than having them roll around on wheels, would presumably *also* want to improve the traffic and car situation so fewer people end up in wheelchairs in the first place. A traditional social model theorist would agree. Of course we should build ramps and make society more accessible to wheelchair users, so that they aren't disabled in addition to being impaired – but we should also improve traffic so that fewer people become impaired in the first place.

Before moving on to psychiatry, I want to stress that I'm really focusing on the *impairment* here, not the *diagnosis*.

I count as perfectly able-bodied by society. I regularly lift heavy weights at the gym and go for long daily walks with my dogs without problem. Nevertheless, it's difficult for me to further improve my stamina through aerobic exercise – I must push myself *much* harder than the average person to see results (see Montero and Lundby, 2017, for research on this physiological difference). This isn't considered a disability in our society, because marathon running and similar activities are entirely optional. However, if society, for some reason, came to demand more and more long-distance running from people in general, I might eventually end up diagnosed with the newly recognized disability Aerobic Low Response Syndrome, and have to ask for various special adjustments. In this hypothetical situation, society would have turned a non-disabled body into a disabled one, but not by changing my body or giving me any new impairments, only by changing its demands and expectations. Analogous things may, of course, happen on the mental level. But I'm here concerned with the mental analogy to car crashes that break people's spines so that they must use wheel-chairs, not the mental analogy to a society where everyone is expected to be a long-distance runner.

Now, let's apply the traditional social disability model to schizo-phrenia. Let's say that schizophrenic people are first impaired by, e.g., frightening hallucinatory experiences and ego disturbances. Second, they are disabled by being stigmatized and excluded from society in various ways. Just like we should build ramps for wheel-chair users, we should try to destigmatize schizophrenia and get better at involving schizophrenics in various ways. However, just as we should make traffic safer so fewer people need wheelchairs in the first place, we should also try to make society, e.g., less racist, so fewer people of colour develop schizophrenia in the first place – research shows that being a person of colour in a racist society dominated by white people is a serious risk factor for paranoid schizophrenia (Bentall, 2004; Halpern, 1993; Boydell *et al.*, 2001).

Despite the tendency in popular science articles to focus on genetics and neurology when discussing mental illness and psychiatric disabilities, there's a large body of research on how both a dysfunctional family life and other kinds of individual trauma (e.g., Popovic *et al.*, 2019; Quide *et al.*, 2018), and society-wide problems like racism and poverty can cause (in conjunction, of course, with genetic and other factors) mental impairments that range from depression to schizophrenia. I've already mentioned research on racism and schizophrenia. Lund *et al.* (2010) also found a strong correlation between common mental disorders and poverty – more specifically, low education, low socio-economic status, food insecurity, lack of housing, and financial stress – in their meta-analysis of 115 studies. They conclude that developmental agencies and international developmental targets should include mental health goals, because this is something that we can plausibly affect.

The causal relations behind the correlation are likely complex – it's possible to first develop a mental disorder, and as a result lose your job and become poor. Perhaps some people become poor because they have a mental disorder whereas others become mentally ill because they're poor, and for some, it's a vicious cycle where it's impossible to determine which came first. Different researchers stress different causal pathways – from poverty to mental illness, or the other way around. Nevertheless, there are also intervention studies looking at the mental health effects of unconditional cash transfers to poor people. Doing so improves well-being and physical markers such as cortisol levels for poor people in general, and improves symptoms in those already diagnosed with mental disorders (e.g., Ljungqvist *et al.*, 2016; Fernald and Gunnar, 2009; Haushofer and Shapiro, 2016). Given all this, it's unlikely that poverty's impact on the frequency of mental disorders in a population is small enough to be dismissed.

However, political discourse tends to treat the frequency of psychiatric disabilities in the population as impossible to influence via political decisions; 'taking the problem seriously' means increased awareness, encouraging people to seek mental health treatment, perhaps increased funding to mental health services, and perhaps some workplace adjustments of the kind discussed above, but nothing more large-scale. This is a serious problem and needs to change. Schizophrenic and otherwise psychiatrically disabled people *should* have access to good mental health care, a destigmatized environment, and any special adjustments we might need to work or study – but we must not forget that we would likely see fewer people getting schizophrenia in the first place if society were less racist, less impoverished, and less fiercely competitive.

5. Relevant Test Environments for Already Disabled People

Environmental factors not only cause impairments to arise in the first place, they can also worsen them and prevent recovery. For instance, T.M. Luhrmann (2007) writes that the best explanation for the vastly different recovery rates seen between American and Indian schizophrenics, in otherwise similar urban populations treated by similar psychiatric systems, is that the former often are homeless whereas the latter usually have homes. Job stress leads to more frequent sick leave and hospitalization for people with mental health conditions (Duchaine, 2020).

It's crucial to see that these problems are often society-wide rather than something that can be fixed locally in the workplace. Suppose that Stina is very stress sensitive, and therefore granted accommodations like a quiet workplace without glaring lights, and the option to work from home a couple of days a week. If she lives in a highly competitive society in which employers have the right to fire anyone anytime they please and often do so, Stina might still be highly stressed due to these background conditions. However, if Stina and/or people around her are so used to living in a competitive society without job security that they never stop to ponder whether things could be different, they might end up thinking of Stina as mentally *impaired* by her stress sensitivity – after all, she *still* suffers, even *after* she got all these accommodations!

When imagining Stina in different test environments, we should also envision her living and working in an overall less competitive and more secure society. As Cooper writes, there's no objective, value-neutral answer as to the range of test environments that would still count as relevant. Perhaps we might think that some highly utopic society that we dream up, or a society where everything revolves around Stina and her needs, isn't realistic or relevant. But shouldn't we, at least, try to imagine how Stina would fare in, say, a social-democratic state with strong labour unions and strong job security (preventing Stina's boss from threatening to fire her or harassing her for not being sufficiently productive) and a strong welfare system (so that even if she were to drop out of the job market, she could live a good life on welfare)?

Perhaps we – or Stina herself – have no way of knowing how well she would fare or function in such a society. If so, we should at least admit as much – not confidently state that Stina's problem is inherent/neurological/medical in nature.

6. Autobiographical Case Study: How I Went from Applying a Medical to a Social Model to Myself when Getting a Better Environment

I think my own case can provide a nice illustration of how difficult it can be to use something like Cooper's 'test environments' in practice to distinguish neurodivergences from impairments, and how easily we might be mistaken about *our own* case.

Since I was a child, I have experienced myself as sliding back and forth between normal reality and a terrifying demon world. I have written about these problems elsewhere (Jeppsson, 2021, 2022b, 2022c, 2022d), and won't go into much detail here; suffice to say that I have spent *so much time* in a state of *absolute terror*. Therefore, I used to think that the social model wasn't really applicable to my own case. Sure, having schizo-something-or-other[4] is stigmatized, and people might give you weird looks if you say that you've been hospitalized for psychosis. Nevertheless, I used to think that stigma accounted for very little of my problems. I used to think, like Alison Jost, that in a hypothetical completely stigma-free situation, I would still suffer horribly from *being chased by demons*. I would still suffer horribly from *the terror*. Intense terror, just like intense pain, is *inherently* bad, regardless of how much other people accept you.

One reason I thought of my problem as medical, not social, was that I imagined myself as I was, with the same terrifying experiences and the same subsequent emotional states, placed in different environments – I failed to foresee that my mental states would change as radically as they did when the environment changed (a common implicit assumption, see Penson, 2015). Another reason is that my environment seemed pretty good. I was married to an incredibly supportive and helpful man, I got to work with philosophy which I found very interesting, most of my colleagues at work knew that I had schizo-something but were tolerant enough, and so on. Sure, I did a long weekly commute to another city which wasn't ideal. My husband had a very stressful job, and I empathized with and felt sorry for him without being able to do anything about his job problems. I constantly searched for permanent jobs at the highly

---

[4]   I have never been precisely diagnosed, beyond 'you're in the ballpark of schizophrenia but doesn't quite tick enough boxes'.

competitive academic job market since I had, so far, only managed to
land fixed-term ones. But none of these problems seemed, in any way,
extraordinary; rather, lots and lots of people have similar struggles.
That's just life.[5]

Then the following happened: I got a permanent philosophy job
with good job security and a good salary, my husband could quit
his job, we moved close to my new university so I didn't have to do
a long commute anymore, we moved to a nice big house, close to
forests and the sea where I take long walks with my dogs – in short,
my life became much less stressful and much more idyllic. In fact,
my life became so good and stable that I managed to quit my anti-
psychotics and other medication and still function without any relapses
into florid psychosis. I saw a therapist who helped me get over some
internalized stigma and shame that I hadn't even been aware of,
which in turn allowed me to freely experiment with various mental
tricks and coping mechanisms until I found ones that worked. I
began writing and publishing about my own madness, *fully* came
out of the madness closet in a way I hadn't dared to do while still on
the job market, and was met with tons of appreciation in response.

Not only do I realize, in hindsight, exactly how stressful my previous life had been – I also realize now that it was a mistake to imagine
myself *still chased by demons and still full of terror* in different scenarios
and then ask whether I would still suffer. It's been five years now since
my life changed to its current idyllic and stable state, and during that
time, my truly horrible and frightening experiences have gradually
subsided. Now, I'm almost never frightened of demons.

This is not to say that I have become *sane* and *normal*. I still experience plenty of little hallucinations and illusions of various kinds, I
still often feel like a tiny creature lodged inside the skull of a body
which I drive but which isn't identical to me, I still experience
sliding in and out of different realities, and so on – but all these experiences are far less frightening, much more benign nowadays.

I'm still mad. I'm also happy to call myself neurodivergent. But
I'm far less *impaired* than I used to be – hardly at all, nowadays.
And this is one important reason why the previously used distinction
between impairment and disability is oversimplified. The environment doesn't just determine how much a given impairment

[5]   I've had these psychiatric problems long before I entered academia,
but it was the same back then – my life seemed pretty fine to me, even
though there were sources of stress too, but nothing extraordinary. So it
didn't seem to me in my pre-academic state either that the environment
might play a major part in my suffering.

becomes an obstacle, it also continuously influences and shapes our impairments – sometimes to the point where they cease *being* impairments and turn into something else.

How many people diagnosed with a serious mental disorder could, hypothetically, experience the same improvement? How many could be neurodivergent rather than impaired if their external environment and overall life situation became *truly* good? I don't think this is possible to say. But we should, at least, *admit* that we don't know, instead of confidently talk of which conditions are always impairing and suffering-causing regardless of environment. Such confidence only betrays a limited imagination when it comes to test environments.

7. Stigma, and Different Environments to Come Out In

I believe that we often focus too much on stigma and not enough on other problems when discussing environmental obstacles that psychiatrically disabled people face. Nevertheless, destigmatization is important. But it's worth asking, with Aftab and Rashed (2021), what it means for an environment to be fully destigmatized. People often assume that there's no stigma if a psychiatrically disabled person can disclose their condition without facing negative reactions or consequences for so doing. However, information campaigns and medical advice sites often take a narrow view on what proper disclosure should look like. Australian government-funded website *Health Direct* advises psychiatrically disabled people on what *they* can do to help decrease the stigma: 'If you have bipolar disorder, say "I have bipolar disorder", not "I'm bipolar". If you convince yourself first that you're a person, not a walking illness, others will find it easier to see you that way too'. This is quite typical advice from this kind of site. You're supposed to explain to people that you're essentially a normal person like everyone else, except that you carry this regrettable illness around.

There's nothing wrong with seeing your psychiatric condition as something you *have* which is distinct from *who you are* if that works for you (Jeppsson, 2022a). But it doesn't suit everyone; an environment in which this is the only way one may disclose without facing backlash is still severely stigmatizing for many people.

I can't honestly say that I'm a pretty normal person who merely *has* schizo-something. I'm mad, that's who I am. I wasn't fully aware of how constricted I felt when I still kept one foot in the closet because I was afraid of discrimination. But since I got job security and fully came out, it's been an enormous relief and boost for my self-esteem.

Sofia Jeppsson

An environment isn't stigma-free until it's perfectly okay, not only to say that you *have* a psychiatric condition, but also okay to *be mad,* to *be neurodivergent,* and, in general, to *be as weird* as you need to be.

8. Conclusion

We may try to determine whether a psychiatrically disabled person's problems are mostly external/social or mostly internal/neurological by placing them and/or imagining them in different environments, exploring whether there is any environment in which they're happy and functional. However, we're often quite unimaginative when thinking of different environments; often, we should widen our scope.

Politicians, corporate leaders, and other people in power often have a vested interest in taking the status quo for granted and label people inherently disabled or impaired if they fail to respond to relatively small, cheap, and local adjustments – it's important that we keep questioning such politically motivated conservative assumptions. Moreover, we should acknowledge how difficult it might be to imagine *oneself* in radically different circumstances. Even if it's true that I would continue to suffer if I, hypothetically, were placed in a great situation but retained the exact same emotions (the exact same hallucinations, *etc.*), we must remember how difficult it may be to predict how this new situation would, in reality, *affect* and *change* my emotional state (my hallucinations, *etc.*).

The fact that we tend to use a narrow range of test environments has important practical implications. There are important implications for assisted suicide/voluntary euthanasia for psychiatrically disabled people, insofar as euthanasia is supposed to be for people whose suffering is inherent/medical only. It also matters for the new eugenics debate, and for claims according to which we should try to eradicate, e.g., schizophrenia from the population. Finally, politicians who claim to take psychiatric disabilities and mental illnesses seriously should be called upon to do more, to improve society, rather than merely promoting anti-stigma campaigns and funding psychiatry.

References

Jonathan Anomaly, Christopher Gyngell, and Julian Savulescu, 'Great Minds Think Different: Preserving Cognitive Diversity in the Age of Gene Editing', *Bioethics*, 34 (2020), 81–9.

Awais Aftab and Mohammed Abouelleil Rashed, 'Mental Disorder and Social Deviance', *International Review of Psychiatry*, 33:5 (2021), 478–85.

Richard Bentall, *Madness Explained: Psychosis and Human Nature* (London: Penguin Books, 2004).

Jane Boydell, J. van Os, K. McKenzie, J. Allardyce, R. Goel, R.G. McCreadie, and R. Murray, 'Incidence of Schizophrenia in Ethnic Minorities in London: Ecological Study into Interactions with Environment', *British Medical Journal*, 323:7325 (2001), 1336.

Robert Chapman, 'The Reality of Autism: On the Metaphysics of Disorder and Diversity', *Philosophical Psychology*, 33:6 (2020), 799–819.

Eli Clare, *Brilliant Imperfection: Grappling with Cure* (Durham: Duke University Press, 2017).

Rachel Cooper, 'Where's the Problem? Considering Laing and Esterson's Account of Schizophrenia, Social Models of Disability, and Extended Mental Disorder', *Theoretical Medicine and Bioethics*, 38:4 (2017), 295–305.

Nancy Doyle, 'Artificial Intelligence is Dangerous for Disabled People at Work: 4 Takeaways for Developers and Buyers', *Forbes*, 10 November 2022.

Caroline S. Duchaine, Karine Aubé, Mahée Gilbert-Ouimet, Michel Vézina, Ruth Ndjaboué, Victoria Massamba, Denis Talbot, Mathilde Lavigne-Robichaud, Xavier Trudel, Ana-Paula Bruno Pena-Gralle, Alain Lesage, Lynne Moore, Alain Milot, Danielle Laurin, and Chantal Brisson, 'Psychosocial Stressors at Work and the Risk of Sickness Absence due to a Diagnosed Mental Disorder: A Systematic Review and Meta-Analysis', *Jama Psychiatry*, 77:8 (2020), 842.

Jill Enright, 'The Social Model of Disability: How this Aligns with the Neurodiversity Paradigm', *Medium*, 24 December 2021.

Lia Fernald and Megan Gunnar, 'Poverty-Alleviation Program Participation and Salivary Cortisol in Very Low-Income Children', *Social Science and Medicine*, 68:12 (2009), 2180–9.

David Halpern, 'Minorities and Mental Health', *Social Science and Medicine*, 36:5 (1993), 597–607.

Johannes Haushofer and Jeremy Shapiro, 'The Short-Term Impact of Unconditional Cash Transfers to the Poor: Experimental Evidence from Kenya', *Quarterly Journal of Economics*, 131:4 (2016), 1973–2041.

Health Direct, 'Mental Illness Stigma', https://www.healthdirect.gov.au/mental-illness-stigma.

Katherine Jenkins and Aness Webster, 'Disability, Impairment, and Marginalised Functioning', *Australasian Journal of Philosophy*, 99:4 (2021), 730–47.

Sofia Jeppsson, 'Psychosis and Intelligibility', *Philosophy, Psychiatry and Psychology*, 28:3 (2021), 233–49.

Sofia Jeppsson, 'Solving the Self-Illness Ambiguity: The Case for Construction over Discovery', *Philosophical Explorations*, 25:3 (2022a), 294–313.

Sofia Jeppsson, 'My Strategies for Dealing with Radical Psychotic Doubt: A Schizo-Something Philosopher's Tale', *Schizophrenia Bulletin,* 30 June 2022 (2022b).

Sofia Jeppsson, 'Exemption, Self-Exemption, and Compassionate Self-Excuse', *International Mad Studies Journal*, 1:1 (2022c), 1–21.

Sofia Jeppsson, 'Radical Psychotic Doubt and Epistemology', *Philosophical Psychology,* 18 November 2022 (2022d).

Alison Jost, 'Mad Pride and the Medical Model', *Hastings Center Report*, 39:4.

Ingemar Ljungqvist, Alain Topor, Henrik Forssell, Idor Svensson, and Larry Davidson, 'Money and Mental Illness: A Study of the Relationship between Poverty and Serious Psychological Problems', *Community Mental Health Journal*, 52:7 (2016), 842–50.

Tanya M. Luhrmann, 'Social Defeat and the Culture of Chronicity: Or, Why Schizophrenia does so Well Over There and so Badly Here', *Culture, Medicine and Psychiatry*, 31 (2007), 135–72.

Crick Lund, Alison Breen, Alan J. Flisher, Ritsuko Kakuma, Joanne Corrigall, John A. Joska, Leslie Swartz, and Vikram Patel, 'Poverty and Common Mental Disorders in Low and Middle Income Countries: A Systematic Review', *Social Science and Medicine*, 71 (2010), 517–28.

David Montero and Carsten Lundby, 'Refuting the Myth of Non-Response to Exercise Training: "Non-Responders" Do Respond to Higher Dose of Training', *The Journal of Physiology*, 595:11 (2017), 3377–87.

Michael Oliver, *Understanding Disability: From Theory to Practice* (Basingstoke: MacMillan, 1996).

William J. Penson, 'Unsettling Impairment: Mental Health and the Social Model of Disability', in Helen Spandler, Jill Anderson, and Bob Sapey (eds.), *Madness, Distress, and the Politics of Disablement* (Bristol: Policy Press, 2015).

David Popovic, Andrea Schmitt, Lalit Kaurani, Fanny Senner, Sergi Papiol, Berend Malchow, Andre Fischer, Thomas

G. Schulze, Nikolaos Koutsouleris, and Peter Falkai, 'Childhood Trauma in Schizophrenia: Current Findings and Research Perspectives', *Frontiers of Neuroscience*, 13 (2019), 274.

Yann Quide, Sarah Cohen-Woods, Nicole O'Reilly, Vaughan Carr, Bernet Elzinga, and Melissa Green, 'Schizotypal Personality Traits and Social Cognition are Associated with Childhood Trauma Exposure', *British Journal of Clinical Psychology*, 57:4 (2018), 397–419.

Tom Shakespeare, *Disability Rights and Wrongs* (London: Routledge, 2006).

Shelley Tremain, 'On the Government of Disability', *Social Theory and Practice*, 4:27 (2001), 617–36.

Shelley Tremain, *Foucault and Feminist Philosophy of Disability* (Michigan: University of Michigan Press, 2017).

Julie Vedder, 'Constructing Prevention: Fetal Alcohol Syndrome and the Problem of Disability Models', *Journal of Medical Humanities*, 26:2–3 (2005), 107–20.

Bouke de Vries, 'Autism and the Right to a Hypersensitivity-Friendly Workplace', *Public Health Ethics*, 14:3 (2021), 281–7.

David Wasserman and Sean Aas, 'Disability: Definitions and Models', in *The Stanford Encyclopedia of Philosophy*, 14 April 2022.

Shula Wilson, 'A Relational Model of Disability', in *Disability, Counselling and Psychotherapy* (London: Palgrave, 2003), 19–40.

Jonathan Wolff, *Ethics and Public Policy: A Philosophical Inquiry*, 2nd edition, (London: Routledge, 2020).

Self-Diagnosis in Psychiatry and the Distribution of Social Resources

SAM FELLOWES

Abstract

I suggest that the diagnosis that an individual self-diagnoses with can be influenced by levels of public awareness. Accurate diagnosis requires consideration of multiple diagnoses. Sometimes, different diagnoses can overlap with one another and can only be differentiated in subtle and nuanced ways, but particular diagnoses vary considerably in levels of public awareness. As such, an individual may meet the diagnostic criteria for one diagnosis but self-diagnoses with a different diagnosis because it is better known. I then outline a potential negative consequence of this. Psychiatric diagnoses can grant access to what I call social resources, namely, political advocacy, campaigning for support, participating in scientific research, building diagnostic cultures, and opportunity for social interactions with people who have the same diagnosis. The strength of the social resources for a particular diagnosis can be made stronger when more people have that diagnosis. As such, inaccurate self-diagnosis can result in the social resources for one diagnosis being strengthened whilst not being strengthened in relation to another diagnosis in comparison to accurate diagnosis. This shows how inaccurate self-diagnosis can alter the distribution of social resources. We need to consider whether this is unfair to people who are diagnosed with less well-known conditions.

1. Introduction

Self-diagnosing psychiatric diagnoses, whereby an individual diagnoses themselves rather than seeks out a medical professional, is a controversial topic. Advocates of self-diagnosis argue that it helps people who cannot access the diagnostic process and that it also helps people who will be misdiagnosed by medical professionals. Critics of self-diagnosis argue that only medical professionals have sufficient expertise to make reliable diagnoses. One important question to consider is the consequences of inaccurate self-diagnosis. What, if any, negative consequences follow from someone self-diagnosing with a condition that they do not actually have? Official diagnoses can play a role in eligibility for medical resources like treatment and support, but self-diagnosis does not typically grant eligibility to these. As such, there is little opportunity for people who self-diagnose to (fairly or unfairly) get access to those limited resources.

doi:10.1017/S1358246123000218

Sam Fellowes

In this paper, I will argue that self-diagnosing individuals have access to an alternative type of resource which I name social resources. Also, I argue that inaccurate self-diagnosis can alter the strength of these social resources for different diagnoses.

Social resources are means of improving engagement with society and getting fair treatment from society. I outline five different social resources relating to psychiatric diagnoses. These are political advocacy, campaigning for support, participating in scientific research, building diagnostic cultures, and opportunity for social interactions with people who have the same diagnosis. People with the same diagnosis can group together to campaign for social changes, for better support, and for better scientific research. They can also form diagnostic cultures whereby they promote their condition as a unique and valuable way to live. Finally, they can meet other people with the same diagnosis, providing a source of social interactions with people who might share similar characteristics.

I argue that the strength of these social resources is influenced significantly by the number of people who have the diagnosis. The more people with that diagnosis means more people to campaign and form cultural movements in relation to the diagnosis, and more people with that diagnosis who can meet one another. The number of people with a diagnosis can have important consequences through strengthening or weakening these social resources. As such, inaccurate self-diagnosis can alter the strength of those resources.

I consider whether self-diagnosing individuals can reliably establish which diagnosis they fit. I provide a detailed example of how different diagnoses can appear superficially different but are only distinguished in subtle and nuanced ways. I then review existing literature on self-diagnosis to establish whether self-diagnosing individuals investigate a range of diagnoses and are aware of how different diagnoses can be distinguished in subtle and nuanced ways. The existing empirical literature gives little reason to believe that they do, but I recognize this might only reflect limitations with that empirical literature. I then outline an additional problem, namely that there is much higher public awareness of some diagnoses compared to others and suggest this can alter the process of self-diagnosis in a manner that increases inaccurate self-diagnosis.

Given that there are hundreds of psychiatric diagnoses it is difficult to make generalizations. The accuracy of self-diagnosis and any negative consequences of self-diagnosis may vary significantly between different diagnoses. I will support my argument with empirical evidence but detailed investigation in relation to specific diagnoses is needed to understand exactly where this issue is applicable.

2. Self-Diagnosis in Psychiatry

There are many barriers to receiving an official diagnosis. Firstly, there are few professionals available to providing an official diagnosis which has led to long waiting times (McDonald, 2020, p. 15; Lewis, 2016; Lewis, 2017, p. 578; Sarrett, 2016, p. 31). Secondly, in some countries there can be significant financial costs to being assessed by an official diagnostician (McDonald, 2020, p. 15; Lewis, 2016; Lewis, 2017, p. 578; Sarrett, 2016, p. 31). Thirdly, some individuals find navigating the healthcare system difficult (Lewis, 2016). Fourthly, some individuals believe they will struggle to describe their symptoms to professionals (Lewis, 2016). Fifthly, there are concerns, typically based on past experience, that medical professionals or institutions may harm the individual seeking the diagnosis (Lewis, 2016; Lewis, 2017, p. 578). Sixth, putting a psychiatric diagnosis on a medical record could harm future prospects, such as employment prospects (Lewis, 2016; Lewis, 2017, p. 578; Sarrett, 2016, p. 31). Seventh, given that there are typically so few services available, it is not always clear if there is much benefit in receiving an official diagnosis (Lewis, 2016; Lewis, 2017, p. 578). Finally, there is concern that the specialist will falsely claim that the individual does not meet the diagnostic criteria (Lewis, 2016; Lewis, 2017, p. 578).

The reliability of self-diagnosis has been debated by diagnosed individuals (the views expressed in this and the next paragraph are from interviews that Sarrett conducted with officially diagnosed autistic individuals). The main reason why self-diagnosis is considered reliable is that someone with the condition knows the condition in a way that someone without the condition does not (Sarrett, 2016, p. 30). This means the self-diagnosing individual has a level of epistemic authority which the official diagnostician lacks. Therefore, someone with the condition is in a better position to judge that they have the condition compared to an outside observer, including medical professionals. A related issue is that the self-diagnosing individual has access to information which is not accessible within a clinical setting. As one autistic individual writes, 'lived experience is more important and complex than clinical assessment' (unnamed autistic individual quoted in Sarrett, 2016, p. 31).

The main reason why self-diagnosis is considered unreliable is that accurate diagnosis is believed to require trained professionals (Sarrett, 2016, p. 27). There is also a concern over self-bias in self-diagnosis. An individual who thinks they have a condition might subconsciously start looking for traits which are not present. This could lead an individual to self-diagnose when they do not meet the diagnostic criteria (Sarrett, 2016, p. 28). An individual might wish to receive a diagnosis because of possible state benefits (Sarrett, 2016, p. 29) or because they think they will feel special (Sarrett, 2016, p. 29). Another potential concern stems from the belief that an individual needs to have a certain level of disability to have a psychiatric diagnosis. This could mean that anyone with that level of disability would have been spotted by medical professionals (Sarrett, 2016, p. 28).

It is important to demarcate between two different approaches to self-diagnosis. Firstly, self-diagnosis can relate to official diagnostic criteria found in the DSM or ICD. A self-diagnosing individual might be better able to establish whether they meet the official diagnostic criteria than a professional diagnostician is able to. For example, the DSM criteria for autism include an intensely focused interest on specific topics. Stereotypical examples of this would be an intensely focused interest on transport or computers. However, some argue that these stereotypical examples are much closer to how some white Western male autistic individuals exhibit intense interests. In contrast, some autistic girls might instead focus more on ponies or boy bands (Moseley, Hitchiner, and Kirby, 2018, p. 2). Consequently, a diagnostician might look for stereotypical notions of autism and consequently miss the way in which an autistic female presents as autistic. In contrast, an autistic female who self-diagnoses might not be influenced by inaccurate stereotypes of autism and thus accurately judge that they are autistic. On this approach the DSM or ICD is taken as providing the standard and the relevant question is whether the diagnostician or the self-diagnosing individual is more likely to accurately assess whether the individual meets the DSM or ICD diagnostic criteria.

Secondly, self-diagnosis can relate to rejecting official diagnostic criteria. For example, the self-diagnosing individual recognises that they do not meet the official diagnostic criteria in the DSM or ICD, but they still consider themselves to have the condition. They consider the official diagnostic criteria to be in some way flawed. The self-diagnosing individual believes they have superior knowledge of at least one psychiatric condition in at least one manner when compared to the DSM and ICD. There is at least one way in which the psychiatric condition can manifest itself which official diagnostic criteria fail to capture but which the self-diagnosing individual has accurately captured. The dispute between the self-diagnosing individual and a potential diagnostician is not about whether the individual meets the official diagnostic criteria but what the correct diagnostic criteria should be.

My argument is applicable to both approaches but will only give examples in relation to the first approach. Presumably, those who reject the DSM still posit that there exist multiple diagnoses and self-diagnosing individuals still need to work out which of those diagnoses they fit. They just reject the notion that the way to diagnose and demarcate between different diagnoses is through consulting the DSM. I focus upon the first approach because I can draw upon detailed empirical examples. To provide examples of how my argument applies to the second approach I would need detailed information of the way in which self-diagnosing individuals alter the diagnostic criteria of multiple diagnoses. To my knowledge, no publication outlines this.

3. The Problem of Alternative Diagnoses

I now consider how self-diagnosing individuals need to consider a range of diagnoses for self-diagnosis to be accurate. Almost all currently employed psychiatric diagnoses cover overlapping symptoms (Kendell & Jablensky, 2003, p. 6; Zachar, 2014, p. 113). Some symptoms on the diagnostic criteria for a particular diagnosis will be present on the diagnostic criteria for a different diagnosis. Diagnoses with symptoms that are exclusive to that diagnosis are extremely rare. I now provide a specific empirical example of how this could occur. I show the similarity and nuanced differences between the diagnoses of autism, schizoid personality disorder, and schizotypal personality disorder.

I first compare autism with schizotypal personality disorder and then consider schizoid personality disorder. The diagnostic criteria of both autism and schizotypal personality disorder include social differences. Both autistic individuals and schizoid personality disorder individuals relate to others in ways which are atypical. They are both considered to struggle in most social situations. Also, both can exhibit restricted and repetitive activities. In these regards, there are significant overlaps between them. They are mainly demarcated by what are known as the positive symptoms of schizophrenia. Schizotypal personality disorder is considered to be on the schizophrenia spectrum. It has some of the positive symptoms of schizophrenia, i.e., the symptoms of schizophrenia which are additional characteristics compared to what typical people exhibit, such as ideas of reference (incorrectly thinking events have significance for themselves), magical thinking, interest in superstition and paranormal phenomena, and paranoid beliefs (as opposed to negative symptoms where characteristics which are usually present in a typical person is absent in the schizophrenic individual) (APA, 2013, p. 656). However, schizotypal personality disorder lacks the hallucinations which are typically present in individuals with schizophrenia.

There are, however, significant complexities in how autism and schizotypal personality disorder overlap and how they are distinct. Firstly, they both have social communication differences. However, there appears to be differences in how and why social behaviour and communication manifest. For example,

> SPD [schizotypal personality disorder] criteria include odd speech that is vague, circumstantial, and metaphorical whereas AD [autism] criteria focus on problematic non-vocal communicative behaviors. While both AD and SPD appear to have communication deficits, the modifiers for SPD odd speech (vague, circumstantial, metaphorical, overelaborate) suggest a highly developed, though disordered, expressive vocal repertoire while the AD criteria suggest a disordered repertoire related to understanding body language. (Hurst *et al.*, 2007, p. 1712)

Also, 'there is an overlap between Asperger [stereotypically considered higher functioning autism] and Schizotypal traits in the expected areas; i.e., social overlaps with interpersonal and communication overlaps with disorganized [but there was less strong overlaps in other areas]' (Hurst *et al.*, 2007, p. 1718).

Secondly, they both have restricted and repetitive behavioural differences. However, there seem to be differences between these because 'repetitive-restricted behaviors domain includes verbal behavior in SPD (e.g., stereotyped thinking and speech), whereas AD criteria include stereotypic, repetitive, inflexible, and persistent patterns of behavior without reference to speech or thinking' (Hurst *et al.*, 2007, p. 1713).

Thirdly, autism and schizotypal personality disorder are demarcated by some of the positive symptoms of schizophrenia. However, '[c]riteria unique to schizotypal PD are those related to psychotic-like experiences and magic thinking, which may well be present in people with PDD/ASD [autism], although not among the core features' (Lugnegård, Hallerbäck, and Gillberg, 2012, p. 337; see also Ford & Crewther, 2014, p. 2).

Whilst they do not appear to be identical, there can be great difficulty in demarcating between autism from schizotypal personality disorder. Two quotes highlight the difficulties of demarcating between them.

> There may be great difficulty differentiating children with schizotypal personality disorder from the heterogeneous group of solitary, odd children whose behaviour is characterized by marked social isolation, eccentricity, or peculiarities of language and whose diagnoses would probably include milder forms of autism spectrum disorders. [DSM-5] (APA, 2013, p. 658)

> [...] it may be that at some point in the developmental course of the two disorders [autism and schizotypal], they may appear almost identical, and in fact, individuals on the two spectra who become "stuck" within this behaviorally similar period may never be able to be differentiated based upon behavioral tests, alone. (Hurst *et al.*, 2007, p. 1719)

I now consider schizoid personality disorder. Schizoid personality disorder is, like schizotypal personality disorder, also considered to be on the schizophrenia spectrum. Schizoid personality disorder differs from schizotypal personality disorder by lacking the positive symptoms of schizophrenia. Thus, both autism and schizoid personality disorder are demarcated in the DSM from schizotypal personality disorder by a lack of magical thinking and odd beliefs (APA, 2013, p. 655) though, as mentioned above, these can be present in autism. Autism and schizoid personality disorder are demarcated by autism having more pronounced social communication difference and more pronounced stereotyped behaviour (APA, 2013, p. 655).

Firstly, autism and schizoid personality disorder both share social communication differences. However, it appears that both differ in how social differences present themselves and what causes them. Autistic individuals often want to socialise but seem to lack an intuitive social sense which is typically employed in social situations. Also, they struggle to read unconscious body language. As such they often struggle in social situations even though many often want to engage in socialising. In contrast, schizoid personality disorder individuals are often taken as having social skills in principle but often choose not to engage in socialising. This can involve a simple lack of desire to socialise but can also relate to not receiving much experientially from socialising, much like how individuals with schizoid personality disorder can often feel little from bodily contact and sexual activity. However, these demarcations between each diagnosis are not clear-cut. It is also well known that some autistic individuals are content with not socialising in principle, as opposed to choosing not to

Sam Fellowes

socialise because they find it difficult. Also, autistic individuals sometimes have both hyper (excessive) and hypo (weak) sensitivity which can lead to socialising being unfulfilling independent of problems caused by innate lack of typical social intuition. Additionally, autistic people often have quite specific interests and are often bored by typical conversations, especially by small talk. This again seems to occur independently of any innate lack of typical social intuition. Finally, whilst schizoid personality disorder individuals may not desire to socialise, their lack of experience at socialising may lead to reduced social skills when they actually attempt to socialise.

Secondly, the repetitive and restricted behaviour in autism is typically quite pervasive, whereas it is typically more delineated in schizoid personality disorder. Autistic repetitive and restricted behaviour covers phenomena like disliking unexpected changes, desire for routines and narrowly circumscribed but intense interests. In contrast, individuals with schizoid personality disorder will typically prefer solitary hobbies which may result in them engaging in more uniform behaviour compared to engaging in non-solitary hobbies which may involve more dynamically changing situations. Also, there can be elements of repetitive and restricted behaviour in relation to thought and speech. For example, 'the stereotyped thinking and speech, a clinical feature observed in patients with schizoid personality disorder, may be taken as "rigid"' (Sugihara, Tsuchiya, and Takei, 2008, p. 1998). However, the demarcation is not clear-cut. Many autistic individuals will also prefer solitary rather than social activities. Also, repetitive thoughts are also common in autistic individuals (same thought reoccurring), but rigid thoughts do not appear to be higher than non-autistic controls (number of different topics of thought) (Cooper et al., 2022, p. 856). Both autism and schizoid personality disorder seem to have repetitive and restrictive aspects but there are both similarities and differences in form.

These similarities mean that it can be difficult to demarcate between autism and schizoid personality disorder in a diagnostic context. These two quotes highlight this:

> There may be great difficulty differentiating individuals with schizoid personality disorder from those with milder forms of autism spectrum disorder. [DSM-5] (APA, 2013, p. 655)

> Children with Asperger's were indistinguishable from "loner" (parent rated schizoid personality traits) children on a schizoid scale (49) suggesting potential misclassification of schizoid PD as Asperger's disorder due to comorbid schizoid trait in "loner" and Asperger's Children. (Ford & Crewther, 2014, p. 3)

62

4. Self-Diagnosing Individuals and Multiple Diagnoses

I have given a detailed example of how autism is demarcated from two other diagnoses in nuanced and subtle ways. I now relate this general issue to self-diagnosis. Do self-diagnosing individuals consider a range of diagnoses when self-diagnosing? Are they aware that some diagnoses are differentiated from each another only in subtle and nuanced ways? Are there any factors that might increase or decrease this awareness? Are they able to apply these subtle and nuanced distinctions to themselves when self-diagnosing? Unfortunately, there is extremely limited empirical data on these questions, but I shall draw upon what is available in the academic literature.

Firstly, a few papers have empirically investigated individuals who self-diagnose as autistic, but none mention those self-diagnosing individuals investigating a range of diagnoses. In relation to individuals who self-diagnose as autistic, 'the more they learned about ASD, the more confident they became in their self-diagnosis' (Lewis, 2017, p. 577) and 'the more they learned about ASD, the less they could doubt their own belief that they had ASD' (Lewis, 2017, p. 577). Similarly, '[m]ost self-diagnosed autistic adults find that, after learning about and researching autism, they have the self-awareness to state confidence in having autism' (Sarrett, 2016, p. 30). These three quotes relate to learning the diagnostic criteria of autism, rather than gaining in confidence when they learned the diagnostic criteria of autism *and also other diagnoses*. Indeed, neither Sarrett (2016) or Lewis (2016, 2017), who both interviewed individuals self-diagnosing as autistic, ever mention a self-diagnosing individual considering any diagnosis other than autism. The notion that an individual has or has not consulted all the relevant diagnoses that they need for accurate self-diagnosis is simply not mentioned in either paper, either by the interviewed participants or the authors of the paper. If the vast majority of individuals who self-diagnose as autistic not only investigate multiple diagnoses but also do so in a manner that appreciates the subtle and nuanced distinctions that I grasped through reading multiple scientific studies, then it is surprising that none of the four empirical papers on self-diagnosis of autism contain even a single sentence mentioning this.

Secondly, portrayals of psychiatric diagnoses have been studied on social media. A recent study looked at the hundred most popular videos on ADHD on TikTok (some exclusion criteria were applied). These videos had a combined total of 283,459,400 views. The study considered 52 of those 100 videos as misleading, with the other 48 videos classified as either useful or personal experience.

Crucially, for my purposes of considering how self-diagnosing individuals relate to multiple diagnoses, '[o]f the 52 misleading videos, 37 videos (71%) misattributed transdiagnostic psychiatric symptoms as being specific only to ADHD, including anxiety, depression, anger, relationship conflicts, dissociation, and mood swings' (Yeung, Ng, and Abi-Jaoude, 2022, p. 91). If this claim is true, then it raises the concern that people who view this content might mistakenly take various behaviours to be instances of ADHD rather than as potentially indicative of a range of conditions. However, even assuming this paper accurately assesses those videos, it only indirectly and tentatively provides evidence about self-diagnosis. We lack information about how many people who self-diagnose with ADHD view such content and how many of those people then believe such content to be reliable. We also lack information about how much reliable information on ADHD they come across and how they weigh inaccurate social media portrayals against accurate information about ADHD. I can only suggest that anyone significantly influenced by such social media posts might have reduced ability to recognise that multiple diagnoses may refer to broadly similar symptoms but are actually demarcated by nuanced and subtle differences.

Another recent study interviews people who view mental health content on TikTok. The article discussed multiple diagnoses, including ADHD, bipolar, and PTSD. Some interviewed individuals were concerned that 'many content creators chase social prestige and vitality, or clout' (Milton *et al.*, 2023, p. 2) through content which described their experience of mental health. This raised the concern that some content creators had self-diagnosed with the conscious or unconscious motive of creating content rather than because they genuinely believed they exhibited the condition. At the same time, the interviewed individuals were concerned about their ability to adequately judge who was faking and who was genuine, showing that at least some individuals who consume mental health content on TikTok are critically reflecting upon the content they see. Another recent paper, which did not interview any social media users, expressed these concerns in a much stronger fashion. It claims that in social media spaces

> [mental health] identities or personas can be claimed at will [...] social and emotional resonances may amplify and reinforce identification with the persona and may even predict later behaviors in line with it [and] may increase the likelihood that the "self-diagnosed" identity is reified and incorporated into one's self-concept. (Haltigan, Pringsheim, and Rajkumar, 2023, p. 5)

My mental health social media experience mainly consists of running an academic account on Twitter, so I am not in a position to judge the accuracy of this claim. Also, even if this is true then there is still the issue of the degree in which such content influences viewers who self-diagnose. I can only suggest that if some individuals who self-diagnose are influenced by social media content produced by individuals who falsely present themselves as having a particular condition, then this could reduce recognition that different diagnoses can appear to cover the same symptoms but that each diagnosis actually has nuanced and subtle differences.

None of the evidence I have offered is conclusive, but I also believe this evidence cannot simply be dismissed. I think it gives us good reason to seek more empirical data on these and related issues, rather than that it shows that we have sufficient empirical data from which we can draw strong conclusions. Also, some of this evidence might be partly true, but this does not then indicate the degree of partial truth. Imagine if the majority of self-diagnosing individuals avoided the above problems, but not all did. This is compatible with, say, 5%, 15%, or 30% of self-diagnosing individuals being significantly influenced by problematic information. Rather than making any firm judgments, I will outline a further factor that could make self-diagnosing individuals less likely to consider multiple diagnoses.

5. Public Awareness of Different Diagnoses Differs Significantly

A significant factor likely influencing which diagnoses someone considers when self-diagnosing is the level of public awareness of different diagnoses. Psychiatric diagnoses differ significantly in how greatly they enter public consciousness. They mainly enter public consciousness through various forms of media. They vary in how often they are mentioned in news articles, how greatly they feature in films or TV programmes, or how often they are mentioned on social media. This can be influenced by many different factors. Diagnoses vary in the degree that symptoms of the condition are observable or prominent, the degree a diagnosis has positive or negative associations, the degree of advocacy relating to the diagnosis, and the degree the relevant condition is present in the population. I shall highlight this by drawing again upon my examples of autism and both schizoid and schizotypal personality disorder.

Sam Fellowes

Autism is typically considered less disabling. The neurodiversity movement has highlighted positive elements of autism. There are many publications where diagnosed autistic individuals claim that autism is either not a bad thing or is a good thing (for example, Kapp, 2020; Walker, 2021). Schizoid and schizotypal personality disorder have more negative associations due to their associations with schizophrenia and the notion of a disordered personality. I cannot locate a single paper relating schizoid or schizotypal personality disorder to neurodiversity. Many people would prefer to think of themselves as having a neurological difference or being neurodivergent rather than being disordered or diseased (which conditions should be considered divergences rather than disordered, and whether this distinction is sustainable, is not an issue I comment upon here).

The level of advocacy is much higher for autism compared to schizoid and schizotypal personality disorder. A glance at social media reveals this. For example, the number of tweets when putting #autism into the search box on Twitter is typically over a hundred times higher over the same time period compared to putting #schizoid, #schizoidpersonalitydisorder, or #schizoidpd into that search box. The same is true in relation to #schizotypal, #schizotypalpersonalitydisorder or #schizotypalpd.

There have been multiple television programmes relating to autism. Putting the phrase 'best tv programmes about autism' (not in quotation marks) into a search engine produces multiple websites listing the latest must-see programmes or films about autism. The same is not true when doing this in relation to either schizoid or schizotypal personality disorder.

Putting the words 'autism advocacy' (not in quotation marks) into Google Scholar produces many papers either discussing autism advocacy or papers engaging in autism advocacy. A similar result occurs when putting in the phrase 'autistic campaign' or the phrase 'autistic culture'. It is easy to find multiple relevant websites relating to campaigning for social change in relation to autism and in relation to producing an autistic culture. Finding similar papers or websites for either schizoid or schizotypal personality disorder is much harder.

Most symptoms of autism are more prominent compared to schizoid or schizotypal personality disorder. Autism typically (though not always) involves individuals who seek social contact whereas the latter two involves individuals who often avoid social contact. Additionally, much of the repetitive and restrictive behaviour of autism relates to physical actions whereas some of the repetitive and restrictive behaviour of schizoid and schizotypal personality disorder relates to speech or thought processes.

It is unclear how common autism is compared to schizoid or schizotypal personality disorder. Autism is estimated to occur in between 1% to slightly under 2% of the population. According to the DSM-5 schizoid personality disorder is estimated to occur in 3.1% to 4.9% of the population (APA, 2013, p. 654) and schizoid personality disorder is estimated to occur in 0.6% to 4.6% of the population (APA, 2013, p. 657). A review of prevalence figures for schizoid personality disorder mentions 1.7%, 0.9%, 0.8%, 4.9%, and 0.6%, and mentions for schizotypal personality disorder 0.6%, 0.6%, 0.06%, 3.3%, and 0.6% (Samuals, 2011, p. 225). I will now consider the consequences of diagnoses varying in public awareness.

6. The Consideration of Multiple Diagnoses and Inaccurate Self-Diagnosis

I now consider how public awareness of different diagnoses may influence self-diagnosis. Firstly, an individual may only investigate some, rather than all, of the conditions that they have the symptoms of. They might not have heard of some conditions they have symptoms of. If they have heard of a condition they might not know enough about the condition, or their information about the condition is too restricted by inaccurate stereotypes to realise they should investigate the condition. They may thus not investigate a psychiatric condition even though they meet its diagnostic criteria. Also, an individual might consider multiple diagnoses, but spend significantly more effort considering some of those diagnoses and less considering others. The individual might feel, for example, after only superficial investigation of each, that they fit one diagnosis better than the other. Consequently, they only focus upon one of those diagnoses and ultimately self-diagnose with one of them when they also meet the diagnostic criteria of the other ones. Additionally, the individual may consider multiple diagnoses and realise they meet the diagnostic criteria of multiple diagnoses. However, they feel that one diagnosis fully accounts for them, so only self-diagnose with one of those diagnoses without realising they can simultaneously be diagnosed with both diagnoses.

Secondly, imagine an individual misunderstands which symptoms they exhibit. They might believe that they exhibit particular symptoms whereas actually they exhibit different symptoms. Based upon the symptoms they believe they exhibit the individual self-diagnoses with one diagnosis. However, when measured by the symptoms the individual actually exhibits, they do not meet the diagnostic criteria of that diagnosis but they do meet the diagnostic criteria of another diagnosis. This possibility has been highlighted when I considered the way in which some symptoms of autism only differ from some symptoms of schizoid or schizotypal personality disorder in nuanced ways. Some symptoms have significant similarities but also some nuanced differences in how they manifest themselves and in the causes for why those symptoms occur.

Thirdly, an individual might accurately assess which symptoms they have, but does not accurately understand the diagnostic criteria of the diagnoses that they do consider. They misunderstand some of the symptoms mentioned on the diagnostic criteria. They incorrectly take themselves as either exhibiting or not exhibiting a symptom of a particular condition based upon misunderstanding the text in the DSM or ICD even though they correctly understand which symptoms they themselves exhibit. For example, an individual accurately assesses that they have repetitive behaviour but fails to realise their repetitive behaviour is closer to the repetitive behaviour associated with one diagnosis than to the repetitive behaviour of another diagnosis because they misunderstand the DSM. This possibility has been highlighted when I considered how there are subtle and nuanced specific differences between some symptoms of autism and some symptoms of either schizoid or schizotypal personality disorder. It is not immediately clear how, based upon the DSM and ICD descriptions, some symptoms listed in the diagnostic criteria for autism differ from some symptoms listed in the diagnostic criteria for schizoid or schizotypal personality disorder. I have drawn on additional psychological or psychiatric literature to highlight the similarities and differences between autism and schizoid and schizotypal personality disorder. This information is not available when simply consulting the DSM and ICD.

I now consider how misdiagnosis can influence social resources that are accessible to both officially diagnosed individuals and self-diagnosed individuals.

7. Self-Diagnosis and the Distribution of Social Resources

I now outline five different social resources. These are social resources in the sense that they all involve engaging with other individuals in a manner that can directly or indirectly improve the well-being of diagnosed individuals.

Firstly, diagnosed individuals can form political advocacy movements. They can argue for increased inclusion through greater understanding of the diagnosis, societal acceptance, or reasonable accommodations. The lives of diagnosed individuals can be improved through changing society (Botha *et al.*, 2022; Ortega, 2013).

Secondly, diagnosed individuals can advocate for more support services and more suitable support services. They can highlight what beneficial support would consist of and then argue existing support is insufficient or even harmful. Improved services could lead to improved lives for diagnosed people (Botha *et al.*, 2022; Ortega, 2013).

Thirdly, diagnosed individuals can advocate for participatory research relating to their diagnosis. They can demand that research on their condition includes diagnosed individuals when setting research topics, designing experiments, and interpreting results. This could potentially improve scientific research and prevent harmful scientific research being done (Buter, 2019; Tekin, 2022).

Fourthly, diagnosed individuals can form part of a diagnostic culture. They can produce art, literature, and media relating to people with a particular diagnosis or relating to people with psychiatric diagnoses in general. This is a means of celebrating an alternative way of living and producing cultural products that people who feel alienated by mainstream culture can potentially relate to (Jaarsma & Welin, 2012; Runswick-Cole, 2014). Note that all these four social resources can benefit a diagnosed individual even if they choose not to be involved in them; for example, successful advocacy could improve services for all autistic people including those who do not take part in the activism.

Finally, individuals with the same diagnosis can find commonalities among one another (Abel *et al.*, 2019; Botha *et al.*, 2022). They can have shared symptoms, shared problems in daily living, and shared interests. This can lead to opportunities to socialising, an important factor given how many people with diagnosed conditions can be very isolated. Even where individuals dislike socialising, they can still engage in online interactions which allows the sharing of information and stories that can enhance self-understanding. Unlike the other four social resources, a diagnosed individual themselves needs to engage in these interactions to benefit from them.

Each of these social resources can exist in a form in which they are not tied to a particular diagnosis or are tied to a particular diagnosis. Some advocacy involves people with different diagnoses working together on a collective aim. However, significant amounts of advocacy are based around people with a particular diagnosis advocating for that diagnosis (McCoy *et al.*, 2020; Seidel, 2020). This is partly because people with a particular diagnosis are considered to have some level of expertise on their own diagnosis. Similarly, some productions of a culture focus on mental health or neurodiversity in general, but some also focus upon specific diagnoses as a particular way of living (Jaarsma & Welin, 2012; Runswick-Cole, 2014). Finally, there are many support groups and internet forums that focus upon a particular diagnosis rather than on psychiatric diagnoses or mental health in general (Abel *et al.*, 2019; Botha *et al.*, 2022).

I now suggest that inaccurate self-diagnosis alters the strength of social resources in relation to particular diagnoses. Each social resource can be performed in a manner that is tied to a specific diagnosis, such as autistic people advocating for autism or autistic people producing an autistic culture. When social resources are tied to particular diagnoses, then the more people who have that diagnosis strengthens the social resource in relation to that diagnosis (strictly speaking, this increase in social resources is probabilistic, so that more people with the diagnosis means more people to engage in these social resources even though not everyone with the diagnosis does engage in the social resources). Both officially diagnosed people and self-diagnosed people can alter the strength of these social resources because both have access to these social resources. The first three resources, those related to different forms of advocacy, are strengthened when more people are involved in advocacy. As such, the greater the number of people with the diagnosis means a greater number of people who may choose to get involved in advocacy. The final two, that of diagnostic cultures and finding commonalities, are also strengthened when more people have the diagnosis because more cultural products are being produced and more chance of interacting with someone with that same diagnosis.

Individuals self-diagnosing, rather than receiving an official diagnosis, can change the number of individuals who have a particular diagnosis. I have outlined how psychiatric diagnoses can overlap with one another and how different diagnoses only differ from one another in nuanced and subtle ways. I have suggested also that public awareness of diagnoses can influence how people self-diagnose when symptoms of different diagnoses overlap with one another. This then means, when measured by the DSM, that someone who self-diagnoses can misdiagnose themselves with a diagnosis of which there is greater public awareness. This then strengthens the social resources in relation to that diagnosis. Meanwhile, this person is not diagnosed with the diagnosis that they actually do fit but of which there is less public awareness. This means that the social resources for the diagnosis that they actually fit are not increased.

Though these are not the only relevant factors, public awareness is significantly related to the strength of the social resources. Stronger social resources help generate public awareness. As such, misdiagnosis risks increasing the strength of the social resources of diagnoses which already have relatively strong social resources, while diagnoses with weaker social resources do not have their social resources made stronger.

This results in a redistribution of the strength of these social resources when compared to accurate diagnosis. People diagnosed with the condition of which there is greater public awareness have the social resources related to this condition strengthened, whereas people diagnosed with the condition of which there is less public awareness do not have their social resources strengthened. This raises important questions about the ideal distribution of social resources in relation to different diagnoses, and about who should decide the relative strength of the social resources for each condition. These important ethical questions will, I hope, be further discussed by bioethicists. I have only sought to show how inaccurate self-diagnosis can alter the strength of social resources related to different conditions, but plausibly there is something unfair about the strength of the social resources being increased for one condition rather than another because one condition is more well known. Also, it seems unfair that conditions that already have relatively strong social resources have higher probability of getting those resources strengthened further compared to diagnoses with relatively weak social resources.

8. Counterargument: Self-Diagnosis Can Be Beneficial Even When Inaccurate

I shall briefly consider whether inaccurate self-diagnosis is beneficial or harmful for the self-diagnosing individual. Psychiatric diagnoses can potentially increase self-understanding (in relation to autism (see Fellowes, 2022; Ortega, 2013). How this relates to inaccurate self-diagnosis is a neglected area of study. It could be argued that self-understanding relates to the symptoms an individual believes they exhibit rather than to the diagnosis. Therefore, two individuals who believe themselves to have the same symptoms will have the same self-understanding even if one self-diagnosed as autistic and the other self-diagnosed as schizoid personality disorder. However, it has been argued that self-understanding provided by psychiatric diagnoses relates less to the particular symptoms an individual considers themselves to have and more to the connotations of psychiatric diagnosis decontextualised away from particular symptom presentation (Fellowes, 2022). Two individuals with identical symptoms will gain different self-understanding if one self-diagnosed as autistic and the other self-diagnosed with schizoid personality disorder. In this situation inaccurate diagnosis might have a more detrimental effect on self-understanding. This issue merits future research. Another area of benefit or harm is how diagnoses vary in the degree of their negative connotations. As such, it could be argued on practical and ethical grounds that inaccurately self-diagnosing with a diagnosis that has positive connotations is beneficial compared to accurately diagnosing with a diagnosis that has negative connotations.

However, benefits to the individual need be weighed against any consequences for the distribution of social resources. Whether the benefits to individuals who inaccurately self-diagnose outweigh any negative consequences from changes to social resources is an ethical question which requires dedicated ethical discussion. In this article I highlight the injustice; I hope this prompts discussion by bioethicists about how best to resolve or balance conflicts between the benefit to one and the harms to another.

9. Counterargument: Official Diagnosis is Also Unreliable

One significant motive for self-diagnosis is that official diagnoses are unreliable. Both those who provide official diagnoses and metal health professionals who are met upon the path towards an official diagnosis may hold misleading views about psychiatric diagnoses. Therefore, official diagnoses result in unfair distribution of social resources.

Like with self-diagnosis, it is also difficult to make generalizations about official diagnosticians and other mental health professionals. They will vary considerably in the degree in which they hold inaccurate stereotypes in relation to any particular diagnosis. For example, one might hold deeply misleading stereotypes in relation to a small number of diagnoses but does not hold any misleading stereotypes in relation to most diagnoses, whereas another might hold misleading stereotypes in relation to almost every diagnosis, but the stereotypes are only slightly misleading in relation to each of those diagnoses. I do not know what percentage of official diagnosticians and medical professionals hold misleading stereotypes, which diagnoses are more likely to be misleadingly stereotyped, or the degree in which any misleading stereotypes which are held are completely false, partly false, or slightly false.

However, the key issue is that the vast majority of official diagnosticians and mental health professionals will have awareness of a significant range of diagnoses. Throughout their training and clinical work they will learn about a variety of diagnoses and meet people with a variety of conditions. Many will likely not have equal familiarity or understanding of all the hundreds of diagnoses in the DSM. Neither will they consider (with justification or not) each of those diagnoses to have equal scientific or clinical legitimacy. However, they are likely to have a baseline awareness of a significant range of diagnoses in a manner in which it might not be present in many self-diagnosing individuals.

10. Conclusion

Self-diagnosis is a topic which generates considerable controversy. There is, unfortunately, limited empirical data on self-diagnosis. Also, the process and the reliability of self-diagnosis may vary considerably across different diagnoses. In this paper, I have outlined how different diagnoses can overlap with one another. Also, I have outlined how they are differentiated in subtle and nuanced ways. I then suggested how the degree of public awareness of different diagnoses may influence self-diagnosis. When self-diagnosing, people are generally more likely to consider diagnoses which have greater levels of public awareness. Also, public awareness can influence how someone interprets themselves and interprets the DSM. There are also concerns about reliability of official diagnosticians, but any responsible official diagnostician will have working knowledge of a range of diagnoses.

I have suggested that inaccurate self-diagnosis can result in altered distribution of social resources. Social resources can be strengthened in relation to a diagnosis when more people have that diagnosis. As such, inaccurate self-diagnosis results in the social resources for one diagnosis being strengthened whilst not being strengthened in relation to another diagnosis in comparison to accurate official diagnosis. This article aims to show this to be a significant possibility and suggests that we need consider whether this is unfair to people who are diagnosed with less well-known conditions.

Some consequences follow from my argument. Firstly, I have raised important bioethical questions about what constitutes a fair distribution of social resources and who should decide on that distribution. These merit further investigation. Secondly, the very few existing empirical studies of individuals who self-diagnose have not outlined the degree to which self-diagnosing individuals consider multiple diagnoses. This seems an important area for future empirical studies. Thirdly, if the concerns I raise are genuine, then this gives further good reason to end the problems that lead people to self-diagnose. If there were not such long waiting lists for diagnostic assessment, if some people did not face such high financial costs getting a diagnostic assessment, and if diagnosticians did not sometimes hold inaccurate stereotypes in relation to diagnoses, then the problem I raise would largely disappear. My argument thus provides an additional reason for our society to remove these and related issues that lead people to self-diagnose.

References

Susan Abel, Tanya Machin, and Charlotte Brownlow, 'Support, Socialise and Advocate: An Exploration of the Stated Purposes of Facebook Autism Groups', *Research in Autism Spectrum Disorders*, 61 (2019), 10–21.

APA. *Diagnostic and Statistical Manual of Mental Disorders* (5th ed.), (Washington, DC: American Psychiatric Association, 2013).

Monique Botha, Bridget Dibb, and David M Frost, '"It's Being a Part of a Grand tradition, a Grand Counter-Culture which Involves Communities": A Qualitative Investigation of Autistic Community Connectedness', *Autism*, 26:8 (2022), 2151–64.

Anke Buter, 'Epistemic Injustice and Psychiatric Classification', *Philosophy of Science*, 86 (2019), 1064–74.

Kate Cooper, Ailsa Russell, Steph Calley, Huilin Chen, Jaxon Kramer, and Bas Verplanken, 'Cognitive Processes in Autism: Repetitive Thinking in Autistic versus Non-Autistic Adults', *Autism*, 26:4 (2022), 849–58.

Sam Fellowes, 'The Value of Categorical Polythetic Diagnoses in Psychiatry', *The British Journal for the Philosophy of Science*, 73:4 (2022), 941–63.

Talitha C. Ford and David P. Crewther, 'Factor Analysis Demonstrates a Common Schizoidal Phenotype within Autistic and Schizotypal Tendency: Implications for Neuroscientific Studies', *Frontiers in Psychiatry*, 5:117 (2014), 1–11.

John D. Haltigan, Tamara M. Pringsheim, and Gayathiri Rajkumar, 'Social Media as an Incubator of Personality and Behavioral Psychopathology: Symptom and Disorder Authenticity or

Psychosomatic Social Contagion?', *Comprehensive Psychiatry*, 121 (2023), 1–5.

Ruth M. Hurst, Rosemery O. Nelson-Gray, John T. Mitchell, and Thomas R. Kwapil, 'The Relationship of Asperger's Characteristics and Schizotypal Personality Traits in a Non-Clinical Adult Sample', *Journal of Autism and Developmental Disorders*, 37 (2007), 1711–20.

Pier Jaarsma and Stellan Welin, 'Autism as a Natural Human Variation: Reflections on the Claims of the Neurodiversity Movement', *Health Care Analysis*, 20 (2012), 20–30.

Steven Kapp, 'Introduction', in Steven Kapp (ed.), *Autistic Community and the Neurodiversity Movement* (Singapore: Palgrave Macmillan, 2020), 1–19.

Robert Kendell and Assen Jablensky, 'Distinguishing between the Validity and Utility of Psychiatric Diagnosis', *American Journal of Psychiatry*, 35 (2003), 139–44.

Laura Foran Lewis, 'Exploring the Experience of Self-Diagnosis of Autism Spectrum Disorder in Adults', *Archives of Psychiatric Nursing*, 30 (2016), 575–80.

Laura Foran Lewis, 'A Mixed Methods Study of Barriers to Formal Diagnosis of Autism Spectrum Disorder in Adults', *Journal of Autism and Developmental Disorders*, 47 (2017), 2410–24.

Tove Lugnegård, Maria Unenge Hallerbäck, and Christopher Gillberg, 'Personality Disorders and Autism Spectrum Disorders: What are the Connections?', *Comprehensive Psychiatry*, 53 (2012), 333–40.

Matthew S. McCoy, Emily Y. Liu, Amy S. F. Lutz, and Dominic Sisti, 'Ethical Advocacy across the Autism Spectrum: Beyond Partial Representation', *American Journal of Bioethics*, 20:4 (2020), 13–24.

T.A.M. McDonald, 'Autism Identity and the "Lost Generation": Structural Validation of the Autism Spectrum Identity Scale and Comparison of Diagnosed and Self-Diagnosed Adults on the Autism Spectrum', *Autism in Adulthood*, 2:1 (2020), 13–23.

Ashlee Milton, Leah Ajmani, Michael Ann DeVito, and Steve Chancellor, '"I See Me Here": Mental Health Content, Community, and Algorithmic Curation on TikTok', *Proceedings of the 2023 CHI Conference on Human Factors in Computing Systems,* (2023), 1–7.

Rachel Moseley, Rachael Hitchiner, and Julie A. Kirkby, 'Self-Reported Sex differences in High-Functioning Adults with Autism: A Meta-Analysis', *Molecular Autism*, 9:33 (2018), 1–12.

Franciso Ortega, 'Cerebralizing Autism within the Neurodiversity Movement', in Joyce Davidson and Micheal Orsini (eds.), *Worlds of Autism* (Minneapolis: University of Minnesota Press, 2013).

Katherine Runswick-Cole, '"Us" and "Them": The Limits and Possibilities of a "Politics of Neurodiversity" in Neoliberal Times', *Disability & Society*, 29:7 (2014), 1117–29.

Jack Samuals, 'Personality Disorders: Epidemiology and Public Health Issues', *International Review of Psychiatry*, 23:3 (2011), 223–33.

Jennifer C. Sarrett, 'Biocertification and Neurodiversity: The Role and Implications of Self-Diagnosis in Autistic Community', *Neuroethics*, 9 (2016), 23–36.

Kathleen Seidel, 'Neurodiversity.Com: A Decade of Advocacy', in Steven Kapp (ed.), *Autistic Community and the Neurodiversity Movement* (Singapore: Palgrave Macmillan, 2020), 89–108.

Genichi Sugihara, Kenji J. Tsuchiya, and Nori Takei, 'Distinguishing Broad Autism Phenotype from Schizophrenia-Spectrum Disorders', *Journal of Autism and Developmental Disorders*, 38 (2008), 1998–9.

Şerife Tekin, 'Participatory Interactive Objectivity in Psychiatry', *Philosophy of Science* (2022), 1–20.

Nick Walker, *Neuroqueer Heresies: Notes on the Neurodiversity Paradigm, Autistic Empowerment, and Postnormal Possibilities* (Autonomous Press, 2021).

Anthony Yeung, Enoch Ng, and Elia Abi-Jaoude, 'TikTok and Attention-Deficit/Hyperactivity Disorder: A Cross-Sectional Study of Social Media Content Quality', *Canadian Journal of Psychiatry. Revue Canadienne de Psychiatrie*, 67:12 (2022), 899–906.

Peter Zachar, *A Metaphysics of Psychopathology* (Massachusetts: Massachusetts Institute of Technology Press, 2014).

In Defence of the Concept of Mental Illness

ZSUZSANNA CHAPPELL

Abstract
Many worry about the over-medicalisation of mental illness, and some even argue
that we should abandon the term mental illness altogether. Yet, this is a commonly
used term in popular discourse, in policy making, and in research. In this paper I
argue that if we distinguish between disease, illness, and sickness (where illness
refers to the first-personal, subjective experience of the sufferer), then the concept
of mental illness is a useful way of understanding a type of human experience, inasmuch as the term is (i) apt or accurate, (ii) a useful hermeneutical resource for interpreting and communicating experience, and (iii) can be a good way for at least some
of us to establish a liveable personal identity within our culture.

1. 'There is No Such Thing as Mental Illness'

There is a family of views that argues against using the term mental
illness to describe distressing mental experiences such as deep
sadness, anxiety, or grief.[1] This family of views includes arguments
from anti-psychiatry (Szasz, 1961; Benning, 2016), critical psychiatry
(Double, 2019; Middleton and Moncrieff, 2019) and the survivor/
ex-patient movement (Chamberlin, 1995; Beresford, 2020), and
less well-articulated versions can be encountered in the media, and
in everyday discourse. Since these views are based on a disparate
range of arguments (Chapman, 2023), it is best to characterise them
as a family resemblance group (Wittgenstein, 1953/2009). The com-
monality between them lies in their rejection of the concept *mental
illness*. This is in stark contrast to the recent worldwide prioritisation
of mental health in public health policy (WHO, 2021). According to
the Global Burden of Disease study, mental illnesses are one of the
largest causes of disability worldwide (Vigo *et al.*, 2016; Arias
et al., 2022). Critics are of course still in favour of reducing

---

[1] I will differentiate between mental illness and mental distress
throughout. One can experience mental distress (e.g., grief) without experiencing mental illness. I will also use the term 'health problems' when I am
not referring to illness specifically as a first-personal experience.

doi:10.1017/S1358246123000267　　© The Royal Institute of Philosophy and the contributors 2023 experiences of mental distress,[2] while believing that people's experiences are wrongly medicalised and should not be regarded as illnesses. I will here argue that we should not abandon the term *mental illness* because it is a useful way of understanding a type of human experience, inasmuch as the term is (i) apt or accurate, (ii) a useful hermeneutical resource for interpreting and communicating experience, and (iii) can be a good way for at least some of us to establish a liveable personal identity within contemporary Western social and political culture.

Over the years I have been told many times that I should not identify as someone who lives with mental illness. At first, the idea seemed to be that this was only a phase of life, that I should not medicalise adolescence. Either I was conflating the usual woes of adolescence with mental illness, or I would 'grow out of' youthful mental illness, just as I grew out of childhood car sickness. Later on, I was told that mental illness is not 'real' because it could not be identified on an MRI brain scan. Finally, some people assume that I have the same mental experiences as everyone else, only I am unwilling to deal with them like everybody else.

We could reframe these three examples as follows. Firstly, by referring to mental illness, we are over-medicalising common life experiences, such as adolescence, and confusing them with illness. Secondly, disease is something that is accessible to the (bio)medical gaze, and to the extent that mental illness is difficult to delineate from mental health and has no biomarkers, it is not a fitting subject for medicine. Thirdly, by referring to mental illness, people are looking to excuse either malingering or acting out. Under this heading, what we think of as mental illness may actually be primarily a moral problem, one of bad behaviour, or of weakness of the will. The writings of anti-psychiatrist Thomas Szasz (1961) offer examples of all three of these arguments (Chapman, 2023).

In this paper, I want to put forward a positive counterargument in favour of the concept of *mental illness*. This counterargument also responds to the kinds of objections to calling myself 'mentally ill' that I have just outlined. Ultimately, I believe that it is important that we continue to accept that mental illness experiences do exist and must be named in order to treat people justly or morally, that is to 'treat persons as persons' (Spelman, 1978), especially as a lack of

---

[2] Although arguably some form of emotionally distressing experiences such as disappointment or grief are important to experience (Olberding, 2023).

recognition of their suffering is very threatening to those who suffer (Wilkinson, 2005).

My argument is that there is a phenomenon that we experience as illness-like (section 3), which is *usefully* described as illness-like within our culture (section 4) and that there are people who can benefit from identifying, either personally or socially, as someone having or living with mental illness. In order to do this, I first need to discuss how *illness* contrasts with *disease* and *sickness* (section 2).

2. Introducing the Disease / Illness / Sickness Triad

While it is frequently used in medical sociology and medical anthropology (e.g., Kleinman, 1988), the *disease / illness / sickness* triad is less frequently employed in philosophy (but see Amoretti and Lalumera, 2020, for a great example). *Disease* is a biomedical, theoretical construct that is identified by the medical gaze; *illness* is the subjective experience of lack of health; and *sickness* is the bundle of social responses and attitudes which are provided to someone who is diagnosed with a disease, or is experiencing illness (e.g., Boyd, 2000). I will argue that continuing to view some mental distress as *illness* is worthwhile, as it is a phenomenological concept which describes a type of suffering from the perspective of the sufferer. By contrast, it is the contemporary notions of *disease / disorder*[3] and *sickness* that accompany experiences of mental *illness* that are the appropriate targets of common objections. In many cases, the target of mental illness critics is actually mental disorder and the accompanying sick role, whether this is explicitly stated, as in the case of the 'Drop the Disorder' campaign (Watson, 2019), or not.

Diseases are pathological processes, seen in the medical gaze and communicated through a diagnosis. They are supposed to be objective representations of what has gone wrong with the body. In philosophy of medicine, one of the key questions is how to conceptualise disease (e.g., Bolton, 2008; Bolton & Gillett, 2019; Wakefield, 1992, 2007). *Diagnosis* is the process through which disease is identified in the individual, named, and applied to them. In the clinician-patient interaction, a key role of diagnosis is to offer an understanding of treatment options, and the likely course of the disease (Jutel, 2011). A diagnosis can validate someone's subjective illness experience

---

[3] In the context of psychiatry, the term *disorder* is used instead of *disease*. The two are conceptually similar enough for my purposes and I will use them more or less interchangeably.

publicly by relating it formally to a disease, while the lack of a diagnosis sometimes calls it into question, as in the case of chronic Lyme disease, which does not exist as a recognised disease entity (Dumes, 2020). Receiving a diagnosis of disease or disorder can also unlock sickness benefits and costs, such as access to treatment, sick pay, legitimate demands for rest, or stigma.

The prototype disease in modern medicine remains one which is diagnosable using standardised techniques, has observable biomarkers, is described through measurable deviations from the normal, and has a clear progression (Marinker, 1975). The ideal medical disease requires that a clear disease mechanism is present (Sontag, 2001) and there is a clear cause for dysfunction. This prototype already struggles with chronic illnesses which require long-term care, rather than cure. In general, modern medicine is based on what Rosenberg (2007) calls disease specificity, which is the 'notion that diseases can and should be thought of as entities existing outside the unique manifestations of illness in particular men and women' (p. 13). Medicine (at least at the theoretical level) treats the disease rather than individual symptoms or the individual person (Foucault, 2010).

Disease specificity, clear causal factors, and a known disease mechanism are all problematic for psychiatric disorders. One of the main aims for successive revisions of the Diagnostic and Statistical Manual of Mental Disorders (current edition: DSM-5-TR, APA, 2022) has been to increase inter-rater reliability for disorders between different clinicians to make sure that different psychiatrists give the same diagnosis to a patient (Tsou, 2019). Psychiatric patients often receive multiple diagnoses, and treatment resistance is relatively common. This means that some of the benefits of diagnosis are not always available: including predictability, self-understanding, or the possibility of hope (Jutel, 2011). Psychiatric disorders are also over-determined, making causal mechanisms difficult to establish. Neither do we fully understand how psychopharmacological interventions work. These are just a few of the many reasons why critical psychologists are right to question the usefulness of psychiatric diagnoses even if the extent of psychiatric exceptionalism is frequently overstated (Chapman, 2023).

In reality, in clinical practice it is often sufficient to treat the symptoms without worrying about an accurate diagnosis. Sociologist of medicine Annemarie Jutel (2011, pp. 122–3) illustrates this with a personal anecdote. She had a chronic cough, which her general practitioner couldn't diagnose, despite numerous tests over a period of months. In the end, she was given anti-inflammatory medication to ease her symptoms, which resolved her complaint immediately. She was no longer ill, even though she never received a diagnosis. At the same time, Jutel acknowledges that as her symptom (an incapacitating cough) was both easily observable and clearly undesirable, there was no danger that her illness account would be dismissed. Equally, a lack of objectively diagnosable mental disorder may not always be a problem, as long as treatment through medication and therapy is effective for many people. Problems often start when diagnosis confers problematic *sickness* costs such as stigmatisation or institutionalisation.

Sickness is the social response to illness and disease. It is the external, public mode of what happens to people when something goes wrong with their health. Individuals acquire a *sick role* (Parsons, 1975). This includes a wide range of provisions, some informal, some formal. Sending someone flowers or a 'get well' card can be seen as informal requirements of the sick role. Formal provisions include statutory sick leave and pay, and social welfare provisions for people with chronic illnesses and disabilities.

Not all aspects of *sickness* are beneficial, as has been amply demonstrated in the case of mental disorders. Treatments for mental disorders have often been punitive. Sufferers have been subject to institutionalisation, forced medication, and even forced sterilisation and other eugenic actions. Unfortunately, this is still an ongoing problem (Saks, 2007; Newton-Holmes and Mullen, 2011; Tickle, 2023; McCurry, 2023), and one which proponents of critical psychiatry and members of the ex-patient / survivor movement are rightly campaigning against.

Informal responses to *sickness* can be equally problematic. Someone can be required to take on a sick role whether they want to or not. People diagnosed with various diseases are often expected to behave or respond to their condition in a socially expected manner. For example, people may learn how to 'do' bipolar disorder (Martin, 2009) or ADHD (Brinkmann, 2016). A prominent negative consequence for many diagnoses is stigma, which has been well documented for mental disorders (e.g., Rüsch *et al.*, 2005). Efforts at eliminating stigma through popularising the idea that mental health problems have biological explanations seem to have resulted in greater unwillingness to engage with the mentally unwell, as their behaviour may now seem to be even further out of their control (Kvaale *et al.*, 2013).

It is important to stress that not all parts of the disease-illness-sickness triad need to be present simultaneously (Wikman *et al.*, 2005). Someone may have a disease without feeling ill, as in the case of asymptomatic Covid-19 infection (Amoretti and Lalumera, 2020). Others might experience illness in the absence of a diagnosable disease, as in the case of Jutel's bad cough (2011). In the case of mental illness, someone feeling ill and with a medical diagnosis may still be seen as undeserving of a sick role due to stereotypes or stigma (Sadowsky, 2021, p. 142). Finally, many people diagnosed with mental disorders do not experience their condition as an illness (Michalak *et al.*, 2011; Thoits, 2016).

In contrast to both the third-personal 'objective' *disease* under the medical gaze and that of the social category of *sickness* as a response to health problems, *illness* (including mental illness) is internal, first-personal experience. Feeling ill spurs people on to seek out medical attention, and can lead to the diagnosis of a disease. Illness adjusts to fit the individual and their circumstances, making it more patient-centred and less alienating than disorder, as it centres individual experience rather than matching signs and symptoms to an ideal-type.

Separating the concept of illness from the concepts of medical disease / disorder and sickness is a necessary first step towards establishing why retaining the concept of *mental illness* is worthwhile. If we deny the existence of mental illness as it lacks clear biomarkers (Szasz, 1961), we are contesting the status of mental disorders as diseases. If we object to treating mental distress with medication, we are calling on aspects of the disease and sickness regimen that accompanies the illness experience. In order to rebut objections which are specifically against using the concept *mental illness* to describe our subjective experience, I will argue for three claims in the rest of this paper. Firstly, that mental illness is a relevantly illness-like experience. Secondly, that calling this experience illness is fitting within our culture. Thirdly, that identifying as someone with such as illness-experience can be beneficial rather than detrimental.

3. Experiencing Mental Illness

Based on the three-fold distinction between disease, illness, and sickness, no matter what kind of illness we are experiencing, there is something phenomenologically 'like' to be ill, a first-personal sense of felt unease, separate from objectively having a disease or occupying a sick role socially. Our way of being-in-the-world when we are ill is different from our way of being-in-the-world when we are healthy (Leder, 1990; Toombs, 1992; Carel, 2016; Reynolds, 2022). The first aim of this paper is to argue that the term *mental illness* is apt, because there exists an experience of mental distress which is fundamentally illness-like.

How we experience the world, (perceptually, cognitively, emotionally, and so on) changes which aspects of that world are most salient to us. Even a minor illness, for example a bad cold, colours how we experience our day. By losing our sense of smell, we cease to perceive aspects of the world we might otherwise take for granted, and bad smells bother us less or not at all. Our activities become more effortful from lack of energy. We cannot concentrate, hence tasks appear harder to complete. We start sneezing, and we become aware of aspects of our environment such as the availability of tissues. Our mood is affected, minor setbacks are more unpleasant than usual.

Illness also changes how we experience our embodied selves, and what features of ourselves we hold salient (Toombs, 1992). Illness alienates us from our bodies in a way that makes them appear not just as objects, but as malfunctioning things which impede our interactions with the world (Toombs, 1992, pp. 71–2). Leder (1990, p. 84) writes about the 'dys-appearance' of the body. The healthy body *disappears* from our attention, we are absorbed in our activities, we move through the world easily. He calls this an ecstatic or outward-focused mode of living. By contrast, an ill body *dys-appears*, appears wrongly, draws itself to our attention to the point that we may not be able to pay attention to anything else. It forces our focus to shift inwards, towards ourselves, and spatiotemporally to the here and now. Standard pain scales track this progress from a background annoyance, through a limitation of normal activities to a complete inability to pay attention to anything other than our pain, making the slightest movement impossible. In her phenomenological study of illness, Havi Carel (2016) argues that the experience of illness involves a series of losses: loss of wholeness, loss of certainty, loss of control, loss of freedom to act, and loss of transparency. For an experience to count as illness, it also needs to be disvalued; whatever else we agree on, in itself illness is a form of suffering we would rather avoid (Chappell and Jeppsson, 2023). Suffering may at times lead to growth, but even if it does, this only gives us reason to value it instrumentally, as a means to an end.[4]

---

[4]   As Kate Finley reminded me, experiences such as psychosis also have aspects other than suffering, whether that is transcendental insight or escape from a bleak reality. These can be very valuable to people and form one of the bases of Mad pride. My argument here only refers to the suffering inherent in the illness experience.

Zsuzsanna Chappell

We may look for proof that mental distress can be experienced as illness-like to the first-personal testimony of people who have experienced it, such as autobiographical accounts (e.g., Saks, 2007; Hornbacher, 2008; Redfield Jamison, 1996). We can also refer to studies in various academic disciplines such as psychology, psychiatry, sociology, anthropology, and philosophy. Since we are concerned with subjective, first-personal experiences, it makes sense to turn to phenomenology as a philosophical tradition and scientific discipline in psychiatry. Phenomenological psychiatry and phenomenology of psychopathology is the study of what it is 'like' to experience mental illness, based on a careful observation of how people describe their experiences (see Stanghellini et al., 2019). One problem is that most people say that it is impossible to accurately describe what these experiences are like (Gipps, 2022). Many mental illnesses are described particularly through this disconnection from others. But accepting that there are limits to our ability to explain if we are ill, or to sympathetically enter into the world of the mentally ill when we are healthy, does not mean that it is completely impossible to describe and comprehend the experience of mental illness (e.g., Jeppsson, 2021; Potter, 2003).

Mental illness is illness-like in that it falls under the wider family resemblance category of illness. Just as in the case of a bad cold, we slip into a different way of experiencing the world[5] through changes to ourselves rather than just our circumstances. The most prominent aspect of these changes is emotional and cognitive in nature; this is why mental illness is primarily 'mental'. This is what marks it out from other illnesses, which are also often accompanied by changes in mood or levels of concentration as a result of unpleasant bodily experiences.[6] In addition, mental illnesses are not simply experiences of unpleasant moods or odd cognitions, but also encompass sensory and somatic elements (Ratcliffe et al., 2013). Body-aches, fatigue, vomiting, and insomnia are common examples. Panic attacks and cases of epilepsy-like seizures are especially dramatic somatic manifestations of mental illness. Mental illness also commonly affects sensory perception, as in hallucination or derealisation (Sass et al., 2017). People may become strangely alienated from

---

[5] The extent of the difference depends on the kind and severity of our illness.

[6] If I am in an irritable mood because I have a bad cold, my illness experience does not centre on my irritability. Instead, it centres on a stuffy nose, a headache, fatigue, and so on. The irritability is the consequence of these, rather than the illness itself.

themselves and others. This alienation negates the usual transparency of these mundane relationships (Lysaker and Lysaker, 2008). None of these aspects of mental illness can be easily separated from each other, and the way they manifest may be to some extent culturally determined. In some cultures, as in China, the somatic symptoms of depression are of primary importance (Ryder *et al.*, 2008).

How can emotions and thoughts become illness-like? Based on the phenomenological characteristics of illness I outlined above (Leder, 1990; Toombs, 1992; Carel, 2016) we would expect this to mean that our thoughts and emotions force themselves on our attention consistently, rather than allow us to navigate the world straightforwardly. In the case of anxiety, we might not be able to distract ourselves from our worries. In the case of depression, we might need to withdraw from the world due to the force of our sadness. In the case of mania, we might be unable to resist our elation to the point of acting foolhardy. In any case, we are driven by our emotions to act in ways which we would not endorse otherwise. Mental illness is often accompanied by the loss of one's world or one's sense of self. The world might become uncanny, transformed so that we can no longer move through our environment with ease. Many people say that mental illness takes away their sense of self (Wisdom *et al.*, 2008); it is profoundly alienating. Delusional beliefs and other aspects of thought can also draw themselves to our attention in an unusual way. Thoughts themselves can become thing-like. Take as an example the 'silent thought echo' (Parnas *et al.*, 2005), whereby thoughts very literally seem to echo around one's head, obscuring newer thoughts. While this may not make thinking impossible, it is very annoying, making the *process* of thinking no longer transparent. Just as in other illnesses, we change in a way that transforms our lifeworld in alienating, limiting ways.

Mental illnesses can be acute or episodic; most people do not experience mental illness as a constant, unchanging state. Some people will experience a period of mental illness once and then fully recover. If the illness returns later in their lives, this is a new instance of illness, just as we can get other illnesses more than once, even chicken pox. Other mental illnesses are more akin to chronic illness. People may experience long periods of remission, but it is more or less guaranteed that the illness will flare up again. While many people experience milder, sub-syndromal illness in the periods in between episodes, even this is experienced as comparative mental health. The illness experiences which map broadly onto the disease concept of bipolar disorder illustrate this point well. The term 'manic-depressive disorder' originated with Kraepelin (1921).

Through years of recording patients' episodes of illness, he built up a large corpus of simple lifetime illness charts (Martin, 2009). On these charts, periods of depression and mania were marked, while periods of relative health in between were only shown through empty stretches. By contrast, contemporary studies often highlight the relatively frequent changes from baseline mood to periods of mild depression or hypomania people with bipolar disorder are prone to, taking this to be part of the illness structure (Martin, 2009; Bonsall *et al.*, 2012). Kraepelin (1921) himself wrote that there are 'slight or slightest colourings of *mood*, some of them periodic, some of them continuously morbid, which on the one hand are to be regarded as the rudiments of more severe disorders, on the other hand pass over without sharp boundary into the domain of *personal predisposition*' (p. 1, emphasis in original).

Thus, whether these periods of remission are experienced as illness or something else is very personal. In her autobiographical meditation on neurodiversity, Antonetta (2014) identifies her experience during periods of remission as a form of neurodivergence. She recognises that her moods and emotional regulation is not how most people experience these things, but she does not believe that these constitute an illness. It may at times make her life harder, but in this she finds it more akin to neurodivergent ways of being such as living with autism, dyslexia, or dyspraxia. It is notable that she wrote her book over a period when she experienced both normality and illness. When she gets worse, she considers herself ill, and seeks medical help. It is an open question whether these in-between periods of remission which are still not 'symptom-free' are seen as mild illness or something else. This may vary from individual to individual and even for the same individual over time; someone who has experienced themselves to be mildly ill in the past may come to rethink this experience as part of how her self usually is. The opposite can happen, not just through medicalisation, but also through a change of circumstances. The burden of being different may feel more like illness when life gets harder; things are stressful and one's ability to function daily becomes more limited. A level of anxiety that one person experiences as an illness may still be an acceptable part of the normal range for someone else. Just as with pain, what is in need of treatment, unbearable, and so on cannot be clearly delineated. I will return to the idea that we need this kind of flexibility in personal illness-identity in order to treat persons as persons in section 5.

4. The Culture of Medicalisation

Since there are forms of mental distress which are relevantly illness-like, we can view the term *mental illness* as a useful hermeneutic tool, i.e, a way of explaining clearly to others and ourselves what is happening to us. Yet it is possible that viewing these phenomena as a form of illness is specific to our culture of Western late modernity, in which case we also need to consider the possibility that this is an undesirable aspect of our culture, which we need to eliminate. Even if calling some phenomena *mental illness* might be an apt description of the experience, we may be misusing this hermeneutic tool through applying it too broadly, or through responding to it in discriminatory ways. This misuse can be an appropriate target for ameliorative action without denying that some people can describe their distressing experience as mental *illness*.

It is commonly seen as problematic if cases of everyday sadness, grief, exclusion, poverty, and other problems of living are treated through medical interventions (e.g., Dowrick and Frances, 2013). While it is impossible to know what proportion of cases are wrongly medicalised, about 80% of psychiatric medications are prescribed without recommendation by a psychiatrist (Rose, 2019). It is a problem if primary care physicians give out these prescriptions just to be doing something to help when nothing else is available. The idea of offering talk therapy to those with such problems of living seems less problematic and more likely to prove to be beneficial, inasmuch as we seek to offer help and support to all who are suffering, even if talk therapy can also have negative effects (Linden and Schermuly-Haupt, 2014). While we commonly alter our biochemistry to suit our needs (drinking coffee and alcohol, taking over-the-counter pain killers, and so on), taking psychopharmaceutical medicines to help with mental distress is sometimes moralised, or seen as inauthentic (Karp, 2006).

By requiring that there should be something illness-like at play, we could guard against over-medicalisation. The promotion of mental health awareness may have led to people overinterpreting their experiences of mental distress as an example of mental disorder (Foulkes and Andrews, 2023). Many disorders, such as generalised anxiety disorder, are dimensional constructs. This means that anxiety can range from ordinary worry to a crippling disorder. Just through being aware that there is such a thing as 'anxiety disorder' people may start to think about their feelings of anxiety as more serious, and more likely to be pathological than it is. Equally, if someone experiences the emotional impact of common events such as the end of a relationship or job loss more intensely than culturally expected, they may think of this as an emotional problem that needs to be 'fixed' through professional intervention (Davis, 2020). As long as we share a common cultural understanding of what *illness* is, it is hopefully still possible to recognise when we are experiencing *illness* instead of other kinds of mental distress.

Medicalisation is also not a straightforward concept. Firstly, people turn to medicine, and indeed are required to do so by pharmaceutical regulators, for many needs which are not disease-related (Jebari, 2016; Bortolotti, 2020). A paradigm example is that of female hormonal contraception. Since hormonal contraceptives can cause side effects and lead to long-term problems for a small proportion of women, it is good practice to monitor their use. This means we provide medical treatment inhibiting fertility, even though fertility is not a disease, illness, or sickness. Secondly, illness experience can exist in the absence of a diagnosis or even a known, recognised disease. In section two, I cited an autobiographical example from Jutel (2011), whose somatic illness was successfully treated even in the absence of a diagnosis. Thus, it is an over-simplification of the role of medicine in our culture to claim that it is necessarily a form of over-medicalisation to turn to medical practitioners to help us with emotional distress in the absence of a well-defined disorder. If pharmaceutical treatments, or even electroconvulsive therapy (Gergel, 2021) help to relieve the suffering of at least some patients, then we should not moralise the medical treatment of mental illness.

This may be all good and well if we accept that the kind of phenomenological experiences I described in section 3 should be labelled *mental illness*. But one could make the stronger objection that even though these cases of mental distress are illness-like, it is still wrong to label them *mental illness*, as this is not their most salient feature. Instead, their most salient feature may lie in spirituality, social injustice, or the kinds of suffering which we can all expect to undergo at some point, such as grief. Thus, it is possible that some distressing experiences are labelled mental illness, either by the person experiencing them or by others, because we lack the appropriate social concepts, skills, and support structures to recognise them for what they are. These types of experience may be described more fittingly using a different concept, like *problems of living* (Szasz, 1961).

Illnesses often have a spiritual dimension. Depression and 'dark night of the soul' (Scrutton, 2020) could both be possible explanations for a prolonged period of mental distress. Yet, it is not necessarily the case that someone experiences *either* depression *or* a spiritual struggle. Instead, we can adopt what Scrutton (2020, p. 115) calls the 'both-and view'; that is, it is possible to experience both mental illness and spiritual struggle simultaneously. Over-spritualising mental distress can be just as problematic as over-medicalising it (Finley, 2023), especially if it discourages sufferers from seeking appropriate help. Just as it would be wrong to overinterpret 'ordinary' anxiety as an illness, it would be wrong to overinterpret mental illness as spiritual in nature, especially if it leads to contentious interpretations based on spirit-possession, or punishment for sin. These examples also show the importance of requiring hermeneutical resources which we all have common cultural access to. Illness is such a resource in our culture, but spirit-possession is not. This would make it a less useful way of understanding and communicating our suffering.

Worries about medicalising everyday emotions, especially grief, are common in philosophy of psychiatry (Wakefield *et al.*, 2007; Horwitz and Wakefield, 2012; Prigerson *et al.*, 2021). Other objections are concerned with social problems (e.g., Beresford, 2020): poverty, unemployment, precarious employment, bullying, and domestic abuse can all lead to a pervading sense of powerlessness and anxiety which could be mistaken for clinical depression or anxiety. Through treating the emotional responses to these problems as illness-like, we might be individualising phenomena that are in need of collective solutions. The interaction between such social ills and mental health is complex. Problems such as poverty or homelessness can be triggers for mental illness, or they can be the consequences of mental illness (Brossard and Chandler, 2022). It is impossible to generalise, we must instead listen to individual stories. Yet, even if mental illness is accompanied by other forms of distress, this does not negate its existence. Scrutton's (2020) 'both-and view' can be helpfully applied outside of the spiritual context as well. It is possible to suffer from social ills, injustice, or discrimination, while also experiencing mental illness.

We see the same mechanism at work with somatic illnesses. People living in poverty often only have access to poor quality accommodation. This type of housing often has serious shortcomings that can lead to illness: mould, damp, poor air quality due to pollution, or the use of solid fuels. Those living in such conditions are more likely to develop asthma and other kinds of respiratory illnesses (Rocha *et al.*, 2019; Simkovich *et al.*, 2019). The fact that the cause of the illness lies in poor living conditions does not mean that we should not treat it medically. But neither is it a satisfactory solution to simply send the patient home with an asthma inhaler, and ignore the non-medical support and policies needed to tackle poor accommodation, poverty, and pollution.

Perinatal mental illness is an interesting contrast to worries about conflating depression with grief. New parents experience a need for physical recovery, sleep deprivation, changes in identity, worries about an increase in responsibility, cognitive problems such as memory loss, and loneliness. All of these can lead to changes in mood. Yet, instead of denying that on top of these difficult experiences (which, in contrast to grief, we are discouraged from acknowledging, as new parenthood is supposed to be a period of unremitting joy), some people may also experience something more problematic and not part of a normal life-stage, we now acknowledge and indeed actively look out for perinatal mental illness. We do this even if many of these problems are due to social factors, such as lack of childcare or inadequate social networks. While we might worry that this is unwarranted medicalisation of ordinary 'problems of living', it is more likely that it is an overdue acknowledgement that some parents do experience mental distress after the birth of a child which goes beyond what would normally be expected. Thus, instead of arguing for a perinatal exemption from diagnoses, we can recognise that this period can be accompanied by specific kinds of mental illness, e.g., depression, anxiety, or psychosis strongly coloured by the context within which it occurs.

Intersectionality plays an important part not just in the creation of identity, but also in correctly identifying lived experiences. According to theories of intersectionality, our identities are not simply additive (Crenshaw, 1989). I do not straightforwardly share the identity 'woman' with a black woman, while diverging in my lived experience of race. I am not a woman and white, I am a white woman. Analogously, someone experiencing grief and depression simultaneously is not just someone who happens to have experienced a loss around the time they experienced mental illness. Instead, the two experiences colour each other fundamentally to the point that they may be hard to separate. The same goes for poverty, new parenthood, and so on. We cannot look at someone's experience of mental illness under these circumstances without also acknowledging other aspects of their mental distress. But equally, we should not deny their experience of mental illness because it is coloured by the experience of another form of mental distress. Neither of these moves would provide appropriate recognition to the suffering of the individual. Furthermore, both circumstances need to be improved simultaneously: it is not enough to offer pills or talk therapy to those with perinatal mental illness without also helping to alleviate loneliness or offering better childcare provisions. If we fail to recognise that someone is not only anxious about unemployment or grieving for a relative, but also experiencing mental illness, we may not be able to offer them appropriate support and we may hurt their interests by not recognising them as they see themselves.

5. Mental Illness Identity

So far, I have argued for two points, based on demarcating the concepts of *disease, illness*, and *sickness* from each other. The concept of *mental illness* is important because it is (i) an apt or accurate term, and (ii) a useful hermeneutical resource for interpreting and communicating experience. In this final section, I will argue that it can also be a good way for at least some of us to establish a liveable personal identity within contemporary Western social and political culture.

We use identities both to make sense of who we are and to help us navigate our social world. Medical diagnoses and illness experiences can lead to the adoption of both internal, personal identities and external, social identities (Jutel, 2011). While identity based on disorder diagnosis can be important to people, a different kind of identity can also be based on identifying with one's subjective experience more congruently, owning one's circumstances and taking appropriate action, from acceptance of one's troubling symptoms to seeking diagnosis, treatment, and other forms of support. Identity in this personal sense is usually incorporated into someone's personal narrative; it is something which defines us and plays some kind of role in why our life is proceeding the way it is. Illness experience can also form the basis of social identities from finding supportive groups of others with similar experiences to engaging in collective action (Jutel, 2011). Illness-identity can be important even if one believes that existing diagnoses are inappropriate, or the illness is dismissed by others, as in the case of medically unexplained symptoms. In these cases disease-identity is simply unavailable, yet illness-identity, and the awareness of the pernicious effect of illness on our life-world remains.

How should we think of the concept of identity? Appiah (2006, p. 16) writes that identity 'X will have criteria of ascription; some people identify as Xs; some people treat others as Xs; and X will have norms of identification'. Thus identities have to be things others can recognise as an identity. This recognition may result in specific behaviour towards such people and one must fulfil minimal norms in order to qualify. Someone cannot identify as a keen runner unless they go running regularly. Others may end up talking to them about running or ask advice about how to take up running themselves. This leaves open the possibility that someone who goes running just as regularly, but views this simply as an accident in their lifestyle (maybe they have no opportunity for another form of exercise) will not identify as a runner at all, much as some people working in philosophy departments do not identify as 'real philosophers'.

Our personal identity is by necessity made up of a large range of identifications. Appiah argues that we use these identities in order to construct our lives and to make sense of our experience. Without this, we cannot pursue *eudaimonia* or the good life. Different aspects of our identity are also important at different times and in different settings. While someone is a patient in a psychiatric hospital, their identity as mentally ill is likely to dominate; but this identity may remain entirely hidden from and unimportant to their identity of being a member of a local sports team. Once we accept this variety and situatedness in our identities, it becomes clear that *mentally ill* may be one useful way for people to make sense of their experiences or seek help within our particular society. Other societies in other places and at other times might offer other concepts based on which to do this, which are not available to us living in our own society. Even in our culture, *mental illness* can be a meaningful multi-dimensional construct: ideas about medical treatment can go hand-in-hand with ideas about spiritual struggle (Finley, 2023). What is of greatest importance here is that there should be multiple ways available for people to identify, beyond a hegemonic narrative.

How can we reconcile this with the idea that one of the phenomenological features of illness is that it alienates us from ourselves? According to psychological research (Strohminger *et al.*, 2017) there is widespread belief in a 'true self' or authentic self which can be obscured by the experience of mental illness (Karp, 2006) in what is known as the problem of self/illness identity (Sadler, 2007; Dings and Glas, 2020; Jeppsson, 2022). If mental illness changes our cognitions and by extension our actions, then it becomes difficult to say what part of what we think and do is 'us' and what part is the distortion introduced by the illness. If an injury stops a keen runner from being able to run, the wish to go running remains theirs. The fact that they are not actually going running is clearly attributable to a cause outside of what they think of as their identity. Of course, if the injury curtails any future ability to go running ever again, then the keen runner will need to re-evaluate their sense of self, as

In Defence of the Concept of Mental Illness

they will no longer be able to identify as someone who runs regularly for pleasure. If the keen runner becomes mentally ill instead, and loses their motivation to go running, it would be much more difficult to tell whether this loss of interest was a symptom of their depression. If someone diagnosed with a severe mental disorder such as 'Sylvia' in Sheehan's *Is There No Place On Earth For Me?* (2014) becomes a devout Christian, their faith may be seen as a symptom of their illness, rather than a genuine, deeply held belief.

In the process it is easy to shift, without noticing, between two kinds of alienation. It may be true that illness makes us feel alienated, but this does not mean that our illness-identity, which signifies that we have *identified* that experience of alienation as illness, need further alienate us from the social world. Just as we should not neglect or even deny a running injury, it might be important for some to name and acknowledge their illness-experience through an illness-identity.

The danger is that too much will be attributed to the illness and, especially in the case of chronic conditions, that one's identity will be subsumed under that of the mental patient. Mental illness is often seen as engulfing: a kind of identity that goes beyond the identity accompanying most other illnesses. If we wrongly define our mental distress as mental illness, we might be guilty of disowning aspects of ourselves which we dislike, distancing ourselves from our problems, and giving up a significant part of our agency as a result. This worry is amplified by the problem of stigma. 'Mentally ill' is a marked identity. Someone with mental illness stands out against the unmarked, sane, and rational majority (Goffman, 1990; Zerubavel 2018). People with mental illness often face the problem of being identified by others in a way which makes the wrong attribute seem salient (Whiteley, 2023). Elyn Saks (2007, p. 255) worries that while 'a woman with cancer isn't Cancer Woman', she might be seen as 'primarily a schizophrenic'.

Yet, these processes are not necessary ones. Maggie Thoits (2011, 2016) identifies a range of responses to a diagnosis of serious mental disorder.[7] Some people may be subsumed under their illness-identity. Others embrace and shape this identity actively, seeking to overcome stigma through pride in their identity and maybe even activism. Yet others choose to deny or renounce their diagnosis. Thoits

---

[7] Thoughtful sociological studies are conducted with people who have been diagnosed with a disease. While I argue that disease is not identical to illness, for my purposes I believe I can use these studies to think about responses to stigma and identity-engulfment.

wonders if the engulfing identity is a result of the way in which we think about or ask questions of the mentally ill. Studies of people with mental illness frequently ask whether their subjects are in employment or in education, but rarely look beyond these common ways of measuring success, such as having a satisfying family life.

Reconciling our illness-identity with other aspects of who we are may be especially difficult if these different identities diverge in ways which can seem radical. Elyn Saks (2007, p. 263) writes about her difficulty of reconciling successful 'Professor Saks' with 'the Lady of the Charts' hospitalised with schizophrenia. Many of these contradictions rely on common prejudices: assumptions such as that it is not possible to be professionally successful, happily married, or a good mother if someone lives with mental illness. This leads us back to the negative social *sick role*, characterised by stigma, that people with mental illness often experience. If this is the case, it is better to eliminate the stigma, rather than to deny people the opportunity to describe their suffering as illness, or identify as mentally ill, if this feels appropriate to them. This might require us to turn towards what Winder (2023) calls unspoiling a spoiled identity; creating alternative narratives around what people with that identity can be. This means working towards changing the common interpretation of an identity: recasting mental illness as more intelligible, with valuable qualities such as being able to see the world through a different lens (Garson, 2023), or writing memoirs like Saks's in order to show that mental illness-identity, intelligence, and success are not incompatible.

All this has three important implications. Firstly, for those who do not identify as mentally ill (e.g., Michalak *et al.*, 2011), other forms of identity should be available which take into account their experiences. In the last few decades, two prominent examples of this have emerged: the neurodiversity paradigm (Chapman, 2020) and Mad identity (Beresford 2020, Rashed 2019). Both of these take a strength rather than deficit-based approach to mental difference. Secondly, no one should be forced into adopting or embodying a fixed or sealed identity against their will (Ahmed, 2014, p. 55). Finally, identities are intersectional and mixed so that it should be possible to adopt both a Mad identity and an illness-identity. My experience is illness-like, and it is important for me personally not to lose sight of or deny the suffering inherent in my mental illness. Yet, I also currently identify as a Mad philosopher, someone who claims to be part of a community of people who experience a wide variety of mental difference and distress. My illness-identity is primarily personal, my Mad identity is primarily social and political.

6. Conclusion

I have argued that the phenomenology of *mental illness* is such that it can be accommodated under the broader, family resemblance category of *illness*, and that we can turn to first-personal, subjective accounts to confirm this. If this is right, then the concept of *mental illness* is apt. It is also a culturally useful hermeneutic tool which we can use to explain what is wrong with us, and to seek help from others. Mental illness frequently co-occurs with other problems of living, whether grief or poverty, but this does not negate its existence. Finally, we need not be afraid that mental illness identity will be engulfing and that it can be one of the many identities we adopt at various times in our lives.

We need our identity to reflect our experience of the world, and the way our life is going. Our identity should also allow us to be understood by others (Bergqvist, 2021). Thus, our identities are positions from which recognition claims can be made about who we are, what our needs are, and how others can treat us as persons. Crucially, by identifying our experience of mental distress as an *illness*, we are putting forward a claim towards a particular caring, affective kind of relationship with others. When I identify my suffering as illness-like, I wish to lay claim to a caring interpersonal relationship, instead of one which negates my experience and my deliberations on my experience by telling me that I have misunderstood the nature of my suffering. It is through responding to such claims that others can offer recognition towards us in illness and treat us as the persons we want to be treated as.

Acknowledgements

I would like to thank Anna Bergqvist, Ray Briggs, Kate Finley, Annie Irvine, Alec Grant, and attendees of the 2021 Philosophy of Psychiatry and Lived Experience workshop for their invaluable comments on this paper.

References

Sara Ahmed, *The Cultural Politics of Emotion*, 2nd edition, (Edinburgh: Edinburgh University Press, 2014).

American Psychiatric Association, *Diagnostic and Statistical Manual of Mental Disorders*, 5th ed., Text Rev. (2022).

Maria Cristina Amoretti and Elisabetta Lalumera, 'The Concept of Disease in the Time of COVID-19', *Theoretical Medicine and Bioethics*, 41 (2020): 203–21.

Susanne Antonetta, *A Mind Apart: Travels in a Neurodiverse World* (New York: Jeremy P. Tarcher, 2014).

Kwame Anthony Appiah, 'The Politics of Identity', *Daedalus* 135:4 (2006), 15–22.

Daniel Arias, Saxena Shekhar, and Stéphane Verguet, 'Quantifying the Global Burden of Mental Disorders and Their Economic Value', *EclinicalMedicine*, 54 (2022).

Tony B. Benning, 'No Such Thing as Mental Illness? Critical Reflections on the Major Ideas and Legacy of Thomas Szasz', *BJPsych Bulletin*, 40:6 (2016), 292–5.

Peter Beresford, '"Mad", Mad Studies and Advancing Inclusive Resistance', *Disability & Society*, 35:8 (2020), 1337–42.

Anna Bergqvist, 'Schizophrenia as a Transformative Evaluative Concept: Perspectives on the Psychiatric Significance of the Personal Self in the Ethics of Recognition', *Philosophy, Psychiatry & Psychology*, 28:1 (2021), 23–6.

Derek Bolton, *What Is Mental Disorder? An Essay in Philosophy, Science, and Values* (Oxford: Oxford University Press, 2008).

Derek Bolton and Grant Gillett, *The Biopsychosocial Model of Health and Disease: New Philosophical and Scientific Developments* (Palgrave Macmillan, 2019).

M.B. Bonsall, S.M.A. Wallace-Hadrill, J.R. Geddes, G.M. Goodwin, and E.A. Holmes, 'Nonlinear Time-Series Approaches in Characterizing Mood Stability and Mood Instability in Bipolar Disorder', *Proceedings of the Royal Society B: Biological Sciences*, 279:1730 (2012), 916–24.

Lisa Bortolotti, 'Doctors without "Disorders"', *Aristotelian Society Supplementary Volume*, 94:1 (2020), 163–84.

Kenneth M. Boyd, 'Disease, Illness, Sickness, Health, Healing and Wholeness: Exploring Some Elusive Concepts', *Medical Humanities*, 26:1 (2000), 9–17.

Svend Brinkmann, *Diagnostic Cultures: A Cultural Approach to the Pathologization of Modern Life* (London: Routledge, 2016).

Baptiste Brossard and Amy Chandler, *Explaining Mental Illness: Sociological Perspectives* (Bristol: Bristol University Press, 2022).

Havi Carel, *Phenomenology of Illness* (Oxford: Oxford University Press, 2016).

Judi Chamberlin, 'Rehabilitating Ourselves: The Psychiatric Survivor Movement', *International Journal of Mental Health*, 24:1 (1995), 39–46.

Robert Chapman, 'A Critique of Critical Psychiatry', *Philosophy, Psychiatry & Psychology*, 30:2 (2023), 103–19.

Robert Chapman, 'Defining Neurodiversity for Research and Practice', in Hanna Rosqvist, Nick Chown, and Anna Stenning (eds.), *Neurodiversity Studies: A New Critical Paradigm* (Abingdon: Routledge, 2020), 218–20.

Zsuzsanna Chappell and Sofia Jeppsson, 'Recovery without Normalisation: It's Not Necessary to be Normal, Not Even in Psychiatry', *Clinical Ethics*, online first (2023).

Kimberlé Crenshaw, 'Demarginalizing the Intersection of Race and Sex: A Black Feminist Critique of Antidiscrimination Doctrine, Feminist Theory and Antiracist Politics', *University of Chicago Legal Forum*, 1989:1 (1989), 139–67.

Joseph E. Davis, *Chemically Imbalanced: The Quest for Self-Mastery in the Age of the Brain* (Chicago: University of Chicago Press, 2020).

Roy Dings and Gerrit Glas, 'Self-Management in Psychiatry as Reducing Self-Illness Ambiguity', *Philosophy, Psychiatry & Psychology*, 27:4 (2020), 333–47.

Duncan B. Double, 'Twenty Years of the Critical Psychiatry Network', *The British Journal of Psychiatry*, 214:2 (2019), 61–2.

Christopher Dowrick and Allen Frances, 'Medicalising Unhappiness: New Classification of Depression Risks More Patients Being Put on Drug Treatment from Which They Will Not Benefit', *BMJ*, 347:f7140 (2013).

Abigail A. Dumes, 'Lyme Disease and the Epistemic Tensions of "Medically Unexplained Illnesses"', *Medical Anthropology*, 39:6 (2020), 441–56.

Kate Finley, 'Narratives & Spiritual Meaning-Making in Mental Disorder', *International Journal for Philosophy of Religion*, online first (2023).

Michel Foucault, *The Birth of the Clinic: An Archaeology of Medical Perception*, A.M. Sheridan (trans.), (London: Routledge, 2010).

Lucy Foulkes and Jack L. Andrews, 'Are Mental Health Awareness Efforts Contributing to the Rise in Reported Mental Health Problems? A Call to Test the Prevalence Inflation Hypothesis', *New Ideas in Psychology*, 69 (2023), 101010.

Justin Garson, 'What Is the Philosophy of Madness?', *The Philosopher's Magazine* (2023), accessed 11 July 2023: https://www.philosophersmag.com/essays/315-what-is-the-philosophy-of-madness.

Tania Gergel, '"Shock Tactics", Ethics, and Fear: An Academic and Personal Perspective on the Case against ECT', *British Journal of Psychiatry*, 220:3 (2021), 109–12.

Richard G.T. Gipps, *On Madness: Understanding the Psychotic Mind* (New York: Bloomsbury Academic, 2022).

Erving Goffman, *Stigma: Notes on the Management of Spoiled Identity* (London: Penguin, 1990).

Marya Hornbacher, *Madness: A Bipolar Life* (Boston: Houghton Mifflin, 2008).

Allan V. Horwitz and Jerome C. Wakefield, *All We Have to Fear: Psychiatry's Transformation of Natural Anxieties into Mental Disorders* (New York: Oxford University Press, 2012).

Kay Redfield Jamison, *An Unquiet Mind: A Memoir of Moods and Madness* (New York: Vintage Books, 1996).

Karim Jebari, 'Disease Prioritarianism: A Flawed Principle', *Medicine, Health Care and Philosophy*, 19:1 (2016), 95–101.

Sofia Jeppsson, 'Psychosis and Intelligibility', *Philosophy, Psychiatry & Psychology*, 28:3 (2021), 233–49.

Sofia Jeppsson, 'Solving the Self-Illness Ambiguity: The Case for Construction Over Discovery', *Philosophical Explorations*, 25:3 (2022), 294–313.

Annemarie Jutel, *Putting a Name to It: Diagnosis in Contemporary Society* (Baltimore: Johns Hopkins University Press, 2011).

David Allen Karp, *Is It Me or My Meds? Living with Antidepressants* (Cambridge, MA: Harvard University Press, 2006).

Arthur Kleinman, *The Illness Narratives: Suffering, Healing, and the Human Condition*, 2nd edition, (New York: Basic Books, 1988).

Emil Kraepelin, *Manic-Depressive Insanity and Paranoia* (Edinburgh: Livingstone, 1921).

Erlend P. Kvaale, William H. Gottdiener, and Nick Haslam, 'Biogenetic Explanations and Stigma: A Meta-Analytic Review of Associations among Laypeople', *Social Science & Medicine*, 96 (2013), 95–103.

Drew Leder, *The Absent Body* (Chicago: University of Chicago Press, 1990).

Michael Linden and Marie-Luise Schermuly-Haupt, 'Definition, Assessment and Rate of Psychotherapy Side Effects', *World Psychiatry*, 13:3 (2014): 306–9.

Paul H. Lysaker and John T. Lysaker, 'Schizophrenia and Alterations in Self-Experience: A Comparison of 6 Perspectives', *Schizophrenia Bulletin*, 36:2 (2010), 331–40.

Marshall Marinker, 'Why Make People Patients?', *Journal of Medical Ethics*, 1:2 (1975), 81–4.

Emily Martin, *Bipolar Expeditions* (Princeton: Princeton University Press, 2009).

Justin McCurry, 'Anger in Japan as Report Reveals Children Were Forcibly Sterilised', *The Guardian*, 22 June 2023, accessed 11 July 2023: https://www.theguardian.com/world/2023/jun/22/anger-in-japan-as-report-reveals-children-were-forcibly-sterilised.

Erin Michalak, James Livingston, Rachelle Hole, Melinda Suto, Sandra Hale, and Candace Haddock, '"It's Something that I Manage but It Is Not Who I Am": Reflections on Internalized Stigma in Individuals with Bipolar Disorder', *Chronic Illness*, 7 (2011), 209–24.

Hugh Middleton and Joanna Moncrieff, 'Critical Psychiatry: A Brief Overview', *BJPsych Advances*, 25:1 (2019), 47–54.

Giles Newton-Howes and Richard Mullen, 'Coercion in Psychiatric Care: Systematic Review of Correlates and Themes', *Psychiatric Services*, 62:5 (2011), 465–70.

Amy Olberding, 'Community Practices and Getting Good at Bad Emotions', *Royal Institute of Philosophy Supplements*, 93 (2023), 9–21.

Josef Parnas, Paul Møller, Tilo Kircher, Jørgen Thalbitzer, Lennart Jansson, Peter Handest, and Dan Zahavi, 'EASE-Scale (Examination of Anomalous Self-Experience)', *Psychopathology*, 38:5 (2005), 236–58.

T. Parsons, 'The Sick Role and the Physician Reconsidered', *The Milbank Fund Quarterly, Health and Society*, 53:3 (1975), 257–78.

Nancy Nyquist Potter, 'Moral Tourists and World Travelers: Some Epistemological Issues in Understanding Patients' Worlds', *Philosophy, Psychiatry & Psychology*, 10:3 (2003), 209–23.

Holly G. Prigerson, Sophia Kakarala, James Gang, and Paul K. Maciejewski, 'History and Status of Prolonged Grief Disorder as a Psychiatric Diagnosis', *Annual Review of Clinical Psychology*, 17:1 (2021), 109–26.

Mohammed Abouelleil Rashed, *Madness and the Demand for Recognition: A Philosophical Inquiry into Identity and Mental Health Activism* (Oxford: Oxford University Press, 2019).

Matthew Ratcliffe, Matthew Broome, Benedict Smith, and Hannah Bowden, 'A Bad Case of the Flu? The Comparative Phenomenology of Depression and Somatic Illness', *Journal of Consciousness Studies*, 20:7–8 (2013), 198–218.

Joel Michael Reynolds, *The Life Worth Living: Disability, Pain, and Morality* (Minneapolis, MN: University of Minnesota Press, 2022).

Vânia Rocha, Sara Soares, Silvia Stringhini, and Sílvia Fraga, 'Socioeconomic Circumstances and Respiratory Function from Childhood to Early Adulthood: A Systematic Review and Meta-Analysis', *BMJ Open* 9:6 (2019), e027528.

Nikolas S. Rose, *Our Psychiatric Future: The Politics of Mental Health* (Cambridge: Polity Press, 2019).

Charles E. Rosenberg, *Our Present Complaint: American Medicine, Then and Now* (Baltimore: Johns Hopkins University Press, 2007).

Nicolas Rüsch, Matthias C. Angermeyer, and Patrick W. Corrigan, 'Mental Illness Stigma: Concepts, Consequences, and Initiatives to Reduce Stigma', *European Psychiatry*, 20:8 (2005), 529–39.

Andrew G. Ryder, Jian Yang, Xiongzhao Zhu, Shuqiao Yao, Jinyao Yi, Steven J. Heine, and R. Michael Bagby, 'The Cultural Shaping of Depression: Somatic Symptoms in China, Psychological Symptoms in North America?', *Journal of Abnormal Psychology*, 117:2 (2008), 300–13.

John Sadler, 'The Psychiatric Significance of the Personal Self', *Psychiatry*, 70:2 (2007), 113–29.

Jonathan Hal Sadowsky, *The Empire of Depression: A New History* (Cambridge: Polity Press, 2021).

Elyn R. Saks, *The Center Cannot Hold: My Journey through Madness* (New York: Hyperion, 2007).

Louis Sass, Elizabeth Pienkos, Borut Skodlar, Giovanni Stanghellini, Thomas Fuchs, Josef Parnas, and Nev Jones, 'EAWE: Examination of Anomalous World Experience', *Psychopathology*, 50:1 (2017), 10–54.

Tasia Scrutton, *Christianity and Depression: Interpretation, Meaning, and the Shaping of Experience* (London: SCM Press, 2020).

Susan Sheehan, *Is There No Place on Earth for Me?* (New York: Vintage Books, 2014).

Suzanne M. Simkovich, Dina Goodman, Christian Roa, Mary E. Crocker, Gonzalo E. Gianella, Bruce J. Kirenga, Robert A. Wise, and William Checkley, 'The Health and Social Implications of Household Air Pollution and Respiratory Diseases', *NPJ Primary Care Respiratory Medicine*, 29:1 (2019), 1–17.

Susan Sontag, *Illness as Metaphor and, AIDS and Its Metaphors* (New York: Picador USA, 2001).

Elizabeth V. Spelman, 'On Treating Persons as Persons', *Ethics*, 88:2 (1978), 150–61.

Giovanni Stanghellini, Andrea Raballo, Matthew Broome, Anthony Vincent Fernandez, Paolo Fusar-Poli, and René Rosfort (eds.),

The Oxford Handbook of Phenomenological Psychopathology (Oxford: Oxford University Press, 2019).

Nina Strohminger, Joshua Knobe, and George Newman, 'The True Self: A Psychological Concept Distinct From the Self', *Perspectives on Psychological Science*, 12:4 (2017), 551–60.

Thomas S. Szasz, *The Myth of Mental Illness: Foundations of a Theory of Personal Conduct* (New York, NY: Harper Perennial, 1961).

Peggy A. Thoits, '"I'm Not Mentally Ill": Identity Deflection as a Form of Stigma Resistance', *Journal of Health and Social Behavior*, 57:2 (2016), 135–51.

Peggy A. Thoits, 'Resisting the Stigma of Mental Illness', *Social Psychology Quarterly*, 74:1 (2011), 6–28.

Louise Tickle, 'High Court Judge "Deeply Frustrated" by NHS Delays in Suicidal Girl's Care', *The Guardian*, 17 February 2023, accessed 11 July 2023: https://www.theguardian.com/society/2023/feb/17/high-court-judge-deeply-frustrated-by-nhs-delays-in-suicidal-girls-care.

S. Kay Toombs, *The Meaning of Illness: A Phenomenological Account of the Different Perspectives of Physician and Patient* (Dordrecht: Springer Netherlands, 1992).

Jonathan Y. Tsou, Şerife Tekin, and Robyn Bluhm, 'Philosophy of Science, Psychiatric Classification, and the DSM', in Serife Tekin and Robyn Bluhm (eds.), *The Bloomsbury Companion to Philosophy of Psychiatry* (London: Bloomsbury Academic, 2019), 177–96.

Daniel Vigo, Graham Thornicroft, and Rifat Atun, 'Estimating the True Global Burden of Mental Illness', *The Lancet Psychiatry*, 3:2 (2016), 171–8.

Jerome C. Wakefield, 'Disorder as Harmful Dysfunction: A Conceptual Critique of DSM-III-R's Definition of Mental Disorder', *Psychological Review*, 99:2 (1992), 232.

Jerome C. Wakefield, 'The Concept of Mental Disorder: Diagnostic Implications of the Harmful Dysfunction Analysis', *World Psychiatry*, 6:3 (2007), 149–56.

Jerome C. Wakefield, Mark F. Schmitz, Michael B. First, and Allan V. Horwitz, 'Extending the Bereavement Exclusion for Major Depression to Other Losses: Evidence from the National Comorbidity Survey', *Archives of General Psychiatry*, 64:4 (2007), 433–40.

Jo Watson, *Drop the Disorder!: Challenging the Culture of Psychiatric Diagnosis* (Wyastone Leys, Monmouth, UK: PCCS Books, 2019).

Zsuzsanna Chappell

Talia Weiner, 'The (Un)Managed Self: Paradoxical Forms of Agency in Self-Management of Bipolar Disorder', *Culture, Medicine and Psychiatry*, 35 (2011), 448–83.

Ella Kate Whiteley, 'A Woman First and a Philosopher Second: Relative Attentional Surplus on the Wrong Property', *Ethics*, 133:4 (2023), 497–528.

Anders Wikman, Staffan Marklund, and Kristina Alexanderson, 'Illness, Disease, and Sickness Absence: An Empirical Test of Differences between Concepts of Ill Health', *Journal of Epidemiology & Community Health*, 59:6 (2005), 450–4.

Iain Wilkinson, *Suffering: A Sociological Introduction* (Cambridge, UK and Malden, MA: Polity Press, 2005).

Terrell J.A. Winder, 'Unspoiling Identity: An Intersectional Expansion of Stigma Response Strategies', *Sociology of Race and Ethnicity*, 9:2 (2023), 195–207.

Jennifer P. Wisdom, Kevin Bruce, Goal Auzeen Saedi, Teresa Weis, and Carla A. Green, '"Stealing Me from Myself": Identity and Recovery in Personal Accounts of Mental Illness', *The Australian and New Zealand Journal of Psychiatry*, 42:6 (2008), 489–95.

Ludwig Wittgenstein, *Philosophical Investigations*, G.E.M. Anscombe, P.M.S. Hacker, and Joachim Schulte (trans.), 4th edition, (Chichester: Wiley-Blackwell, 2009).

World Health Organization, *Comprehensive Mental Health Action Plan 2013–2030* (Geneva: World Health Organisation, 2021).

Eviatar Zerubavel, *Taken for Granted: The Remarkable Power of the Unremarkable* (Princeton: Princeton University Press, 2018).

'The Hermeneutic Problem of Psychiatry' and the Co-Production of Meaning in Psychiatric Healthcare

LUCIENNE SPENCER AND IAN JAMES KIDD

Abstract
'The co-production of meaning' is a phrase that has become entrenched in the field of public mental health, adopted almost as a slogan within the literature. But what does it actually mean? Current definitions gesture toward the very broad idea that co-production involves a collaboration between 'service users' and healthcare professionals, each contributing their knowledge to better understand and treat mental health problems. Yet, terms such as 'equal' 'reciprocal', and 'partnership' fail to clarify the nature of this 'co-production', and how it can be achieved.

To better understand the co-production of meaning, we shall attempt to develop an account of co-production through phenomenological psychopathology. Through Hans Georg Gadamer's remarks on 'the hermeneutic problem of psychiatry' two key obstacles to 'co-production' emerge: 1) contingent problems, and 2) intrinsic problems. In calling attention to these obstacles, we problematise the concept of 'co-production' in public mental health, revealing it to be more complex than originally thought. We conclude by arguing that new developments in phenomenological psychopathology can be used to overcome the limitations of 'co-production'.

1. Introduction

'The co-production of meaning' is a phrase that has become entrenched in the field of public mental health, adopted almost as a slogan within the literature. This ambiguous terminology has been inconspicuously ushered into public discourse; however, the term too often seems too narrowly or broadly defined. The Centre for Coproduction in Mental Health and Social Care at Middlesex University describes 'co-production' in terms of 'the principle that people who use services have valuable knowledge and expertise' and understands it to be a means of 'developing equal and reciprocal relationships between professionals, people using services, and communities to produce knowledge and services that are potentially more effective overall'.[1] Similarly, the

---

[1] Middlesex University London, *Centre for Coproduction in Mental Health and Social Care*, accessed 5 June 2023: https://www.mdx.ac.uk/our-research/centres/centre-for-coproduction-in-mental-health.

doi:10.1017/S135824612300019X © The Author(s), 2023. Published by Cambridge University Press on behalf of The Royal Institute of Philosophy

103

Lucienne Spencer and Ian James Kidd

Royal College of Psychiatrists defines co-production as 'an ongoing partnership between people who design, deliver and commission services [and those] who use the services and people who need them'.[2] Moreover, the National Development Team for Inclusion claims co-production 'should seek to achieve equality and parity by bringing together people who can work as equals, to develop a shared understanding of what needs to change and a commitment to bringing that about'.[3]

Such definitions emphasise collaboration, reciprocity, parity, and similar values, all of which understand 'co-production' as a means of bringing different groups into more productive contact. Unfortunately, the definitions are often aspirational in character and fail to define their terms, some of which might be mutually inconsistent. Take the emphases on equality and parity: we assume that one main reason people need to work with and learn from others is because of differences between (or inequalities in) their skills, knowledge, and understanding. 'Co-production', more generally, is consistent with the idea of (i) equally capable people working on a common task and of (ii) unequally capable people working on a common task. The assumption is that co-producing will result in something that one single group cannot, by itself, achieve, but that could mean we have equal abilities and knowledge or unequal abilities and knowledge. But this latter option is more complex and contentious, even if it gestures to an important epistemic and moral ideal.

In this paper, we make a start on developing an account of 'co-production' that uses the resources of phenomenological psychopathology. We focus on the ideal of the co-production of meaning and start with Hans-Georg Gadamer's remarks on the 'hermeneutic problem of psychiatry'. From here, we identify two kinds of obstacles to the co-production of meaning – *contingent* and *intrinsic* – and suggest that the latter poses serious problems for the ideal of a co-production of meaning in the context of psychiatric healthcare. Fortunately, those problems could, in principle, be addressed using a phenomenological approach.

---

[2] National Collaborating Centre for Mental Health, *Working Well Together: Evidence and Tools to Enable Co-production in Mental Health Commissioning* (London: National Collaborating Centre for Mental Health, 2019).
[3] Sarah Carr and Meena Patel, *Progressing Transformative Co-Production in Mental Health* (National Development Team for Inclusion, 2016).

2. 'The Hermeneutic Problem of Psychiatry'

In his 1996 book, *The Enigma of Health*, the phenomenologist and hermeneuticist Hans-George Gadamer offered a rich account of 'the art of healing' centred on the dialogues of doctors and patients. The medical encounter, he argued, should essentially be a practice of interpretation. A doctor should 'set in motion once again the communicative flow of the patient's life experience and to re-establish that contact with others from which the person is so tragically excluded' (Gadamer, 1996, p. 138). In line with Gadamer's hermeneutically sophisticated philosophy, these dialogical medical encounters should go beyond the patient simply offering testimonies that their doctor dutifully receives and affirms. There is an ongoing exchange and exploration of the different kinds of meanings that saturate those experiences reported by the patient. Those meanings are subjected to different kinds of activities, such as interpreting, challenging, contextualising and questioning. Indeed, the richness and dynamism of our experiences should be matched by the complexity and energy of our interpretive practices. Gadamer speaks of an 'ongoing process', a 'relationship', that includes disorientation, as well as 'the experience of regaining equilibrium' (Gadamer, 1996, p. 137). In the course of these processes, there can be – to quote Gadamer's famous slogan – a 'merging of horizons', which denotes the coming together of the first-person and third-person perspective (Gadamer, 1996, p. 112). The product is a deeper and richer understanding of the patient's experiences than would be possible through mere monodirectional analysis and the static reception of the doctor.

The aspiration of *The Enigma of Health* to offer an 'art of healing' might lead one to think that this account of dialogical interpretation would apply across all forms of medicine and healthcare. In the final chapter, however, Gadamer distinguishes psychiatry and asks if his hermeneutical approach could be applied in that domain. While the psychiatrist must try to draw out the meanings of a patient's psychiatric illness[4], they will find in many cases 'an unbridgeable divide' (Gadamer, 1996, p. 171). This should worry a psychiatrist on two fronts. First, encountering that divide disrupts the dialectical activity of interpretation and, worse, the realisation of its unbridgeable character confirms the existence of permanent limitations to interpersonal

---

[4] We acknowledge that the term 'illness' can be controversial in this field, as it suggests that all forms of psychiatric 'difference' are necessarily pathological. We recognise the limits of this terminology, as one may be neurodiverse and not 'ill' in any way.

understanding. Some obstacles are temporary and removable, while others are permanent and unchangeable. A further epistemological problem is that of determining with confidence whether an obstacle is contingent or intrinsic, and whether the sense of the obstacle being resistant to removal is correct. In these cases, argues Gadamer, a psychiatrist encounters the 'hermeneutic problem of psychiatry' (Gadamer, 1996, p. 169).

We want to use Gadamer's remarks on the hermeneutic problem of psychiatry to think about the co-production of meanings within psychiatric healthcare. Gadamer offers general insights, of course, not least the complicated issues inherent in the very idea of 'producing' meanings, what it means for experiences to be meaningful, how the meanings we experience relate to one another, and so on. There are also complicated issues about different kinds of meaning and how they relate to one another, the conferral of meanings versus the identification of meanings, and the ways our practices and interests shape meaning. A crucial issue for our discussion is whether meanings *can* be 'produced' by two or more people; if not, then the idea of a 'co-production of meaning' will be a non-starter. Meanings could be *discovered* or *conferred*, but these seem quite different, and in many cases, it may be better to say that two people come to *discover* meanings: what is produced is not the *meaning* but rather its *discovery* or *articulation*. What are produced in many cases are ways of *discovering*, describing, and *appreciating* meanings: hermeneutic practice is productive if it enhances our experience of meanings. The activity is essentially an act of revelation – an activity of exploration that brings into view new kinds of meanings, previously unrealised ways that those meanings connect to one another and to one's habits, concerns, relationships, and life-projects. Of course, acts of exploration can be obstructed or disrupted by all sorts of factors. Experiencing and responding to obstacles seems integral to the activity of exploration. In what follows, we describe two general obstacles to a hermeneutically explorative kind of psychiatric healthcare practice. We start with *contingent obstacles* and then go on to *intrinsic obstacles*.

2. Contingent Obstacles

Gadamer understands the hermeneutical endeavour in medicine as a complex, sustained, and necessarily interpersonal practice. We seek understanding with, and of, other people and the wider structures and concerns of our shared social world. Within psychiatric dialogue, a primary obstacle is what Gadamer calls 'the fundamentally unequal relationship that prevails between doctor and patient', which dialogue and discussion can 'humanise' (Gadamer, 1996, p. 112). The immediate problem is that the kind of dialogue described by Gadamer requires resources that are usually scarce, such as time, trust, empathy, and freedom from distraction. Moreover, resources are typically conditioned by power structures, institutional barriers, negative prejudices and biases, and a wider set of epistemic and moral deficiencies. These factors, individually or collectively, can impede even sincere and well-motivated efforts to co-produce meanings. The conditions for rich interpersonal interactions aimed at mutual understanding rarely obtain in an optimal form and often we must make do; the richly authentic 'I-Thou' encounters so well described by Martin Buber are precious in part because they are rare and fragile (Buber, 2000).

The term *contingent* suggests something that was not inevitable and which could have been different. A sense of contingency sustains a sense that there are alternative possibilities, other ways that something could be, other ways that it can develop, and therefore meaningful possibilities for intentional agency. Many experiences can involve a loss of this sense of contingency. This includes many of the predicaments we typically associate with diagnoses of depression, but also includes cases in which possibilities are being blocked by material, interpersonal, social, or cultural conditions (we return to cases of psychiatric illness in the next section).

Consider some of the contingent features of psychiatric healthcare practices that can obstruct the kinds of interpersonal hermeneutical practices described by Gadamer. We have already mentioned the power imbalances latent in the psychiatric encounter, including what the feminist philosopher Miranda Fricker calls *social power*: 'a practically socially situated capacity to control others' actions, where this capacity may be exercised (actively or passively) by particular social agents, or alternatively, it may operate purely structurally' (Fricker, 2007, p. 13).

Control, here, can mean commanding or prohibiting certain actions, and determining if, how, and when another acts, which can reflect various motivations. Within psychiatry, there is usually more social power in the psychiatrist, achieved not only by their training, skills, and expertise, but also by the institutional certification of those epistemic-practical achievements (Carel and Kidd, 2014, p. 530). For instance, healthcare professionals have legal authority under the Mental Health Act to use their expert judgment to detain a person, thereby infringing on their liberty. They can define the state of mind of their patient, position them within some

Lucienne Spencer and Ian James Kidd

diagnostic category, and prescribe medical treatments, including some which may transform the patient's mental state significantly. Such medico-legal systems transform epistemic status into practical and social power.

The analysis of how medico-legal structures relate to epistemic systems was famously pioneered by Michel Foucault and continued by those who adopt his genealogical exposures of the implication of psychiatric classifications into systems of power/knowledge (cf. Foucault, 1961). *Madness and Civilization*, for instance, describes a transition in the nineteenth-century asylum, whereby chains and other instruments of restraint that bound those committed were swapped for the 'abstract, faceless power' of authority (Foucault, 2001, p. 238). Kinds of physical restraint became redundant once the norms of those systems were internalised: 'the absence of constraint in the nineteenth century is not unreason liberated, but madness long since mastered' (Foucault, 2001, p. 239). Whatever the historical merits of these analyses, there is an important insight into the dynamics of epistemic and social power. Foucault describes how a patient suffers a diminution of their epistemic role: their participant role is replaced by a more limited status as 'the observed', entrapped within a systems of surveillance. Foucault also argues that psychoanalysis continues this tendency: psychoanalysis 'doubled the absolute observation of the watcher with the endless monologue of the person watched' (Foucault, 2001, p. 238). The narrative of the patient is not truly speech expression, or at least not speech expression with any power. It is, rather, 'endless monologue', functioning to elicit further behaviour which can, in turn, sustain further expert scrutiny, 'thus preserving the old asylum structure of non-reciprocal observation but balancing it, in a non-symmetrical reciprocity, by the new structure of language without response' (Foucault, 2001, p. 238).

The historical and institutional conditions may change, but the generalised tendencies to exclude an interactive dialogical model with a narrower one of monologue and scrutiny persists. Earlier forms of epistemic constraint and self-restraint have been replaced by newer and more sophisticated ones. For instance, there has been a significant shift away from sectioning under the Mental Health Act towards deinstitutionalised therapeutic practices. *Madness and Civilization* describes a certain stage in an ongoing process, inviting us to identify later developments: the earlier conceptual, administrative, and moral structuring of madness (Gutting, 1989, pp. 84ff.). Outside of sectioning, the healthcare professional no longer has the same level of control over the patient's liberty, but there are different, subtler kinds of control now at work, including systems of epistemic control. The epistemic control involves a range of interpersonal, scientific-medical, and social components – sanist attitudes, taboos, systematic epistemic injustices, deficient economies of credibility, pharmacogenetic regimes, and the systematic stigmatisation and social and material disadvantaging of those diagnosed with psychiatric conditions (Mental Health Foundation, 2016; Kidd, Spencer, and Carel, 2023).

Let us turn back to the phenomenon of epistemic injustice. Defined broadly, these involve cases where a person is unfairly and harmfully subjected to a denial or disruption of their epistemic abilities. The paradigmatic cases are testimonial injustices and hermeneutical injustices, those being the two main kinds of epistemic injustice described by Miranda Fricker which became central to the scholarly literature (Fricker, 2007; Kidd, Medina, and Pohlhaus Jr., 2017). Fricker explains that the concept is an attempt to 'delineate a distinctive class of wrongs [...] in which someone is disingenuously downgraded and/or disadvantaged in respect of their status as an epistemic subject' (Fricker, 2017, p. 53). As epistemic subjects, the activities of creating and sharing knowledge and achieving understanding of our own and others' social experiences are essential to our everyday functioning and our overall flourishing. Our epistemic capacities are interwoven with our practical interests, moral comportment, interpersonal relations, and social relations. Thus, being wronged epistemically can be seriously problematic and sometimes even fatal. When our testimonies are denied credibility, our ability to convey our goals, represent our interests, voice our concerns, and explain our preferences is impaired. If we are prevented from making ourselves intelligible to others, we lose the intelligibility which sustains meaningful interpersonal connection and engagement. Across the various forms of testimonial and hermeneutical injustice, the epistemic, moral, practical, and political harms and wrongs are made vivid.

Consider the following example of *hermeneutical marginalisation* within a university. Participants at a conference discuss what a good academic conference looks like. Those welcome to participate in the exchange may discuss the importance of inviting renowned keynote speakers, selective reviewing for submitted talks, and how best to advertise the event. Following multiple exchanges across many universities over time, an interpretive framework develops to capture 'what makes a good academic conference'. Historically, most women's inputs to academia were denied proper roles in these informational exchanges, if a woman was included at all. What occurs are unjust denials of due credibility that sustain kinds of 'unequal hermeneutical participation', resulting in the construction of social-interpretive frameworks that marginalise and disadvantage certain groups (see Fricker, 2007, p. 152). Within that framework, the significance of certain actions goes unrecognised, like the importance of gender-balanced line-ups; particular needs, like offering childcare support to those who need it, go unrecognised and unmet. Important things are not understood because those who understand them are not properly included, and these hermeneutical lacunae are often difficult to close because they lack visibility or urgency (Fricker, 2007, p. 151). When these hermeneutically defective conditions persist, the experiences and testimonies of dissonant or marginalised groups will be rendered unintelligible, eccentric, or trivial.

It is worth adding that a total gap in the hermeneutical resources is a rare occurrence. Although Fricker uses terms such as 'lacuna' or 'gap', we suggest that it is better to consider the 'pool of shared ideas' (to borrow Fricker's metaphor) as being more or less depleted (and in rare cases, there may even be a complete drought). Only the hermeneutically privileged can contribute towards, alter, and remove resources from the pool of shared ideas. The hermeneutically marginalised do not have this power and are forced to contend with ill-fitting concepts (Fricker, 2017, p. 54; Medina, 2017, pp. 42–3).

Fricker further develops the concept of hermeneutical injustice by stipulating that a group can be limited not only by *what* they can express but also *how* they can express it: 'the characteristic expressive style of a given social group may be rendered just as much of an unfair hindrance to their communicative efforts as an interpretive absence can be' (Fricker, 2007, p. 160). In this context, a speech expression may be disregarded as unreliable or unintelligible due to the subject's style of speech. Rebecca Tsosie provides a useful example of such hermeneutical injustice inflicted upon Indigenous groups in Northern California. In *Lying vs Northwestern Indian Cemetery Protective Association,* the court permitted the extension of a logging road through a site that the Indigenous groups of Northern California called 'sacred'. The court ruled that the government was not harming the Indigenous groups as they did not 'coerce the Indigenous peoples into giving up their "belief" that the land was "sacred"' (Tsosie, 2017, p. 361). The word 'sacred' was not seen to hold any legal weight, evaluated to be a concept held 'in the mind' at an individual level (*ibid.*). Therefore, although the Indigenous groups had the means to articulate the harm they encountered, such spiritual language is structurally barred by the legal system. As such, the Indigenous interpretation of the events was rejected.

Unlike testimonial injustice, Fricker understands hermeneutical injustice as a 'somewhat indirect' discrimination because 'the injustice will tend to persist regardless of individual efforts' (Fricker, 2017, p. 54). In other words, it is grounded in *structural* hermeneutical marginalisation. The injustice lies in the wider social structure, as certain groups are excluded from contributing to a shared interpretative framework. Accordingly, hermeneutical injustice typically endures despite the hearers' attempts to understand the speaker, as the interpretive framework renders the marginalised speaker almost unintelligible. The marginalisation of the victims is built into the very structure of the interaction and has a scope that extends beyond the given interaction. Nevertheless, Medina clarifies that the agent's responsibility is not diminished in a case of hermeneutical injustice. As Medina points out, there is collective culpability for hermeneutical injustice as 'an entire culture can be held responsible for not trying to understand a particular kind of experience or a particular kind of subjectivity' (Medina, 2017, p. 42). For this reason, Medina claims 'we can identify degrees of complicity in how individuals respond to lacunas and limitations in the hermeneutical resources they have inherited and in how they participate (or fail to participate) in expressive and interpretive dynamics' (Medina, 2017, p. 42–3).

Testimonial and hermeneutical injustices relate to psychiatric healthcare practice, particularly encounters between patients and psychiatrists. Testifying and interpreting are integral to all interpersonal interactions but have a special significance within contexts where interpersonal understanding is especially difficult and complex. 'Co-producing meaning' depends on our ability to initiate and sustain richer testimonial interactions and to engage in complex reciprocal hermeneutical practices. If so, epistemic injustice is a powerful obstacle. Consider a specific harm of hermeneutical injustice – *cognitive disablement* – which Fricker defines as follows:

> [A] cognitive disablement prevents her from understanding a significant patch of her own experience: that is, a patch of experience which it is strongly in her interests to understand, for without that understanding she is left deeply troubled, confused, and isolated, not to mention vulnerable to continued harassment. (Fricker, 2007, p. 51)

Cognitive disablement means our epistemic energies cannot be directed effectively since we remain, to some degree, obscure to ourselves; our goals, reasons for action, preferences and sense of the world cannot be understood in ways that provide confidence and

Lucienne Spencer and Ian James Kidd

satisfaction, a state often correlated with anxiety, fear, self-estrange-
ment, and uncertainty. Moreover, if an individual is cognitively disabled, they may misidentify the source of it as some failure of their
own. In this case, our understanding of our relationship to the
social world is distorted. A whole dense structure of social-epistemic
norms, prejudices, constraints, and practices goes unrealised as a
person lacks the vital ability to perceive and understand oppressive
structural realities. Under these conditions, the co-production of
meaning would inevitably fail since it is blocked by individual, interpersonal, and institutional conditions.

To develop this claim, consider the inequalities inherent in
forming, legitimating, and maintaining socially and epistemically authoritative interpretive frameworks. It is insufficient for a patient to
simply *talk* to the healthcare professional. Interactions always take
place in some framework, however tacit and unsystematic, that sustains our sense of relevance, credibility, and plausibility, and supplies
some sense of typical interactive styles and possibilities. A patient
must understand the framework, if they are really to authentically
and successfully communicate their experiences, and that understanding will be more likely if they were involved in the construction
of the framework. The key interpretive framework found in psychiatry is that of diagnostic manuals such as the DSM (Diagnostic
and Statistical Manual of Mental Disorders) and a main criticism
has been their failure to properly include the perspectives of patients
(Cooper, 2005; Pickersgill, 2014; Schaffner and Tabb, 2015; Tabb,
2015). Indeed, patient input into the DSM seems to have been de-
prioritised from the outset. Robert Spitzer, chair of the task force
behind the DSM-3, once argued that it is 'politically correct non-
sense' to suggest that psychiatric patients and their family members
could provide any valuable insight into diagnostic criteria, which
he felt should be developed only by 'committees of mental health
professionals who are chosen because of their expertise in some
aspect of psychiatric diagnosis' (Sadler and Fullford, 2004).

Such blunt assertions of hermeneutical exclusion are apparent, but
many other sources will be less obvious or, at least, better concealed.
Moreover, claims about contributions which patients can make must
always be cashed out and justified, and how easy this will be depends
on the nature of the contribution. Tasia Scrutton, for instance, notes
that many persons who experience auditory hallucinations as positive
and important life events do so by appealing to spiritual interpretations; interpretations that conflict with the medical interpretations
urged by, and much more intelligible to, their doctors (Scrutton,
2017). However, spiritual understandings of auditory hallucinations

112

are not included in the DSM, meaning that this kind of perspective – which is common and often deeply culturally-sustained – will be excluded (Scrutton, 2017, p. 350). In this case, unequal hermeneutical participation denies certain people and communities from a practice that would have value for them and one that would, in some sense, enable richer meaning-making (Fricker, 2007, p. 153). Moreover, the inclusion of religious interpretations of auditory hallucinations might strain the more general metaphysical frameworks that shape scientific epistemic practices. These frameworks perpetuate an implicit scientific naturalist conception of the world which denies the existence of gods and other supernatural beings and acts at a profound level as an economy of credibility. Such frameworks make it hard to find credible accounts of auditory hallucinations as, for instance, aural encounters with God (cf. Kidd, 2017). In these cases, a Gadamerian 'merging of horizons' could be impossible, because the horizons are too different in their basic ontological presuppositions to be merged.

We have described some individual, interpersonal, and structural obstacles that might generate and sustain testimonial and hermeneutical injustices in ways that will tend to block the sorts of collaborative practices involved in the 'co-production of meaning'. We think they are contingent in the sense that they (a) are products of historical events, decisions, and developments that could have been different and which (b) in principle could be different in the future because (c) workable alternatives to them either exist, even if in underdeveloped forms, or could be developed. The study of these contingent obstacles is a multidisciplinary project – encompassing philosophy, sociology, history, and other disciplines – and identifying and developing alternatives to our current practices is a task for all those concerned with our psychiatric healthcare systems. Nevertheless, sensitivity to contingent factors comes with the risk of undue optimism. Contingent obstacles can still be deeply entrenched, and many people will resist their removal, not least because principled cases can be made for retaining current arrangements and rejecting proposed alternatives. A further risk is that our focus on contingent obstacles occludes the possibility that some obstacles are *intrinsic* – ones which would emerge and persist even if all the social and epistemic challenges were eliminated or had never existed in the first place.

In the following sections, we develop the idea that some real obstacles to 'co-producing meaning' in psychiatric healthcare may reside in the predicaments experienced by patients, rather than more contingent interpersonal or structural realities. To do this, we will appeal to phenomenological psychopathology.

3. Intrinsic Obstacles

There has been a particular focus in the literature on the inherent link between psychiatric illness and communication difficulties. For instance, a person with a psychiatric disorder may be wilfully silent due to a newfound apathy towards the hearer and towards communication itself, or even a desire to keep one's audience at a distance. In the case of schizophrenia: 'the interviewee may be much less aware of or concerned with the needs of the interviewer, potentially due to the intensity of other symptoms or a significant lack of connection with conventional reality, including conventional uses of language (Pienkos *et al.*, 2021, p. 61; see also Sass, 2017, p. 53). Indifference towards language and communication has also been found to be a core theme in depression (Kendler, 2016). Indeed, this indifference toward communication may result from the overall distraction of this illness itself. In the words of Styron: 'the ferocious inwardness of the pain produced an immense distraction that prevented my articulating words beyond a hoarse murmur; I sensed myself turning wall-eyed, monosyllabic [...]' (Styron, 2010, p. 17).

Language difficulties may also be a product of 'an unfocused or vacillating cognitive style that prevents topics from being carried through to closure' (Sass, 2017, p. 53). For example, patients with psychosis have described a state of chaotic thinking: 'My head is "swarming" with thoughts or "flooding". I become overwhelmed by all the thinking going on inside my head. It sometimes manifests itself as incredible noise' (Fusar-Poli *et al.*, 2022, p. 176). This, too, has been found in cases of anxiety, whereby 'the mind jumps from one random thought to another, resulting in speech patterns that are sped up, disorganized, and incoherent' (Aho, 2018, p. 262).

Some studies suggest that deficiencies in the 'theory of mind' (briefly, the capacity to recognise distinct mental states in other people) may also lead to communication impairment. Such difficulties are common in ADHD (Çiray *et al.*, 2022) and ASD (Andreou and Skrimpa, 2020). Finally, a further cause of communication breakdown, commonly found in schizophrenia, 'can be the sense or belief that words and language are absurd or arbitrary' (Pienkos *et al.*, 2021, p. 58).

To further understand language impairment in psychiatric illness, we may turn to phenomenology, which characterises psychiatric illness as a profound alteration of the lived world. Most people move through the world with what R.D. Laing calls an 'ontological security':

> [...] he can live out into the world and meet others: a world and others experienced as equally real, alive, whole, and continuous. Such a basically ontologically secure person will encounter all the hazards of life, social, ethical, spiritual, biological, from a centrally firm sense of his own and other people's reality and identity. (Laing, 1964, p. 33)

This is to say that the ontologically secure person is irrevocably intertwined with the world and has confidence in the predictable way it is presented. Due to this confidence and predictability, the manner in which the ontologically secure moves through the world does not even come to their attention. They perceive the world pre-reflectively as 'perception [...] is the background against which all acts stand out and is thus presupposed by them' (Merleau-Ponty, 2012, p. lxxiv). The philosophy of psychiatry, however, identifies a breakdown in the subject-world synthesis in the case of psychiatric illness. R.D. Laing refers to this as an 'ontological *insecurity*', although it has also been dubbed a 'death of possibilities' (Ratcliffe and Broome, 2012), an 'anomalous world' (Madeira *et al.*, 2019) and 'unworlding' (Sass, 1990).

An ontological breakdown may disrupt a number of phenomenological factors. First, there may be a disruption in one's sense of Self. This is a common report for people with psychosis: 'I thought I was dissolving into the world; my core self was perforated and unstable, accepting all the information permeating from the external world without filtering anything out' (Fusar-Poli, *et al.*, 2022, p. 172). This is a particular focus of Laing, who states that '[the ontologically insecure person] may not possess an over-riding sense of personal consistency or cohesiveness [...]. It is, of course, inevitable that an individual whose experience of himself is of this order can no more live in a "secure" world than he can be secure in himself' (Laing, 1964, p. 37).

Second, there may be a disruption in one's experience of space. The lived space is the space in which a person pre-reflexively orientates themselves and moves through. In cases of agoraphobia, the illness imposes upon the person an inability to leave the realm of 'home' or the familiar: 'the centrality of the physical home, with its borders and boundaries, marks a threshold from agoraphobic embodiment to non-agoraphobic embodiment' (Trigg, 2013, p. 418). This too has been identified as a feature of depression: 'distancing is experienced as loss of spatial depth and things become dull and flat as in everything is out of reach, living as static objects; not integrated into a landscape, occupying places and not regions' (Tatossian, 2019, p. 87)

Third, there may be a disruption in one's experience of time. The embodied being is necessarily positioned in 'time', and every experience receives its meaning against the background of its temporal profile. The experience of a slowing down of time has been identified as a core feature of depression (Minkowski, 1933; Binswanger, 1960; Fuchs, 2013; Gallagher, 2012; Vogel *et al.*, 2018). People with depression may report that '[time] goes very, very slowly. Like I remember lying awake at about 4am in my [...] room and it was going so slowly, all I had to do was get through to the morning so I could get some help and it seemed almost impossible just to get through those few hours because it was taking so long' (Ratcliffe, 2015, p. 175). In contrast, anxiety is typically experienced as an acceleration of time: 'Sufferers experience this temporal quickening through a number of bodily sensations including "palpitations", "accelerated heart rate", "sweating", "trembling or shaking", and "shortness of breath"' (Aho, 2018, p. 262).

Fourth, there may be a disruption in one's relation to one's body. By this we do not refer to the physical, objective body ('I have a body') but the lived body ('I *am* a body'). This refers to the body as experienced from within, in the first-person perspective. The lived body is at the centre of all experience, yet a breakdown in one's relation to one's body is characteristic of a number of psychiatric illnesses. This is particularly common in Anorexia Nervosa. Drawing upon Sartre, Svenaeus argues that those with anorexia adopt the objectifying gaze of the Other, thus causing them to experience their body as uncanny (Svenaeus, 2018, 44–50). Abnormal body experiences may also be reported in schizophrenia: 'I didn't feel [my body]. I didn't feel alive. It didn't feel mine [...]. I never felt a feeling of fusion or harmony between "me" and "my" body: it always felt like a vehicle, something I had to drive like a car' (Fusar-Poli, *et al.*, 2022, p. 171).

Fifth, there may be a breakdown in one's perceived possibilities to interact with the world. The objects in the world that motor intentionality is directed toward appear to the embodied subject as offering certain opportunities for interaction, known as 'affordances' (Gibson, 1968). People with depression, however, report that objects in the world no longer offer possibilities for interaction in the way they once did. While a kettle once offered the affordance of making a cup of tea, that object no longer appears to offer possibilities for engagement: 'it takes an enormous amount of effort to engage with the world and your own life' (cited by Ratcliffe, 2015, p. 33) So too, in schizophrenia:

> People and things are no longer encountered as 'ready-to-hand'[5]—as affording a range of immediately perceived interactive possibilities (the way a friendly smile affords conversation or a chair sitting) specified by the norms and conventions tacitly governing the context in which they're encountered. Instead, everyday encounters and projects are experienced as puzzling or devoid of meaning. (Krueger, 2020, p. 602)

Finally, there may be a breakdown in one's intersubjective capacities. Phenomenology recognises that a fundamental aspect of our experience of the world is that we find ourselves in a shared world. One's experience of the Other is thus necessary for one's sense of a meaningful world. Objects in the world only make sense in relation to a shared world; for example, my understanding of a telephone only has meaning in a world of Others. However, the manner in which one relates to the Other has been found to be transformed in some forms of psychiatric illness. This breakdown of intersubjectivity is a symptom of PTSD: 'the traumatized individual is unable to perceive the affordances the other offers because their ability to empathize is impacted: the girl in the café might be perceived as a potential threat, as someone who could hurt me' (Wilde, 2019, p. 144). Wilde identifies that this difficulty to engage with the Other drives 'a sense of alienation, of being cut off, and not being at home in the world' (*ibid.*). A disruption of intersubjectivity has also been found in depression (Ratcliffe, 2018), schizophrenia (Laing, 1964), and agoraphobia (Trigg, 2013).

However, it is worth noting that these profound alterations in one's sense of Self, space, time, body, and possibilities for action naturally lead to a difficulty in engaging with the Other. In the words of Laing, for the ontologically insecure person:

> The whole 'physiognomy' of his world will be correspondingly different from that of the individual whose sense of self is securely established in its health and validity. Relatedness to other persons will be seen to have a radically different significance and function. (Laing, 1964, p. 37)

---

[5] 'Ready-to-hand' is a term coined by Heidegger to capture the way in which objects in the world offer themselves for practical use, e.g. the cup of tea is 'ready-to-hand' as it calls to be drunk.

In other words, the breakdown in relationship with the Other is because the person with psychiatric illness has a radically different lifeworld. These breakdowns in intersubjectivity make for further disruptions in co-production. Co-producing meaning presupposes an ability to engage in certain kinds of interpersonal practices, such as discussing, trusting, and empathising. Through psychiatric illness, there is a loss (or at least a barrier to) interpersonal abilities, without which co-production cannot be achieved.

A further interruption of co-production comes with the inexpressibility of one's lived experience while in a position of ontological insecurity. As one patient with psychosis describes: 'There are things that happen to me that I have never found words for, some lost now, some which I still search desperately to explain, as if time is running out and what I see and feel will be lost to the depths of chaos forever' (Fusar-Poli, 2022, p. 168). In *Darkness Visible*, William Styron describes depression as 'so mysteriously painful and elusive in the way it becomes known to the self [...] as to verge close to being beyond description. It thus remains nearly incomprehensible to those who have not experienced it in its extreme mode' (Styron, 2010, p. 5). So too, in describing her experience of bipolar disorder, Nancy Tracey claims emotional pain is even harder to express than physical pain:

> Language is insufficient to express emotional pain and turmoil. We have good words for describing physical pain: radiating, hot, throbbing, sharp, achy and so on. But when it comes to emotional pain we're "sad." [...] It's not surprising that people don't get what we're talking about. (Tracey, 2016, p. 74)

Indeed, the ineffable nature of psychiatric illness motivates Gadamer's pessimism for a hermeneutic approach to psychiatric healthcare. He states that 'the patient's insight into their own illness is disturbed' (Gadamer, 1996, p. 168). A (perhaps) uncharitable reading of Gadamer may dismiss this claim as more epistemic injustice, as Gadamer underestimates the patient's ability to understand their own illness experience. However, it seems that Gadamer is instead attempting to touch upon a profound disturbance in the patient's lifeworld, leading to a struggle to make sense of one's experience.

Therefore, even if hermeneutical injustice were eliminated from the psychiatric encounter, entrenched communication problems are an aspect of the illness itself. This infringes upon the co-production of meaning, as the illness itself inhibits the patient's capacity to discuss their lived experience. In what follows, we argue that in order to overcome Gadamer's 'Hermeneutical Problem' and achieve co-production in meaning we need to turn to phenomenological psychopathology.

4. Co-Production through Phenomenological Psychopathology

In the search for alternative approaches to psychiatry, there has been a reignited interest in phenomenological psychopathology: an approach that uses the phenomenological method to highlight the lived experience of the person with mental ill-health and invites a person-centred approach to diagnosis and treatment. Advocates of the phenomenological method recognise that it is impossible to conduct an isolated investigation on the 'mind' or 'brain' of a psychiatric patient because embodied subjectivity is irreducible to a mere mind, and that we need a rich account of experience to understand what we are seeking to explain scientifically.

At the heart of phenomenological psychopathology is the work of Karl Jaspers. Jaspers marries the phenomenological tradition of early Husserl with the psychology of his contemporaries, such as Wilhelm Dilthey, Max Weber, and Georg Simmel, to form a revolutionary approach to psychiatric practice. As Zahavi and Loidolt observe, Jaspers' goal was to transform psychiatry with the insights of philosophy: 'Jaspers passionately defended the need for methodological pluralism, emphasizing the extent to which methods and viewpoints from philosophy had a special value for psychiatry' (Zahavi and Loidolt, 2022, p. 58).

Jaspers begins by distinguishing between the objective and the subjective symptoms one can examine in a psychiatric patient. Objective symptoms can be observed on the surface and deduced through sense perception and 'rational thought' (Jaspers, 1968, p. 1314). Objective symptoms include 1) 'concrete events that can be perceived by the senses' (e.g., physical gestures and speech expression), 2) 'all measurable performances' (e.g., whether the patient can work, or learn, or retain memory), 3) 'the rational content of what the patient tells us' (e.g., reports of delusion) (*ibid.*). These objective symptoms were the main focus of the psychotherapists in Jaspers' day (and arguably continue to dominate modern psychiatry).

In contrast, Jaspers recognises that the psychiatric patient also has subjective symptoms, which are not as easily assessed. Drawing on Husserl's phenomenological tradition, Jaspers understands subjective symptoms as the elusive inner life of the psychiatric patient.

Lucienne Spencer and Ian James Kidd

This can be understood as the emotional, temporal, spatial, and intentional style of one's embodied experience in the world. In the context of psychiatry, Jaspers applies the phenomenological method to examine the patient's lifeworld in a state of psychiatric illness. This is at the centre of phenomenological psychopathology – understanding psychiatric illness through the lifeworld of the patient.

5. Overcoming the Contingent Obstacles

Phenomenological psychopathology challenges the contingent obstacles of communication in psychiatric practice, first and foremost by redressing the unequal power structures in psychiatric healthcare and developing a patient-centred approach. By inviting the patient into an informational exchange that prioritises their own expression of their lived experience, the clinician is no longer the arbiter of meaning-making. This shift in epistemic authority is one of the key benefits of a phenomenological approach to psychopathology: meaning-making is centred not around the clinician but the patient.

As we have seen, in a clinical exchange, the meaning the psychiatric patient places on aspects of the world may not be taken seriously and may be dismissed as irrational or a product of illness itself. This can be understood as a form of testimonial injustice. Through phenomenological psychopathology, on the other hand, the patient's interpretation is placed at the centre of the therapeutic process. Phenomenological psychopathology can be understood as the development of 'a framework for approaching mental illness in which theoretical assumptions are minimized, and the forms and contents of the patient's subjective experience are prioritized' (Stanghellini et al., 2019, p. 3). Phenomenological psychopathology surpasses the limited scope of pre-structured interviews and diagnostic criteria by examining the patient's lifeworld. After all, in the words of Stanghellini et al.: 'we, as clinical psychiatrists, do not usually sit in front of a broken brain – we sit in front of a suffering person' (Stanghellini et al., 2019, p. 4). This shift in epistemic authority is one of the key benefits of a phenomenological approach to psychopathology: meaning-making is centred not around the clinician but the patient.

Moreover, as a 'quest for meaning', phenomenological psychopathology strives to overcome the hermeneutical inequality perpetrated by traditional interpretive frameworks. By casting aside the often ill-suited hermeneutical resources of the diagnostic manual, phenomenological psychopathology seeks to articulate the world as it appears to the person with psychiatric illness, 'including all those details that resist standard semiological classification' (Stanghellini *et al.*, 2019, p. 959).

Indeed, the rejection of pre-given interpretive frameworks is at the heart of phenomenological psychopathology, as it plays a key role in Jaspers' 'General Psychopathology'. Jaspers identifies 'theoretical prejudice' in the work of his predecessors, whereby clinical examination was skewed in order to fit within a dominant theoretical framework: 'anything that supports it or seems relevant is found interesting; anything that has no relevance is ignored; anything that contradicts the theory is blanketed or misinterpreted' (Jaspers, 1997, p. 17). As such, Jaspers calls for a suspension of 'all outmoded theories, psychological constructs or materialist mythologies of cerebral processes' and 'basic constructs or frames of reference' (Jaspers, 1968, pp. 1315–6). This bracketing includes the taxonomy and classification pre-established in psychiatry, as well as all inherited, obsolete psychological theories that may unduly influence the psychiatrist.

Although some advocates of the method have attempted to devise a psychiatric classification that is rooted in a phenomenological approach (see Fernandez, 2019), the most common view held amongst phenomenological psychotherapists is that, given the world-disrupting nature of psychiatric illness, there is no straightforward, universal translation for any psychiatric experience. Rather than a one-size-fits-all approach, phenomenological psychopathology strives to facilitate reflective awareness and communicability of the patient's first-person account through doctor-patient dialogue.

Therefore, the phenomenological psychopathologist is sensitive to the communicative hurdles the patient faces and demonstrates a reflexive awareness that the language of the diagnostic manual may be an ill-fitting hermeneutical resource for the patient's lived experience. Through phenomenological psychopathology, the clinician not only exercises a hermeneutical openness to the patient's interpretation but rejects the dominant interpretive framework in order to foster the patient's alternative understanding of their illness experience.

While such an emphasis on the first-person perspective may tackle the contingent communication problems in psychiatric practice, what is less evident, is how phenomenological psychopathology can help us tackle the intrinsic obstacles. These problems are far more challenging to overcome, as they are part of the very nature of the illness itself. In what follows, we consider how useful phenomenological psychopathology can be for overcoming inherent communication problems in co-production.

6. Overcoming Intrinsic Obstacles

Phenomenological psychopathology goes beyond a mere description of 'what it is like' to have a certain psychiatric illness; phenomenological psychopathology concerns an in-depth examination of the interpersonal, intentional, temporal, spatial, and affective structure of the patient's lifeworld. In collating these valuable first-person descriptions, the clinician and patient can, over time, paint a picture of the lifeworld of a given psychiatric illness by drawing out the prevalent core structures in each account. Consequently, phenomenological psychopathology 'provides tools that can facilitate successful clinical diagnosis as well as the revision of our diagnostic categories' (Stanghellini *et al.*, 2019, p. 4).

However, how does the phenomenologist initially attain meaningful first-person descriptions when faced with intrinsic obstacles to expression? Many of the burgeoning resources in phenomenological psychopathology focus on developing new interview techniques to extract the first-person narrative from the patient. The most popular include the PHD method of interview (Stanghellini *et al.*, 2019), The Examination of Anomalous World Experience (EAWE) (Pienkos, Silverstein, and Sass, 2017) and the Examination of Anomalous Self Experience (EASE) (Parnas *et al.*, 2005). These interview techniques acknowledge the inherent problems in conveying complex illness experiences. For example, Parnas *et al.* observe:

> The experiences may be *fleeting*, perhaps even verging on something *ineffable*. They are *not* like material objects that one can 'take out of one's head' and describe them as if they were *things* with certain properties, or redescribe the experience at different occasions in exactly the same terms. The patient may be short of words to express his own experience. (Parnas *et al.*, 2005, p. 237).

Advocates of phenomenological psychopathology go on to recommend techniques for the clinician to employ in order to encourage meaningful dialogue. These include taking metaphorical language seriously, establishing a good rapport with the patient, and 'a patient-doctor mutually interactive reflection' (Parnas *et al.*, 2005). The latter involves a back-and-forth between patient and clinician, where the clinician reformulates the question, provides examples, and slowly extracts the meaning from the patient in the style of a semi-structured interview (*ibid.*). An account of how best to extract a meaningful account of the patient's lived experience can also be found in Stanghellini and Mancini's 'toolbox': 'the family of tools in use during the interview' (Stanghellini and Mancini, 2017, p. 3). This includes 1) phenomenological unfolding, 2) hermeneutic analysis, and 3) dynamics analysis (Stanghellini, 2016).

A further technique is that of guiding a self-narrative from the patient. Anna Bortolan emphasises that the narrative aspect of phenomenological psychopathology offers the patient not only epistemic insight but is also part of the recovery process. She argues that, by putting one's phenomenological experience into words, the patient has command over the ambiguous and overwhelming change in her lifeworld: 'This increased sense of control, in turn, inclines us to be more proactive in regulating our feelings, which results in less overwhelming emotions and an increased sense of empowerment' (Bortolan, 2019, p. 1059). In some cases, however, the collapse of the possibility of meaningful narration may be integral to the experience. Certain experiences of grief and depression, for instance, may involve the loss of an orientation towards the future that narrative practice presupposes (Ratcliffe and Broome, 2012).

Nevertheless, phenomenological psychopathology in its current form only offers resources for the *clinician* to mediate successful meaning-making. It does not currently offer resources for those with lived experiences to tackle the intrinsic obstacles to communication. For this reason, we turn to the phenomenology of illness more broadly and to Havi Carel's 'phenomenological toolkit' (Carel, 2012, 2016). Stanghellini's phenomenological 'toolbox' shares many similarities with Carel's 'phenomenological toolkit': both advocate employing the epoche, drawing out the meaning structures of illness and examining the patient's being-in-the-world. However, Carel's phenomenological toolkit is first and foremost 'a patient resource' and only secondly 'aimed at training clinicians' (Carel, 2016, p. 199).

Carel argues that a phenomenological method is an essential tool for the expression of illness, and for the develop of a rich (or 'thick') account of the illness experience: 'a philosophical framework that views cognition as embodied, focuses on subjective experience, and provides a robust existential account of selfhood is well suited to understanding the experience of illness' (Carel, 2012, p. 100). While phenomenological psychopathology advocates for phenomenology as an ideal resource for clinicians, Carel recognises that it is also an ideal tool for patients to communicate their experiences. Carel's opts for a 'flexible individual tool which patients can use to develop their understanding of their illness', instead of focusing on the clinician's understanding (Carel, 2012, pp. 106–7).

Indeed, Carel even extends the process beyond the bounds of the patient-clinician dialogue, and transforms the hermeneutical process into a collaborative effort between patients, clinicians, and family members in a workshop setting:

> The small-group structure of the workshop and the fact that participants all suffer from an illness, or aim to care for ill persons, provide a safe environment that will allow participants to share the idiosyncrasies of their experiences with no pressure for these to fit into a pre-given mould. (Carel, 2016, p. 202)

Given the ineffability of illness, a collective attempt at expression may be more effective with more participants contributing their knowledge. This is reminiscent of Fricker's account of Wendy Sanford, who is introduced to the term 'postpartum depression' after participating in a university-based workshop. In a 'life-changing forty-five minutes', she can make sense of her own experience of postpartum depression. Consequently, a 'hermeneutical darkness' is 'suddenly lifted from Wendy Sandford's mind' (Fricker, 2007, p. 149).

Moreover, Carel's phenomenological toolkit attempts to provoke meaningful reflection, not merely through language and text, but through 'visual and sensual samples' (Carel, 2012, p. 109). In the words of Carel, 'The evocative force of images and sounds will enable participants to explore possibly unnamed emotions and experiences. The phenomenological dimension of the workshop is amplified by this use of varied media, which will appeal to the experiential and perceptual, rather than restrict exploration to already formulated ideas' (*ibid.*). As the ineffable experiences of illness seem to defy everyday language, it may indeed be more promising to appeal to expression beyond language.

It is worth qualifying here that such phenomenological approaches are by no means simple and fail-safe methods for tackling intrinsic communication problems. Overcoming intrinsic obstacles to communication is no mean feat. However, we propose that through a phenomenological toolkit, we can go some way towards finding new ways of expressing the near inexpressible.

7. Conclusion

This chapter began with Gadamer's 'hermeneutic problem of psychiatry', which identifies an 'unbridgeable divide' between clinician and patient in the psychiatric encounter (Gadamer, 1996, p. 171). This poses a problem for the co-production of meaning in mental health research, as a collaborative effort in meaning-making is an essential aspect of co-production. In considering Gadamer's 'hermeneutic problem of psychiatry', two key obstacles to successful co-production emerge, the first being contingent barriers to communication. The genuine dialogue described by Gadamer requires scarce resources – time, trust, empathy – and runs up against power structures, institutional barriers, negative biases, and general deficiencies in shared moral energies. These contingent factors result from historical events, decisions, and developments that could have been different. One key contingent factor is hermeneutical marginalisation, whereby communication is inhibited due to gaps in the interpretive framework, caused by a lack of inclusion of marginalised voices in the meaning-making process. Contingent factors such as these inhibit the co-production of meaning.

These structural issues must be redressed to ensure a reciprocal dialogue between clinician and patient, whereby both parties can participate in meaning-making. The study of these contingent factors is ever-growing in the philosophy of psychiatry. Nevertheless, sensitivity to contingent factors should not occlude the possibility that some obstacles are intrinsic. In other words, even if all the social and epistemic challenges were eliminated, or had never existed in the first place, some intrinsic factors would persist no matter what the social world or the psychiatric care system is like. Difficulties in co-producing meaning in psychiatric healthcare may result from the illness itself. We refer to these as the intrinsic obstacles to communication. Communication difficulties may arise due to a newfound chaotic way of thinking or indifference towards the clinician. However, in turning to phenomenology, it becomes apparent that communication difficulties can arise from a profound alteration in one's lifeworld. A transformation of the way one experiences their body, their sense of self, time, space, objects in the world and others can lead to ineffability. Thus, even if a hermeneutically just psychiatric context could be constructed, the illness itself may inhibit successful meaning-making in co-production.

In calling attention to the contingent and intrinsic obstacles to communication, we problematise the concept of 'co-production', revealing it to be more complex than originally thought. We conclude by arguing that new developments in phenomenological psychopathology can be used to overcome the contingent obstacles to co-production and can go some way towards ameliorating the intrinsic obstacles too. Phenomenological psychopathology redresses the uneven power structures in psychiatry by prioritising the patient's experience. Moreover, it rejects the interpretive frameworks traditional to psychiatric healthcare, and attempts to develop a new framework from the expressions of the patients themselves. As such, phenomenological psychopathology is hermeneutically just, as the patient plays a central role in the meaning-making process.

When tackling the intrinsic problems of co-production, we found that phenomenological psychopathology fell short. While it provides clinicians with resources for extracting the narratives of lived experience from the patient, the method fails to provide resources for the patient to better express the inexpressible. Thus, we turn to Havi Carel's 'phenomenological toolkit', which helps patients voice their illness experience in phenomenological terms. The phenomenological toolkit also attempts to provoke expression through visual and sensual stimulations, as Carel recognises that our day-to-day language is ill-equipped for transformative experiences. While intrinsic problems still obstruct successful co-production, we believe Carel's phenomenological toolkit lends itself towards the expression of ineffable experiences.

Gadamer's hermeneutic problem of psychiatry should trouble those who propose to co-produce meaning in psychiatric healthcare. By highlighting the contingent and intrinsic obstacles of expressing the lived experience of psychiatric illness, we hope that those intending to co-produce meaning may reflect upon ways of overcoming these hurdles. We suggest the phenomenological method as a promising approach for ameliorating these communication difficulties. Ultimately, we hope to find new ways of bridging the so-called 'unbridgeable divide' in psychiatric healthcare.

References

Kevin Aho, 'Temporal Experience in Anxiety: Embodiment, Selfhood, and the Collapse of Meaning', *Phenomenology and the Cognitive Sciences*, 19 (2020), 259–70.

Maria Andreou and Vasileia Skrimpa, 'Theory of Mind Deficits and Neurophysiological Operations in Autism Spectrum Disorders: A Review', *Brain Sciences*, 10:6 (2020), 393.

Ludwig Binswanger, *Mélancolie et Manie: Études Phénoménologiques*, Jean-Michel Azorin and Yves Pélicier (trans.), (Paris: Presses Universitaires de France, 2011 [1960]).

Anna Bortolan, 'Phenomenological Psychopathology and Autobiography', in Giovanni Stanghellini, Matthew Broome,

Anthony Vincent Fernandez, Paolo Fusar-Poli, Andrea Raballo, and René Rosfort (eds.), *The Oxford Handbook of Phenomenological Psychopathology* (Oxford: Oxford University Press, 2019), 1053–64.

Martin Buber, *I and Thou*, Ronald Gregor Smith (trans.), (New York: Scribner Classics, 2000).

Havi Carel, 'Phenomenology as a Resource for Patients', *The Journal of Medicine and Philosophy*, 37:2 (2012), 96–113.

Havi Carel, *Phenomenology of Illness* (Oxford: Oxford University Press, 2016).

Havi Carel and Ian James Kidd, 'Epistemic Injustice in Healthcare: A Philosophical Analysis', *Medicine, Health Care and Philosophy*, 17 (2014), 529–40.

Sarah Carr and Meena Patel, *Progressing Transformative Co-Production in Mental Health* (National Development Team for Inclusion, 2016).

Remzi Oğulcan Çiray, Gonca Özyurt, Serkan Turan, Ezgi Karagöz, Çağatay Ermiş, Yusuf Öztürk & Aynur Akay, 'The Association Between Pragmatic Language Impairment, Social Cognition and Emotion Regulation Skills in Adolescents with ADHD', *Nordic Journal of Psychiatry*, 76:2 (2022), 89–95.

Rachel Cooper, *Classifying Madness: A Philosophical Examination of the Diagnostic and Statistical Manual of Mental Disorders*, (New York: Springer, 2005).

Anthony Vincent Fernandez, 'Phenomenological Psychopathology and Psychiatric Classification', in Giovanni Stanghellini, Matthew Broome, Anthony Vincent Fernandez, Paolo Fusar-Poli, Andrea Raballo, and René Rosfort (eds.), *The Oxford Handbook of Phenomenological Psychopathology* (Oxford: Oxford University Press, 2019), 1016–30.

Michel Foucault, *Madness and Civilization*, 2nd edition, (Abingdon: Routledge, 2001 [1961]).

Miranda Fricker, *Epistemic Injustice: Power and the Ethics of Knowing* (Oxford: Oxford University Press, 2007).

Miranda Fricker, 'Evolving Concepts of Epistemic Injustice', in Ian James Kidd, José Medina, and Gaile Pohlhaus Jr (eds.), *The Routledge Handbook of Epistemic Injustice* (London: Routledge, 2017), 53–60.

Thomas Fuchs, 'Depression, Intercorporeality, and Interaffectivity', *Journal of Consciousness Studies*, 20 (2013), 219–38.

Paolo Fusar-Poli, Andrés Estradé, Giovanni Stanghellini, Jemma Venables, Juliana Onwumere, Guilherme Messas, Lorenzo Gilardi, Barnaby Nelson, Vikram Patel, Ilaria Bonoldi,

Massimiliano Aragona, Ana Cabrera, Joseba Rico, Arif Hoque, Jummy Otaiku, Nicholas Hunter, Melissa G Tamelini, Luca F. Maschião, Mariana Cardoso Puchivailo, Valter L. Piedade, Péter Kéri, Lily Kpodo, Charlene Sunkel, Jianan Bao, David Shiers, Elizabeth Kuipers, Celso Arango, and Mario Maj, 'The Lived Experience of Psychosis: A Bottom-Up Review Co-Written by Experts by Experience and Academics', *World Psychiatry*, 21:2 (2022), 168–88.

Hans-Georg Gadamer, *The Enigma of Health: The Art of Healing in a Scientific Age* (Stanford: Stanford University Press, 1996).

Shaun Gallagher, 'Time, Emotion, and Depression', *Emotion Review*, 4:2 (2012), 127–32.

J.J. Gibson, *The Senses Considered as Perceptual Systems* (London: Allen & Unwin, 1968).

Gary Gutting, *Michel Foucault's Archaeology of Scientific Reason: Science and the History of Reason* (Cambridge: Cambridge University Press, 1989).

Karl Jaspers, *General Psychopathology*, Julius Hoenig and Marian W. Hamilton (trans.), (Baltimore, MD: Johns Hopkins University Press, 1997 [1913]).

Karl Jaspers, 'The Phenomenological Approach in Psychopathology', *The British Journal of Psychiatry*, 114:516 (1968), 1313–23.

Kenneth S. Kendler, 'The Phenomenology of Major Depression and the Representativeness and Nature of DSM Criteria', *The American Journal of Psychiatry*, 173:8 (2016), 771–80.

Ian James Kidd, *Epistemic Injustice, Healthcare, and Illness: A Bibliography*, (2017), accessed 6 June 2023: https://ianjameskidd.weebly.com/epistemic-injustice-healthcare-and-illness-a-bibliography.html.

Ian James Kidd, José Medina, and Gaile Pohlhaus Jr (eds.), *The Routledge Handbook of Epistemic Injustice* (London: Routledge, 2017).

Ian James Kidd, Lucienne Spencer, and Havi Carel, 'Epistemic Injustice in Psychiatric Research and Practice', *Philosophical Psychology*, ahead-of-print (2023), 1–29.

Joel Krueger, 'Schizophrenia and the Scaffolded Self', *Topoi*, 39 (2020), 597–609.

Ronald David Laing, *The Divided Self: An Existential Study in Sanity and Madness* (London: Penguin Books, 1964).

Luis Madeira, Elizabeth Pienkos, Teresa Filipe, Mariana Melo, Guilherme Queiroz, João Eira, Cristina Costa, Maria Luísa Figueira, and Louis Sass, 'Self and World Experience in Non-Affective First Episode of Psychosis', *Schizophrenia Research*, 211 (2019), 69–78.

José Medina, 'Varieties of Hermeneutical Injustice', in Ian James Kidd, José Medina, and Gaile Pohlhaus Jr (eds.), *The Routledge Handbook of Epistemic Injustice* (London: Routledge, 2017), 41–52.

Mental Health Foundation, *Stigma and Discrimination*, (2016), accessed 6 June 2023: https://www.mentalhealth.org.uk/a-to-z/s/stigma-and-discrimination.

Maurice Merleau-Ponty, *Phenomenology of Perception*, Donald A. Landes (trans.), (Abingdon: Routledge, 2012).

Middlesex University London, Centre for Coproduction in Mental Health and Social Care, accessed 5 June 2023: https://www.mdx.ac.uk/our-research/centres/centre-for-coproduction-in-mental-health.

Eugene Minkowski, *Le Temps Vécu: Études Phénoménologiques et Psychopathologiques*, Yves Pelicier (ed.), (Paris: Presses Universitaires de France, 2013 [1933]).

National Collaborating Centre for Mental Health, *Working Well Together: Evidence and Tools to Enable Co-Production in Mental Health Commissioning* (London: National Collaborating Centre for Mental Health, 2019).

Josef Parnas, Paul Møller, Tilo Kircher, Jørgen Thalbitzer, Lennart Jansson, Peter Handest, and Dan Zahavi, 'EASE: Examination of Anomalous Self-Experience', *Psychopathology*, 38:5 (2005), 236–58.

Martyn D. Pickersgill, 'Debating DSM-5: Diagnosis and the Sociology of Critique', *Journal of Medical Ethics*, 40:8 (2014), 521–5.

Elizabeth Pienkos, Steven Silverstein, and Louis Sass, 'The Phenomenology of Anomalous World Experience in Schizophrenia: A Qualitative Study', *Journal of Phenomenological Psychology*, 48:2 (2017), 188–213.

Elizabeth Pienkos, Borut Škodlar, and Louis Sass, 'Expressing Experience: The Promise and Perils of the Phenomenological Interview', *Phenomenology and the Cognitive Sciences*, 21:1 (2021), 53–71.

Matthew Ratcliffe, *Experiences of Depression: A Study in Phenomenology*, (Oxford: Oxford University Press, 2015).

Matthew Ratcliffe, 'The Interpersonal Structure of Depression', *Psychoanalytic Psychotherapy*, 32:2 (2018), 122–39.

Matthew Ratcliffe and Matthew Broome, 'Existential Phenomenology, Psychiatric Illness, and the Death of Possibilities', in Steven Galt Cowell (ed.), *The Cambridge Companion to Existentialism* (Cambridge: Cambridge University Press, 2012), 361–82.

John Z. Sadler and Bill Fulford, 'Should Patients and Their Families Contribute to the DSM Process?', *Psychiatric Services*, 55:2 (2004), 133–8.

Louis Sass, 'The Truth-Taking-Stare: A Heideggerian Interpretation of a Schizophrenic World', *Journal of Phenomenological Psychology*, 21:2 (1990), 121–49.

Louis Sass, *Madness and Modernism: Insanity in the Light of Modern Art, Literature, and Thought* (Oxford: Oxford University Press, 2017).

Kenneth F. Schaffner and Kathryn Tabb, 'Varieties of Social Constructionism and the Problem of Progress in Psychiatry', in Kenneth S. Kendler and Josef Parnas (eds.), *Philosophical Issues in Psychiatry III: The Nature and Sources of Historical Change* (Oxford: Oxford University Press, 2015), 85–106.

Anastasia Philippa Scrutton, 'Epistemic Injustice and Mental Illness', in Ian James Kidd, José Medina, and Gaile Pohlhaus Jr (eds.), *The Routledge Handbook of Epistemic Injustice* (London: Routledge, 2017), 347–55.

Fredrik Svenaeus, *Phenomenological Bioethics: Medical Technologies, Human Suffering, and the Meaning of Being Alive* (London: Routledge, 2018).

Giovanni Stanghellini, 'Phenomenological Psychopathology and Care. From Person-Centered Dialectical Psychopathology to the PHD Method for Psychotherapy', in Giovanni Stanghellini and Massimiliano Aragona (eds.), *An Experiential Approach to Psychopathology: What is it Like to Suffer from Mental Disorders?* (Berlin: Springer, 2016), 361–78.

Giovanni Stanghellini, 'Phenomenological Psychopathology and Psychotherapy', in Giovanni Stanghellini, Matthew Broome, Anthony Vincent Fernandez, Paolo Fusar-Poli, Andrea Raballo, and René Rosfort (eds.), *The Oxford Handbook of Phenomenological Psychopathology* (Oxford: Oxford University Press, 2019), 952–71.

Giovanni Stanghellini and Milena Mancini, *The Therapeutic Interview in Mental Health: A Values-Based and Person-Centered Approach* (Cambridge: Cambridge University Press, 2017).

William Styron, *Darkness Visible: A Memoir of Madness* (New York: Open Road Integrated Media, 2010 [1990]).

Kathryn Tabb, 'Psychiatric Progress and the Assumption of Diagnostic Discrimination', *Philosophy of Science*, 82:5 (2015), 1047–58.

Arthur Tatossian, *La Fenomenologia delle Psicosi*, Riccardo Dalle Luche and Giampaolo Di Piazza (eds.), (Roma: G. Fioriti, 2019 [1979]).

Nancy Tracey, *Lost Marbles: Insights into My Life with Depression and Bipolar* (2016).

Dylan Trigg, 'The Body of The Other: Intercorporeality and the Phenomenology of Agoraphobia', *Continental Philosophy Review*, 46:3 (2013), 413–29.

Rebecca Tsosie, 'Indigenous Peoples, Anthropology, and the Legacy of Epistemic Injustice', in Ian James Kidd, José Medina, and Gaile Pohlhaus Jr (eds.), *The Routledge Handbook of Epistemic Injustice* (London: Routledge, 2017), 356–69.

David H. Vogel, Katharina Krämer, Theresa Schoofs, Christian Kupke, and Kai Vogeley, 'Disturbed Experience of Time in Depression – Evidence from Content Analysis', *Frontiers in Human Neuroscience*, 12 (2018), np.

Lilian Wilde, 'Trauma and Intersubjectivity: The Phenomenology of Empathy in PTSD', *Medicine, Health Care and Philosophy*, 22 (2019), 141–5.

Dan Zahavi and Sophie Loidolt, 'Critical Phenomenology and Psychiatry', *Continental Philosophy Review*, 55:1 (2022), 55–75.

Co-Production and Structural Oppression in Public Mental Health

ALANA WILDE

Abstract

Co-production, in the field of mental health, aims to bring together academic and clinical researchers and those with lived experience. Often, research projects informed by this methodology involve the meeting of opposing attitudes, whether to the legitimacy of psychiatry, determinants of mental ill health, or the most appropriate interventions. This has meant that whilst some have reported positive experiences of co-production, many people with lived experience of mental ill health, sometimes referred to as 'experts by experience' (EbE), report harms which have taken place or been perpetuated during co-produced research projects. In the literature, nearly always, this is understood as a kind of epistemic injustice in Miranda Fricker's sense. In this paper, I argue that whilst Fricker's view does provide a plausible explanation of what's at play, we can gain more insight into the structural factors which exclude EbE by applying a framework of epistemic oppression. By highlighting the systemic and structural factors which work to keep certain knowers and their contributions out of our collective epistemic resources, we begin to understand the enormity of the task required to redress injustices in our knowledge production systems.

1. Introduction

Co-production, as a relatively nascent research methodology in public mental health, aims to bring together academic and clinical researchers and those who have lived experience of mental ill health. It is posited as a revolutionised approach to research by including those who have traditionally been research*ed* as equal members of the research team. These research projects take place across mental health disciplines such as public health, primary care design, digital mental health interventions, *etc.*, and bring together opposing attitudes to the legitimacy of psychiatry, to the determinants of mental ill health, and to what we ought to value. This has meant that whilst some have reported positive experiences of co-production, many people with lived experience of mental ill health, sometimes referred to as 'experts by experience' (EbE), report harms which have taken place or been perpetuated during co-produced research

doi:10.1017/S1358246123000231

projects. In the literature these harms are almost always described as being a kind of epistemic injustice, drawing upon the work of Miranda Fricker (2007). In this paper, I'll explain how epistemic injustice provides a plausible explanation of the harms done to experts by experience in their capacity as authoritative knowers. I'm going to argue, though, that we might better understand such exclusionary and harmful practices through the lens of epistemic oppression. Epistemic oppression, in Kristie Dotson's (2014) sense, provides a distinct epistemic perspective which allows us to highlight systemic and structural factors which work to keep certain knowers, and their contributions out of our collective epistemic resources. The harms, I'll argue, are still epistemic in nature, but by extending beyond individual-level prejudice, we're able to see what would be required so that co-production is done well.

2. Epistemic Injustice: An Obvious Framework?

Oftentimes, discussions of harms perpetuated by the research environment are understood as a kind of *epistemic injustice*, in as much as experts by experience are often not treated as the right kind of knowers, despite being believed to have valuable knowledge of research foci. And this sense of a harm being done to someone in their capacity as a knower perhaps seems apt, given the focus of this paper. Co-production invites individuals with lived experience – understood as 'experts by experience', in many cases – to contribute to research from the earliest stages based upon their first-hand knowledge of the topic that is examined. Attempts to further and to deepen our knowledge of some topic or other, just are epistemic in nature.

Miranda Fricker (2007) developed what is the most widely accepted framework of *epistemic injustice* to explain the phenomenon of individuals, often from marginalised social positions or groups, routinely being dismissed or disbelieved. For epistemic injustice to occur, a judgement of an individual as a less credible knower (either relative to the credibility I assign to myself or compared to a competing source of information) is made, based on a prejudicial stereotype. Typically, this stereotype takes the form of a negative identity prejudice. On Fricker's view, we routinely use heuristic aids, such as stereotypes, as psychological shortcuts that aid our judgement and reasoning (Fricker, 2007). Consider the following example. If someone is invited to testify at a trial as an 'expert witness' and begins their testimony with a list of their academic achievements, I may assign what they say a greater level of importance

134

than if they were a 'bystander', due to my prejudicial belief that academic qualification makes one particularly well suited to evidence-giving. In Fricker's terminology, I rely on my own heuristic aid concerning expert witnesses, which assigns high levels of credibility to academic 'experts', and take what the expert witness says at face value. What goes 'wrong' in cases of epistemic injustice, is that the stereotypes upon which I rely are almost always negative or ethically noxious in nature. These stereotypes are inversely correlated with judgements regarding competence and credibility. If my interlocutor belongs to a 'group' against whom I hold a negative identity prejudice (whether conscious or not) I may deflate or decrease the level of legitimacy I assign to what they say (Fricker, 2007).

Being perceived as 'ill' in any sense, whether physical or mental, can heighten susceptibility to experiencing this deflation of one's credibility as a knower. Carel and Kidd have argued that individuals with physical illnesses are more vulnerable to epistemic injustices than those in good health (Carel and Kidd, 2014, 2016). And mental ill health remains a topic subject to particularly pernicious and deeply entrenched negative stereotypes, such that vulnerabilities to being undermined or dismissed as a credible 'knower' are compounded (Crichton, Carel, and Kidd, 2017). Perceptions of individuals with mental ill health as being dangerous, unreliable, or irrational seem inextricably at odds with widely accepted *epistemic virtues* of honesty, and reliability.[1] These perceptions are not restricted to only one particular kind of psychiatric illness or diagnostic category. Decreased perceptions of the reliability of individuals with schizophrenia (Angermeyer and Matschinger, 2005; Corrigan *et al.*, 2001), PTSD, and of mental health on a broad scale (Wahl, 1999; Guidry-Grimes, 2015) are well documented, to name only a few. Being invited to participate in research as an expert in one's own circumstance whilst simultaneously being open about having received a psychiatric diagnosis, then, may well render much of what an 'expert by experience' has to say vulnerable to scepticism or dismissal.

In fact, the very concept of epistemic injustice seems to have afforded some relief to those who have been treated by the psychiatric system, as one service user who now takes part in co-production explains:

---

[1] For more on reliability and honesty as epistemic virtues, see, for example, Greco (2010), Goldman (1999), Lycan (1988), Sosa (2007), and Zagzebski (1996).

I stumbled across the concept of epistemic injustice on Twitter
[...]. It helped me to make sense of my experiences of harm
within psychotherapy and mental health services. I realised
I was taught to dismiss my own knowledge and this had deeply
affected my trust in myself and my confidence in what I know.
From being disbelieved about my experiences to being told
I should ignore what my body and mind were telling me [...]
epistemic injustice was everywhere [...]. I have lost count of
how many times I have told someone something about my
mental health, only for them to turn to the 'experts' to confirm
what I have said, as if I am an unreliable narrator of my own
mind. What often happens is that service-user knowledge is
only trusted if it is backed up by a researcher or professional.
(Coproduction Collective, 2023)

Just as individuals have spoken of relief at realising there are established conceptual frameworks that make sense of their experiences
in other areas,[2] the notion of epistemic injustice can be a useful tool
for experts by experience to understand how and why their testimony
has failed to gain the uptake intended.

I've focused here mainly on the testimonial 'kind' of epistemic
injustice that experts by experience face as this has received the most
attention and seems most apt for current discussions. What I think
interesting about the application of epistemic injustice to cases
where expert by experience testimony is excluded or afforded less
credibility in co-production approaches to mental health research,
is that the very reason individuals with lived experience are invited
to participate in these spaces is *because of* their direct, first-hand acquaintance with mental ill health. This is not to say that the transpos-
ition of negative identity prejudices to the research context is all that
surprising – we often allow biases to affect our epistemic conduct,
even when we have strong intentions to the contrary – but rather, dismissal of expert by experience testimony in a research endeavour designed to
include such testimony seems to be a particular instance of what Fricker
calls 'ethically bad affective investments' (2007, p. 35).

In the domain of public mental health, the goal of co-production is
not always to assess legitimacy or efficacy of existent approaches to
psychiatric recovery or service design, but often to understand the

[2] For instance, the concepts of neurodiversity (Grandin and Panek,
2014), gaslighting (Stern, 2007), imposter syndrome (Feenstra *et al.*,
2020), and heteronormativity (Butler, 1990) have also been discussed as
comfort-giving for those in minoritised groups as a way of making sense
of one's experiences.

etiological, psychopharmacological, or even socially driven bases of mental ill health. A holistic research picture, which is the aim of co-production, must take on board perspectives of those with experience and with lived insight. This makes the negative identity prejudices which carry over to the research context seem that much more pernicious, and make them instances of bad epistemic practice on the part of those deflating the credibility of experts by experience. Service users, carers, and those who have been subject to psychiatric treatment are known to have had, or perhaps to still have, direct acquaintance with mental ill health. Dismissal of their accounts as inconvenient, as illegitimate, or as unduly unreliable seems to go against the entire motivations for conducting this kind of research. In §3, I'll discuss in more detail the ways in which expert by experience testimony routinely fails to enter into our shared pools of knowledge.

Fricker's view, then, gives us one way of making sense of what's happening in such cases. Negative and prejudicial attitudes to mental ill health affect the heuristics upon which we all rely in judgement-making. In the context of co-production, those experts by experience who have been open about their illness or diagnosis, despite having been invited to participate in research based on their lived experience of that illness or diagnosis, routinely find that their words do not get the right sort of uptake to shift norms or to affect research conversations. The focus upon the ways in which social injustices lead to epistemic injustices captures nicely many of the facets of the discrimination faced in relation to mental health. What I think, and what I'll go on to say (in section 4), is that understanding the exclusion of expert by experience testimony or knowledge only gets us a narrow understanding of the picture. On Fricker's view, I, as an epistemic agent in my own right, am responsible for negative identity prejudices that I hold and the effects that these prejudicial beliefs have on the credibility assignments that I make. I can either rely on the faulty heuristic aids I possess and give short shrift to evidence of those I take to be members of particular categories on that basis; or, I can accept counterevidence, and revise the beliefs I hold, attempting to assign due weight to testimony of my interlocutors, and strive to be epistemically just in my interactions. This is a perfectly plausible way of making sense of how, in individual interactions, expert by experience testimony is subject to deflationary credibility assessments or is perhaps otherwise subverted. But, in the research environment, we are not only focusing upon individual interactions, and as such, the adage 'it's not about me' becomes relevant. The academic or clinical experts here have, presumably, committed themselves to undertaking a co-produced research project. We might expect that this means not all members of the research team hold negative identity prejudices toward those they plan to partner with, or at least that not all of the academic and/or clinical research team are making such ethically bad affective investments, repeatedly. To cast such an aspersion would be to assume that such research projects are undertaken in bad faith. And I don't think that's what's going on in these sorts of pictures. In order that research be done effectively and achieve any kind of advancement in what we take ourselves to understand or to do, there are norms, conventions, and broader requirements at play such that knowledge gains uptake and enters into shared understanding. It is not just what I, *qua* epistemic agent, do, but in order to advance knowledge, I must be able to affect a system level shift, or, at the very least, have my research findings enter into shared epistemic resources. Fricker's view may well accommodate this, as a series of repeated instances of credibility deficit assignment which undermine the legitimacy of knowledge offered up by experts by experience. But, in what follows, I'm going to say that making sense of the exclusion of experts by experience using an alternative framework of epistemic harm might help us to understand what's happening in these cases at a system level.

3. The Tensions at Play: Failures of Uptake

Prior to providing an alternative analysis of epistemic harm, it may be helpful to understand a little more about the tensions that are manifest in the research process. Understanding these instances, at the level of individual interaction as epistemic injustice is I think, as I've indicated, a correct appraisal. What I'm going to go on to say, though, is that we can similarly make sense of these sorts of exclusionary research practices at a broader systemic level by understanding them as *epistemic oppression*. The latter concept, I'll say in §4, allows us to understand why co-production as an approach to research is rife with epistemic harms. But on either view, understanding the ways in which testimony fails to gain uptake or to be received as legitimate knowledge helps to paint a fuller picture of the phenomenon this paper attempts to make sense of.

(i) Testimony received as anecdote

First, there is a purported tension between what is deemed 'hard science', that is, evidence-based and deriving from medical professionals, and anecdotal contributions to knowledge. Co-production, as a methodology which does not require those with lived experience to possess the same academic or clinical expertise as the research team *qua* accepted experts, is often seen as an 'additional' dimension of knowledge, bolted on to research projects rather than integral to them. Being invited to participate in research on the basis of your lived, experiential (and sometimes phenomenological) insights is often received as being invited to speak about those experiences. But experiences and recounting of thoughts and feelings on a personal level are not afforded the same level of scientific credence as the results of a pharmacological trial or a population level ethnographic study (Rose and Kalathil, 2019; Johnson and Martínez Guzmán, 2013). In fact, as Diana Rose and Jayasree Kalathil recount, in their (2019) article 'Power, Privilege and Knowledge: The Untenable Promise of Co-Production in Mental "Health"', individuals with lived experience are often invited to speak in the very spaces in which their 'illnesses' or 'disorders' are discussed in derogating or distressing terms by more typical academic researchers only moments later. This, they go on to say, is akin to being a subaltern in the research team and to having one's knowledge rendered unspeakable (2019).[3] Even if you are sympathetic to the value of experiential knowledge and would agree that instances like those Rose and Kalathil describe are harmful and ought not to constitute the way research is done, you may also agree that present research hierarchies tend to privilege the quantitative or the 'evidence-based' as opposed to the qualitative or narrative kinds of knowledge (Crichton, Carel, and Kidd, 2017). 'Lay' research members (those who are often invited on the basis of their lived experience) are simply not afforded the power or control of research that would allow them to influence research's direction, or to challenge chosen methodologies such that their contributions 'count' in meaningful ways (Slade *et al.*, 2010). Methods that are viewed as value-free and objective remain privileged over and above subjective or first-hand accounts of distress or service use (Faulkner, 2017). Knowledge that is not deemed objective and is thus value-rich or rooted in experience is – understood in a Foucauldian sense – 'subjugated' (Foucault, 1980; Brown and Strega, 2005, p. 11). The tendency to prefer 'hard' evidence over 'soft', then, and the habit of categorising expert by

---

[3]   Spivak's notable 'Can the Subaltern Speak?' (1988) outlines the ways in which one's voice can become subjugated such that one's speech is rendered incapable of gaining uptake.

experience testimony as the latter, predisposes researchers to dismiss or distort the content of such testimony.

The harm, here, derives from experts by experience being recruited to such projects under the guise of equitable and significant involvement. Co-production is designed for that very purpose.[4] By inviting an individual with lived experience to participate in research on the basis of their first-hand acquaintance with mental ill health, there is a (not unreasonable) expectation that their contributions will be valued. Accordingly, giving testimony relating to experience the status of 'other' or second-class knowledge seems particularly harmful as this testimony forms the very basis for the involvement of such individuals.[5]

(ii) Subversion of message – psychiatrisation or lacunas in understanding

Second, there is a tendency of clinical or professional members of the research team to, intentionally or otherwise, water down or otherwise subvert or pathologise the contributions of those with lived experience. This may (as we'll see later in section §4) have more to do with ingrained societal (mis)conceptions relating to the epistemic virtues, vices, and traits of those with mental ill health.

Typically, this may take the form of the individual with lived experience asserting 'S' in discussions, but the clinical or academic research partners on the project interpreting this as 'S^*'. Power dynamics carried over to the research environment often mean that experiential knowledge is offered up by those with lived experience but is ultimately defined by the 'experts' in the room. This is in many ways unsurprising when we consider the power that psychiatric professionals have over determining the rights, or removal of rights (in some cases) of their patients. Residual and engrained power

[4] Tracing the histories of co-production and the multitude of definitions of the concept highlight the onus that is placed upon equal and fair participation.

[5] This point might be viewed as contentious by those currently undertaking research given the onus that higher education institutions, research funders, and public sector bodies place on co-producing knowledge. It's plausible that academic and clinical research teams are strongly opposed to recruiting experts by experience but must do so in order to secure funding to undertake their project. However, to then see the testimony of experts by experience as almost a sub-class of knowledge remains harmful, if that is not clearly communicated to those recruited.

dynamics transferring from the clinical setting over to the research setting may well affect which testimonies are assigned credibility, and conversely, which are not. Whoever is responsible for the writing up of meetings, the research progression, or the evidence-gathering aspects of the research process may find themselves reading into an individual's testimony a meaning that simply is not, or was not, that. And whilst this interpreting of testimony is in itself a harm, what compounds this particular harm is the way in which such testimony is routinely sanitised or made to fit dominant societal conceptions of mental ill health (Jones and Kelly, 2015). For instance, someone with lived experience might say that they 'value the community which they have gathered around them during periods of ill health' but this could, understood through the lens of psychiatric practice, be interpreted as 'patient is unmotivated to stay well due to the care and attention they receive when less able to go about their day-to-day activities'. Such a subversion of meaning *could* be due to the habits of psychiatric practitioners in interpreting what patients say to them. This is often based upon habitual practices (not dissimilar to Fricker's heuristic aids mentioned earlier) whereby shortcuts are taken based upon experience: often patients demonstrate trait T and this could be an instance of T, despite the content of the utterance literally meaning S. Alternatively, this subversion could be due to a failure of shared frameworks of reference possessed by the expert by experience and the clinician.

As Luvell Anderson (2017) notes, often – and particularly when marginalised individuals or identities are at play – some conceptual resources simply aren't shared. Two conversational parties may believe they are talking along the same lines, but the more privileged party makes sense of what they hear based upon their understanding of the world. If this understanding doesn't quite track the understanding that the original speaker had, the end result can be that both feel as though they understand and have been understood by one another, however a gap in hermeneutic horizons leads to a lacuna in meaning or sense making (Anderson, 2017). Simply put: neither party can articulate or take away from an utterance something which they don't relate to. If a clinician or academic has not had the positive experience of finding oneself understood by a particular community in ways which differ (positively) from routine social interactions, that may not be the sense that they take from the above statement. However, they may feel as though they have understood it, through the lens of patient interactions previously had, and the expert by experience may have no reason to suppose that their words will take on a new meaning. And it is not only the words we

Alana Wilde

say, and the way they are received that can affect the experience of co-production for those with first-hand acquaintance of mental ill health. Bee *et al.* (2015) take a similar kind of hermeneutic gap as being the cause of many failures in service user-involvement, stating that:

> [...] service user involvement fails because the patients' frame of reference diverges from that of providers. Service users and carers attributed highest value to the relational aspects but [...] planning is typically operationalised as a series of practice-based activities compliant with auditor standards. (Bee *et al.*, 2015, p.104)

Here, the hermeneutic gap relates to the most valued elements, either of a service or of the research process itself. Where the focus of academic or clinical experts is procedural, service-users involved can experience exclusion and disempowerment (Carr, 2016).

Further, individuals whose first-hand experience of psychiatric systems, or of forms of marginalisation in the social sense which are not shared by clinical or academic research partners, may be viewed as hostile or overly-critical of psychiatry as a branch of medicine. Mad Studies, and the anti-psychiatry movement, have gained a wealth of traction since the 1970s/80s and whilst criticisms of psychiatric practices are by no means restricted to these movements, they are dominant within them. Should an individual with lived experience report their believed illegitimacy of, say, psychiatric diagnosis in a research endeavour designed to interrogate the use of control and restraint in psychiatric inpatient settings, and the testimony of 'lay' researchers be overwhelmingly negative (as might be expected), this could be sanitised or subject to reinterpretation or subversion. The perceived hostility of those with lived experience – in that their testimony challenges accepted practices and standards – might lead to that testimony being omitted, altered, or otherwise changed (Hodge, 2005; Lewis, 2014).

Ultimately, what *can* be expressed is often determined by those in more traditional positions of power. The 'rules of research', as Marian Barnes (2002) notes, have not been transformed thus far and these rules 'define both the way in which deliberation is conducted and who is considered to be legitimate participants in the process' (Barnes, 2002, p. 329). Thus, traditional researchers retain the power to determine whose knowledge makes it into shared spaces and what narratives might be able to influence dominant understandings of research processes.

(iii) Duality of roles – legitimate knower, or mentally ill and lacking credence?

Thirdly, there are a multitude of roles which those with lived experience must simultaneously occupy. As Rose and Kalathil (2019) note, being positioned as an expert on the basis of one's lived experience in many ways renders one's legitimacy unstable and subject to variance on the basis of perceived mental state. As an individual with lived experience, whose lived experience is widely known in the research team, any expression of emotion or distress can serve to make one appear irrational, unwell, or unstable. And, of course, this has the effect of undermining the legitimacy of the knowledge conveyed in the same way that being perceived as mentally unwell affects the credibility or reliability you may be presumed to have in social and political spaces. Whilst the inviolability of professional knowledge is a given, or is received as a given, the degree of credibility the testimony or knowledge contributed by an individual with lived experience has depends upon the presentation of that testimony or knowledge. Becoming distressed, angry, or even appearing less animated than at previous meetings can result in the credibility your testimony is assigned being lowered, as there is an inverse (presumed) relationship between credence and legitimacy and heightened emotional states. This can also lead to what Liegghio calls 'psychiatrization' (Liegghio, 2013), where, like testimony subversion I outlined in (ii) above, what an expert by experience *says* is attributed to or presumed to be affected by their mental (ill) health. Heightened emotional state, or clinical assessment of the rationality or sanity of experts by experience can lead to either them or their testimony being pathologised.

Again, this can – almost equally – be attributed to societal attitudes to mental ill health and to the requirement for rationality in empirical science. Neither party views mental ill health as compatible with our 'norms' of epistemically virtuous practice. Mental ill health is viewed as in tension with rationality almost universally, and whilst it is not the goal of this paper to unpack such a tension, it is something which will be returned to in the following discussion.

4. Understanding Epistemic Harm as Epistemic Oppression

What the above scenario illustrates is a variety of ways in which the knowledge of experts by experience is simultaneously (mis)understood and undermined: either as not scientific enough, as a veiled disclosure of symptoms, or else as being lacking in authority or scientific legitimacy. These can all be explained in various ways, with various causes or reasons being pointed to, as the preceding section has shown. Whilst all of this can be explained at the level of individual interaction, I'll now move to more of a system-level view of epistemic harm, appealing to Kristie Dotson's framework of *epistemic oppression* (2014).[6]

4.1 Epistemic oppression: resilient systems

Dotson defines epistemic oppression as being 'a persistent and un-warranted infringement on the ability to utilize persuasively shared epistemic resources that hinder one's contribution to knowledge pro-duction' (2014, p. 116). Akin to the harm done to Fricker's epistemic agent in her capacity as a knower, an individual facing epistemic oppression is being undermined in her epistemic agency. However, Dotson's view specifically expands beyond the level of individual interaction and focuses upon the ability of an individual *qua* epistemic agent, to draw upon, contribute to, and shift shared epistemic resources (Dotson, 2014, p. 115). Whilst she acknowledges that (like instances of epistemic injustice) there are often social and political factors which undermine or impede the ability of an agent to make use of such epistemic resources, what differentiates Dotson's view from Fricker's is an account of third-order epistemic oppression.

---

[6] There is potential, depending on one's views regarding egalitarian dis-tribution of goods – including knowledge and perhaps credibility – to argue that *distributive epistemic injustice* would be an equally appropriate frame-work to apply given the unjust imbalances in power and privilege which I'll go on to discuss in section 4. I'm sympathetic to this argument, though think there are real reasons to avoid categorising knowledge or cred-ibility – in this particular context – as something which experts by experi-ence lack. For more on distributive epistemic injustice, see for example Coady (2017) and Nikolaidis (2021). Relatedly, Dotson's concept of *con-tributory injustice* (Dotson, 2012; Miller Tate, 2019) could be appealed to as a means of explaining how testimony subversions occur. Again, I think there's merit in this argument in some senses, but I do not think contribu-tory injustice applies here: experts by experience do not lack concepts that the dominant majority share, nor have they developed resources to explain their own experiences. Rather, the problems here lie in the ways in which the knowledge fails to enter into shared epistemic resources because of our epistemological systems norms of research and our social misconceptions re-garding mental ill health. I'm grateful to Paul Giladi for pressing me on these points.

The central claim of Dotson's account of third-order epistemic oppression is that this kind of epistemic oppression is not wholly reducible to social and political factors, but 'follows from a feature of epistemological systems themselves [...] epistemological resilience' (2014, p. 116).

Epistemological systems are, broadly speaking, systems which contain all of our epistemic habits, norms, and attitudinal beliefs. They also, following Taylor (2004) and Medina (2011), contain operative and instituted social imaginaries. Social imaginaries can be understood as shared collective understandings of what normal and desirable ways of living are. In the United Kingdom, our attitude to free healthcare as underpinned by equality of access, and the belief that one of the duties of the state is to provide public services, might be considered a social imaginary. They also help us to share common understandings of frequent dichotomies: acceptable/unacceptable beliefs or ways of living, normality and deviance, values and undesirable traits. Operative social imaginaries are those which tacitly govern our understandings and assumptions, influencing our perceptions and behaviour without us ever necessarily becoming aware of their presence. By contrast, an instituted social imaginary is more of an explicit, regulatory framework such as a legal Act, agreed terms of reference, or another codified behavioural schema; an instituted social imaginary may govern our actions and behaviour in much the same way as operative imaginaries, but we are much more cognisant of the latter (Taylor, 2004). Both operative and instituted social imaginaries partly comprise our epistemological systems. These systems, taken as a whole, affect what promotes or conversely what detracts from knowledge production (Dotson, 2014, p. 121). Whilst epistemological systems are by no means fixed or immutable, uncovering flaws in the system which governs your worldview of knowledge is a sort of meta-epistemic challenge. As such, revisions of entire epistemological systems are difficult to bring about. Dotson describes this as 'experiencing the impossible as possible and, correspondingly, viewing the limit of one's epistemological systems that designate the possible as impossible' (2014, p. 132). Bartunek and Moch similarly describe the incredulity one experiences when encountering the limits or drawbacks of one's own epistemological governance as being somewhat 'mystical' (1994, p. 28). And given the challenges associated with even identifying the limits of one's own epistemology, let alone the degree of paradigm shift required to remediate or redress injustices which are entrenched into the fabric of that system, or perhaps the imaginaries which it contains, our epistemological systems are highly resilient. Resilience, in this sense, relates to the degree of counterinformation which can be absorbed into the system itself without requiring a revision of the resources the system is comprised of (Dotson, 2014). Prudent epistemic practice, according to Medina, requires that 'epistemic friction' – the counterevidence mentioned above – be sought out frequently, such that epistemological systems be updated as alternatives appear and are established as credible (Medina, 2011, p. 29). Yet, when the counterevidence is such that it threatens to topple a well-established hierarchical view of knowledge, the tendency to dismiss or ignore the counterevidence, however credible it may appear, can obscure the limits of the system and be absorbed as anomalous.

Third-order epistemic oppression, then, occurs when an individual – either due to their social or institutional position, or to social and political factors which undermine their credibility – is unable to create sufficient 'epistemic friction' within the epistemological system that the research takes place in (Dotson, 2014). This friction would arise, should they be able to gain uptake, because of the incompatibility of their offered testimony with the system itself. However, possessing neither the power nor the epistemic virtues recognised by the system within which knowledge production is taking place, to gain uptake sufficient to make visible the limits of the dominant operative imaginary renders their knowledge incapable of entering in to the shared epistemic resources. We can thus present a range of reasons which might lead to the dismissal of testimony. Epistemic oppression, I'll explain below, occurs when (a) and either (b) or (c) apply:

(a) The position the utterer occupies is marginalised either socially or in a domain specific context such that their contributions are routinely met with suspicion;
     and either,
(b) the content of an individual utterance is at odds with commonly held beliefs or challenges norms of epistemic practice supported by the epistemological system;
     or,
(c) incorporating the content of the utterance into the epistemological system would render the system unstable.

If both (b) and (c) are the case, then, due to the revisions which would be required should the testimony be received as knowledge, it will likely be explained away. Instances of (a) and (b) or (a) and (c) will likely ensure that the individual contribution is delegitimised or otherwise viewed as irrelevant, misguided, or lacking in credibility. These latter scenarios relate not just to the marginalised position the individual holds as rooted solely in social and political system inequalities, but to the lack of power these individuals are perceived to possess in relation to the shifting of content of epistemological systems. I maintain that structural positionality and power are essential features of epistemic oppression, which is why (a) must be satisfied. The reasons I have stipulated that at least two of the three criteria must apply relates to what I term a 'threshold for epistemic oppression'. To see why this threshold requires at least two of the three listed criteria, consider the following.

Taking (a) alone just gets us to an understanding of epistemic injustice, in Fricker's sense, based upon negative identity prejudices. If only (b) as a reason for dismissal of one's testimony were constitutive of epistemic oppression, then any belief or disagreement with a majority view might be considered an infringement upon your capacity as an epistemic agent. Maintaining the stability of the epistemological system as a reason for dismissal or taking some evidence less seriously alone, as in (c), doesn't necessarily constitute oppression either; the contents of such information, or who is providing it, would be required such that (c) is relevant. This is not to say, of course, that routinely reasons like (c) suffice to disregard evidence; on the contrary, I think many of us have dismissed something that doesn't 'fit' with all else we know to be true or that we value. As Dotson explains, epistemological systems can withstand a great deal of disruption. In actuality, I think it likely that all three of the above criteria will likely be present in most or all cases of epistemic oppression. Epistemic oppression then, occurs when information that you have, because of some fact about who you are, and the shifts to dominant epistemic resources that would be required if you were taken seriously (either due to their unsuitability in practice, or to the content of your utterance being at odds with what is commonly accepted) fail to enter into or bring about a shift in the epistemological system.

What makes this a distinctly epistemic kind of harm lies in what is required to redress the oppressive practice. As we're thinking at a system level, epistemic vices, virtues, and habits are all in play, and the norms we rely upon (which kinds of knowledge are privileged), the authorities we recognise as epistemically superior (whose knowledge is privileged), and the barriers to expanding our conceptions of good epistemic practice (what counts as good knowledge) can all be understood in distinctly epistemic terms. An individual might be marginalised based on socio-political inequalities and this may drive the misperceptions that affect the knowledge of that specific person entering into the collective domain, but the epistemic features of the epistemological system are such that challenging one's own (mis)perceptions would not suffice to redress system level epistemic oppression: our entire epistemological system would require revision.

4.2. Failure of design? Applying the framework of epistemic oppression to co-production

Thus far, then, I've explained what third-order epistemic oppression is and have given some illustration of the sorts of scenarios in which testimony might be subject to epistemic oppression – by requiring a shift or revision of epistemological systems, which an individual operating within the system is unable to bring about. What I've yet to explain is why the exclusion of experts by experience is especially well understood using this framework. What, for instance, makes our epistemological systems resistant to revision based on the testimony of individuals with lived experience of mental ill health? To begin, let's remind ourselves of the three ways I have outlined where testimony is dismissed or accorded less credibility: (i) testimony received as anecdote; (ii) subversion of message by those more powerful in the research context; and (iii) duality of roles.

In discussions of (i) I outlined the tensions between 'hard' and 'soft' science or evidence. Hard evidence is considered more robust, arising from the positivist mode of social research where fact takes precedent over value, and quests for knowledge focus upon that which is 'invariable' and 'universal' (Durkheim, 1982). As Vaditya outlines: 'Qualities such as rationality, reason, objectivity, and impartiality are privileged over, and opposed to, irrationality, emotion, subjectivity and partiality' (Vaditya, 2018, p. 274). Alternative forms of knowledge, such as those from the perspectives of marginalised people, were squeezed out of common accepted research practice during the growth of positivist modes of advancing knowledge (Kovach, 2005). As such, the academe, as the respected source of knowledge advancement, also tends to privilege fact and objectivity over and above opinion or values-led hypotheses. Our epistemological systems, and our operative social imaginaries, then, are established such that they prefer and uphold specific ways of doing research or arriving at new or expanded knowledge. And these constraints mean that testimony received as anecdote, such as first-hand accounts of distress, simply aren't afforded the status of 'knowledge' (Faulkner, 2017).

Consider also the ways in which Vaditya (2018) has characterised the qualities privileged in the research environment and how these map on to our social conceptions of mental health or, conversely, mental wellness. The epistemically more virtuous qualities of rationality, reason, objectivity, and impartiality not only indicate robustness in research, but good epistemic practices. Coincidentally, these also happen to be the very qualities presumed lacking if you happen to have lived experience of mental ill health. The negatively valenced qualities Vaditya highlights of 'irrationality, emotion, subjectivity' (2018, p. 274) are precisely those which are presumed inextricably linked to mental ill health. It just so happens that, according to dominant epistemologies, they also make for bad science and less than desirable epistemic practices. Being an expert by experience then, appears to bestow upon an individual in what Townley describes as 'an epistemically disadvantageous social identity, akin to being given a version of the curse of Cassandra' (Townley, 2003, pp.105–6). Townley is of course, not talking about research into mental ill health. But whilst in Greek mythology Apollo bestowed Cassandra with the prophetic ability to foresee the future, but simultaneously cursed her such that no one would ever believe her testimony (Townley, 2003), in cases of co-production, the phenomena at play are much less mystical. Rather, experts by experience are invited to participate in co-production because of their insights, but routinely have those insights fail to enter into the collective epistemic domain of knowledge, as that knowledge, and their very identity, fail to meet the positivist requirements of good science. This could be understood as an illustration of (a) or (b) as above, or perhaps some combination of the two. The content of testimony may be dismissed because of perceived inadequacies in the robustness of the evidence it contains because the expert by experience is not an academic or clinician themselves; lay persons cannot offer up hard scientific evidence, and testimony may be deemed too subjective. It could also be dismissed due to the perceived relationship between mental ill health and the epistemic virtues that the dominant epistemological system recognises as authoritative; irrational individuals cannot offer up rational evidence, as it were. Or, it could be that the content of expert by experience testimony is viewed, against the contents of the epistemological system, as being incompatible with accepted views and norms (in the case of anti-psychiatry, Mad studies, or other views which either disagree with or argue against curative interventions). Any of these scenarios would vastly affect when and to what degree expert by experience testimony gains uptake. I suspect it does not happen often.

In the rare circumstance where expert by experience testimony is received as truthful and reliable (though still anecdotal to a degree) but is deemed at odds with the existing and widely utilised epistemological system, it likely will still fail to gain the uptake required to act as a catalyst for revision of the shared epistemic resources into which she attempts to have her knowledge enter (Dotson, 2014, p. 130). And this, again, can be attributed to the extreme resilience dominant epistemological systems display, particularly when it comes to histories of social oppression, marginalisation, and injustice. Mental health, and psychiatric illness, have been subjugated categories in Westernised cultures throughout history, and thus anti-psychiatry or Mad Pride type views cannot be assimilated into the epistemological system without the resultant need to examine our entire worldview of mental health. The more ingrained into culture, institutions, and social understandings a view becomes, the more difficult it can be to challenge. Similarly, our research paradigms, funding processes, evaluative mechanisms, and the economy of academic education, which serve to further the successes of those who produce knowledge in accordance with the epistemic virtues and rules of the governing epistemological system, mean that conceptions of research are also entrenched (Vaditya, 2018). By taking this system-level appraisal of the harm perpetuated by co-production when experts by experience are excluded in research paradigms, and by understanding it as a kind of epistemic oppression, we're able to lay out this systemic injustice. Given the incompatibility, if my arguments here are accepted, between the variance in understandings of mental ill health with our dominant epistemologies, it is unsurprising that co-production has received criticism for dismissing the very knowledge it seeks out.

Thinking about the ways testimony is subverted, watered down, or misunderstood, as in (ii), we might also make sense of this phenomenon using Dotson's view. In her paper 'Conceptualizing Epistemic Oppression', she recreates the *Allegory* crafting an image of a row of fettered persons, facing to the left, who increase in their position of privilege from left to right. The furthest left individual is the only person able to see the remainder of the open cave, yet is also the most marginalised in terms of social position (Doston, 2014, p. 130). She has a unique position. When she attempts to share knowledge, using dominant epistemic resources she shares with others, e.g., language, conceptual frameworks, and so on, but which those further to the right have no direct experience of, she is met with ridicule. She occupies the most marginalised position in the cave hierarchy of power (Dotson, 2014, p. 130). Now her assertions may be met with mere disbelief, and those to the right of her might determine she does not occupy a social position commensurate with enough authority to enter knowledge (uncorroborated by more superior individuals) into the collective epistemic resources. Or, as I think more likely in practice, it's possible that those to the right of her attempt to make sense of what she says, based on their own experiences – their hermeneutic horizons. In either case, the content of testimony is changed or determined by others as lacking in credibility. And this is in addition to, or is perhaps compounded by, those features of the epistemological system outlined when discussing (i), which we might say are the basis for our expert by experience being situated in the position of greatest marginalisation. Similar arguments could be given for (iii). Positionality, as a non-expert research team member with expertise understood in terms of positivist qualities either exemplified by research methods or outputs, or by the individuals undertaking said research, will affect what an expert by experience is able to have taken seriously. The degree to which the knowledge she tries to share would create epistemic friction within the epistemological system will also determine whether she is able to enter what she knows into the shared epistemological resources. Whilst our conceptions of science, of research, of traditional ways of conducting these things, and our pernicious attitudes toward mental ill health remain integral parts of both the operative and the instituted social imaginaries which govern our epistemic practices, it is easy to paint a pessimistic picture of co-production.

5. Concluding Remarks: Why Appeal to System-Level Oppression?

Having explained how Dotson's epistemic oppression helps us to understand exclusionary practice in research, we might begin to question what this view offers over and above identity-based prejudice. Both pictures provide a plausible account of the sorts of factors affecting which individuals are deemed capable of knowing, and how that knowledge translates (or doesn't) to collective understanding.

On my view, Dotson's account doesn't necessarily explain what's at play more effectively, but it does help to capture two important nuances. First, as a system-based framework, epistemic oppression helps us to understand how knowledge is precluded from entering collective resources even in incredibly well-intentioned research environments. Individual researchers might be amenable to altering their research practices and may be sympathetic to views which would require significant shifts in epistemological systems that are dominant. But those individuals, too, are working within the same framework of epistemological systems, and in order that their research be taken seriously, and their outcomes be delivered in accordance with the terms of their funding, they cannot reinterpret or shift the system alone, nor can they step outside of the dominant epistemological system and continue to do research. Just as experts by experience face a series of double-binds, so too do the academic and clinical researchers. They also operate within the bounds of epistemological systems insofar as their own cognition and epistemic habits are concerned and are unlikely to have awareness of the limits of that system when it comes to the incompatibility of mental ill health with virtuous epistemic practice.

Epistemic oppression, then, gets us an understanding of an entrenched system of injustice, for which no one individual is culpable, but in which most of us are complicit. We may not even recognise this system as oppressive, and co-production in particular, as a research methodology designed to empower those with lived experience as active research partners, may be taken as a quest for epistemic justice, rather than a mode likely to perpetuate harm (Okoroji *et al.*, 2023; Russo, 2023). And, there are accounts of co-production done well, where the issues I have laid out here are side-stepped, and experts by experience are able to participate as valued and respected partners (Faulkner *et al.*, 2019). What this framework 'gets us' is an understanding of prejudices that run deeper than the level of individual interactions or personally held biases. It also goes some way to setting out the enormity of the task ahead, for to truly include individuals with lived experience in research, the epistemological systems governing research and epistemic habits in the academe would require substantial revisions. Co-production as a methodology is not one which is inherently designed to gatekeep knowledge, quite the opposite in fact. What this paper has demonstrated though, if the arguments I have given are accepted, is that for mental health in particular changes to research paradigms and social understandings of psychiatric illness are what would bring about change, rather than active participation of the typically research*ed* in existing research culture. Epistemic oppression as an alternative to epistemic injustice merely helps us to understand how the system is stacked against those with lived experience of mental ill health.

References

Luvell Anderson, 'Hermeneutical Impasses', *Philosophical Topics*, 45:2 (2017), 1–19.

Matthias C. Angermeyer and Herbert Matschinger, 'Causal Beliefs and Attitudes to People with Schizophrenia: Trend Analysis Based on Data from Two Population Surveys in Germany', *The British Journal of Psychiatry*, 186:4 (2005), 331–4.

Co-Production and Structural Oppression

Marian Barnes, 'Bringing Difference into Deliberation? Disabled People, Survivors and Local Governance', *Policy & Politics*, 30:3 (2002), 319–31.

Jean M. Bartunek and Michael K. Moch, 'Third-Order Organizational Change and the Western Mystical Tradition', *Journal of Organizational Change Management*, 7:1 (1994), 24–41.

Penny Bee, Owen Price, John Baker, and Karina Lovell, 'Systematic Synthesis of Barriers and Facilitators to Service User-Led Care Planning', *The British Journal of Psychiatry*, 207:2 (2015), 104–14.

Leslie Brown and Susan Strega (eds.), *Research as Resistance: Critical, Indigenous, and Anti-oppressive Approaches* (Toronto: Canadian Scholars' Press, 2005).

Judith Butler, *Gender Trouble: Feminism and the Subversion of Identity* (New York: Routledge, 1990).

Havi Carel and Ian James Kidd, 'Epistemic Injustice in Healthcare: A Philosophical Analysis', *Medicine, Health Care and Philosophy*, 17:4 (2014), 529–40.

Havi Carel and Ian James Kidd, 'Epistemic Injustice and Illness', *Journal of Applied Philosophy*, 34:2 (2016), 172–90.

Sarah Carr, *'Position Paper: Are Mainstream Mental Health Services Ready to Progress Transformative Co-Production? Discussion Paper'* (2016), accessed 21 February 2023: https://eprints.mdx.ac.uk/20267/.

Paul Crichton, Havi Carel, and Ian James Kidd, 'Epistemic Injustice in Psychiatry', *Psychiatry Bulletin*, 41 (2017), 65–70.

David Coady, 'Epistemic Injustice as Distributive Injustice', in Ian James Kidd, José Medina, and Gaile Polhaus Jr (eds.), *The Routledge Handbook of Epistemic Injustice* (Abingdon-on-Thames: Routledge, 2017), 61–8.

CoProduction Collective, *Epistemic Injustice and CoProduction*, accessed 1 May 2023: https://www.coproductioncollective.co.uk/news/epistemic-injustice-and-co-production.

Patrick W. Corrigan, L. Philip River, Robert K. Lundin, David L. Penn, D, Kyle Uphoff-Wasowski, John Campion, James Mathisen, Christine Gagnon, Maria Bergman, Hillel Goldstein, and Marry Anne Kubiak, 'Three Strategies for Changing Attributions about Severe Mental Illness', *Schizophrenia Bulletin*, 27:2 (2001), 187–95.

Kristie Dotson, 'A Cautionary Tale: On Limiting Epistemic Oppression', *Frontiers: A Journal of Women Studies*, 33:1 (2012), 24–47.

Kristie Dotson, 'Conceptualizing Epistemic Oppression', *Social Epistemology*, 28:2 (2014), 115–38.

153

Emile Durkheim, *The Rules of Sociological Method*, translated edition, Steven Lukes (ed.), (New York: The Free Press, 1982).

Alison Faulkner, 'Survivor Research and Mad Studies: The Role and Value of Experiential Knowledge in Mental Health Research', *Disability Society*, 32 (2017), 500–20.

Alison Faulkner, Sarah Carr, Dorothy Gould, Christine Khisa, Trish Hafford-Letchfield, Rachel Cohen, Claudia Megele, and Jessica Holley, '"Dignity and Respect": An Example of Service User Leadership and Co-Production in Mental Health Research', *Health Expectations*, 24:1 (2019), 10–19.

Sanne Feenstra, Christopher T. Begeny, Michelle K. Ryan, Floor A. Rink, Janka I. Stoker, and Jennifer Jordan, 'Contextualizing the Impostor "Syndrome"', *Frontiers in Psychology*, 11 (2020), accessed 22 May 2023: https://frontiersin.org/articles/10.3389/fpsyg.2020.575024/full.

Michel Foucault, *Power/Knowledge: Selected Interviews and Other Writings, 1972–79*, Colin Gordon (ed.), (New York: Pantheon, 1980).

Miranda Fricker, *Epistemic Injustice: Power and the Ethics of Knowing* (New York: Oxford University Press, 2007).

Temple Grandin and Richard Panek, *The Autistic Brain: Thinking Across the Spectrum* (London: Rider Books, 2014).

John Greco, *Achieving Knowledge: A Virtue-Theoretic Account of Epistemic Normativity* (Cambridge: Cambridge University Press, 2010).

Alvin Goldman, *Knowledge in a Social World* (Oxford: Oxford University Press, 1999).

Laura Guidry-Grimes, 'Modelling Psychiatric Disability', *Journal of Evaluation in Clinical Practice*, 21 (2015), 490–5.

Suzanne Hodge, 'Participation, Discourse and Power: A Case Study in Service User Involvement', *Critical Social Policy*, 25:2 (2005), 164–79.

Katherine Johnson and Antar Martínez Guzmán, 'Rethinking Concepts in Participatory Action Research and their Potential for Social Transformation: Post-Structuralist Informed Methodological Reflections from LGBT and Trans-Collective Projects', *Journal of Community and Applied Social Psychoogy*, 23 (2013), 405–19.

Nev Jones and Timothy Kelly, 'Inconvenient Complications: On the Heterogeneities of Madness and their Relationship to Disability', in Helen Spandler, Bob Sapey, and Jill Anderson (eds.), *Madness, Distress and the Politics of Disablement* (London: Polity Press, 2015), 43–57.

Margaret Kovach, 'Emerging from the Margins: Indigenous Methodologies', in Leslie Brown and Susan Strega (eds.), *Research as Resistance: Critical, Indigenous, and Anti-oppressive Approaches* (Toronto: Canadian Scholars' Press, 2005), 19–36.

Lydia Lewis, 'User Involvement in Mental Health Services: A Case of Power Over Discourse', *Sociological Research Online*, 19:1 (2014), accessed 1 May 2023: http://www.socresonline.org.uk/19/1/6.html.

Maria Liegghio, 'A Denial of Being: Psychiatrization as Epistemic Violence', in Brenda A. LeFrancois, Robert Menzies, and Geoffrey Reaume (eds.), *Mad Matters: A Critical Reader in Canadian Mad Studies* (Toronto: Canadian Scholars' Press, 2013), 122–9.

William, G. Lycan, *Judgement and Justificatio*, (Cambridge, MA: Cambridge University Press, 1988).

José Medina, 'The Relevance of Credibility Excess in a Proportional View of Epistemic Injustice: Differential Epistemic Authority and the Social Imaginary', *Social Epistemology*, 25:1 (2011), 15–35.

Alex James Miller Tate, 'Contributory Injustice in Psychiatry' *Journal of Medical Ethics*, 45 (2019), 97–100.

Alexandros C. Nikolaidis, 'A Third Conception of Epistemic Injustice', *Studies in Philosophy and Education*, 40 (2021), 381–98.

Celestin Okoroji, Tanya Mackay, Dan Robotham, Davino Beckford, and Vanessa Pinfold, 'Epistemic Injustice and Mental Health Research: A Pragmatic Approach to Working with Lived Experience Expertise', *Frontiers in Psychiatry*, 14 (eCollection 2023).

Diana Rose and Jayasree Kalathil, 'Power, Privilege and Knowledge: The Untenable Promise of Co-Production in Mental "Health"', *Frontiers in Sociology*, 4 (2019), accessed 1 May 2023: https://frontiersin.org/articles/10.3389/fsoc.2019.00057/full.

Jasna Russo, 'Psychiatrization, Assertions of Epistemic Justice, and the Question of Agency', *Frontiers in Sociology*, 8 (2023), accessed 20 April 2023: https://frontiersin.org/articles/10.3389/fsoc.2023.1092298/full.

Mike Slade, Victoria Bird, Ruth Chandler, Jo Fox, John Larsen, Jerry Tew, and Mary Leamy, 'The Contribution of Advisory Committees and Public Involvement to Large Studies: Case Study', *BMC Health Services Research*, 10:323 (2010), accessed 19 March 2023: https://bmchealthservres.biomedcentral.com/articles/10.1186/1472-6963-10-323.

Ernest Sosa, *A Virtue Epistemology: Apt Belief and Reflective Knowledge* (Oxford: Oxford University Press, 2007).

Alana Wilde

Gayatri Chakravorty Spivak, 'Can the Subaltern Speak?', in Cary Nelson and Lawrence Grossberg (eds.), *Marxism and the Interpretation of Culture* (Illinois: University of Illinois Press, 1988), 271–316.

Robin Stern, *The Gaslight Effect: How to Spot and Survive the Hidden Manipulation Others Use to Control Your Life* (New York: Broadway Books, 2007).

Charles Taylor, *Modern Social Imaginaries* (Durham, NC: Duke University Press, 2004).

Cynthia Townley, 'Trust and the Curse of Cassandra (An Exploration of the Value of Trust)', *Philosophy in the Contemporary World*, 10:2 (2003), 105–11.

Venkatesh Vaditya, 'Social Domination and Epistemic Marginalisation: Towards Methodology of the Oppressed', *Social Epistemology*, 32:4 (2018), 272–85.

Otto F. Wahl, 'Mental Health Consumers' Experience of Stigma', *Schizophrenia Bulletin*, 25:3 (1999), 467–78.

Linda T. Zagzebski, *Virtues of the Mind: An Inquiry into the Nature of Virtue and the Ethical Foundations of Knowledge* (Cambridge: Cambridge University Press, 1996).

Co-Production is Good, but Other Things are Good Too

EDWARD HARCOURT AND DAVID CREPAZ-KEAY

Abstract

The world of mental health has become used to the notion of co-production as a good thing. While the paper is not a critical analysis of co-production, the authors make the case that while it is a good thing, it is not the only good thing; and it is neither sufficient, nor necessary for good things to happen in mental health services. Alternative concepts of progressive innovation in this field are introduced. Real world case studies (most of them previously unpublished) are then worked through to test which concept(s) – co-production, or the alternatives, or neither – are the better fit, bearing in mind the complex relationships to be negotiated, not just between service users and mental health professionals, but between service users and members of other professions, and of the general public. Finally, the question is raised as to whether there is anything (such as the flattening of hierarchies or stigma reduction) which all these innovations – co-production and the alternatives – have in common.

1. Introduction

There is a complex political dynamic – that's small-p political – between mental health service users[1] and philosophers. A number of service users have for a long time felt disempowered relative to a (relatively) high-prestige profession – psychiatry. So the prospect of having an ally in the shape of another (relatively) high-prestige profession – philosophy – is understandably attractive. At the same time philosophers often feel disempowered relative to government funding policies which put pressure on them to generate 'impact' from their work, and an alliance with service users offers the hope of impact. Thus while (some) service users feel they need philosophers, (some) philosophers also need to be needed. A similar

---

[1] The same could also be said of some people with mental health difficulties who have successfully avoided services ('survivors': Kalathil and Jones, 2016), but since the focus of this paper is on services and how and by whom they are produced, we stick to 'service users', while acknowledging the complex pressures on terminology choice in this area.

doi:10.1017/S1358246123000255 © The Author(s), 2023. Published by Cambridge University Press on behalf of The Royal Institute of Philosophy dynamic may be presumed to affect other academic disciplines too, and indeed stakeholders beyond the academy. But there is a risk involved in such a mutual dependence: the risk of forming an uncritical alliance, an alliance in which key concepts or terms are waved through without due critical scrutiny.

The aim of this paper is to ask whether an uncritical alliance has formed round the concept of *co-production* in mental health services. Please note: the aim of the paper is *not* to launch a critique of co-production. On the contrary, the concept of co-production has been a useful banner under which many campaigns by and on behalf of service users have been fought. The question is not whether co-production is a good thing – we agree it is – but rather whether, thanks to an uncritical alliance – never mind who the partners are – the label has been over-used. Are all the things (including all the good things) put in place or being campaigned for as making a positive difference to service users instances of co-production, or are they good for some other reason?

Our methodology is both conceptual and empirical. As with many cases of interdisciplinary work, what's needed are both concepts and real-world examples: real-world examples sharpen concepts and then concepts sharpen our description of the world. We sharpen our concepts by thinking about whether or not they're fit to capture what we encounter on the ground, and thanks to that, end up with more accurate and critically refined descriptions of it.

2. Co-Production

Mental health services have traditionally been provided by mental health professionals to patients, with little or no input from the patients themselves.[2] However, the concept of co-production has gained prominence in the UK mental health system over the last decade, with the publication of several key policy documents, such as the NHS Five Year Forward View and the Five Year Forward View for Mental Health (NHS, 2014; Mental Health Taskforce, 2016). These documents highlighted the need for greater user involvement and co-production in mental health services and set out a vision for transforming mental health care in the UK. This has been reinforced by more recent policy developments, such as the

---

[2] The same points apply *mutatis mutandis* to patient involvement in research, but mental health services are our focus here.

NHS Long Term Plan and the Mental Health Act Review (NHS, 2019; Wessely *et al.*, 2018).

That said, terminology can be difficult here. In some places, service user involvement and 'co-production' mean one and the same thing. In others, 'co-production' contrasts with 'mere' service-user involvement, on the grounds that you can truthfully say you are 'involving' someone while in fact giving them a very marginal role, thereby confirming their subordinate status in a knowledge or power hierarchy (Baklien and Bongaardt, 2014; Voronka, 2016). In such contexts, 'co-production' is a kind of gold standard, where clinicians and service-users are equal partners. While we recognise that service user involvement comes in degrees and can be more or less thoroughgoing, we use 'co-production' to refer to any approach that aims to empower patients by giving them a voice in the decision-making process, as well as to improve the quality and effectiveness of mental health services by drawing on the knowledge of both mental health professionals and patients.

One of the key benefits of co-production in mental health services is that it can help to address the power imbalance between service users and healthcare professionals. Co-production can also help to promote recovery and well-being by empowering service users and carers to take an active role in their own care and support. This can improve engagement and reduce stigma, which are both key factors in promoting mental health and well-being (Needham, 2009).

To the extent that we argue that certain attempts to change mental health services for the better don't exemplify 'co-production', that's not because we think they don't live up to the label in the 'gold standard' sense – that's a different problem. Our point is rather that, granted that co-production has the benefits described, it doesn't follow that anything and everything that has these benefits constitutes co-production.

3. Other Good Things...

Notwithstanding the emergence of co-production as a powerful approach to service improvement, it is important to be open to the multiplicity of ways of achieving improvements in services (and other positive outcomes). There are other ideas of progressive patient-focused care and/or services which have recently appeared in the literature and some that predate co-production, and this paper will discuss four: evidence-based practice, service user-led service development, community involvement, and user-centred design. However, the fact that they are known by different names does not prove that they are not, in an underlying way, the same as what is intended to be captured by 'co-production'. So we will introduce each in turn, and then discuss with reference to some real cases whether or not they are genuinely different and which of them, naming conventions apart, it is illuminating to describe as co-production as opposed to some other concept. To the extent that they do not all fit the co-production model, we will then ask whether there is anything more general – beyond being broadly beneficial – that they all have in common.

The four other progressive approaches to mental health services we will consider are evidence-based practice, service user-led services (*etc.*), community involvement, and user-centred design (UCD). *Evidence-based practice* involves using the best available research evidence to inform decision-making about service design, delivery, and evaluation. By using evidence to inform decisions, practitioners can ensure that services are based on the latest research and have the best chance of being effective. In *service user-led services*, service users take control of their own care, rather than simply being partners with healthcare professionals. This approach recognises that service users have a unique perspective on their own needs and experiences, and that they are best placed to make decisions about their own care. Service users take the active role in decision-making processes, such as service planning, policy development, and resource allocation. They also take the lead in the recruitment and training of staff, and the development of interventions. *Community involvement*, meanwhile, is an approach to service provision that emphasises the participation and engagement of communities in the design, delivery, and evaluation of services. It recognises that communities are experts in their own needs and experiences, and that involving them in the service provision process can lead to more effective and sustainable outcomes. Community involvement can take many forms, depending on the needs and priorities of the community. For example, community members may be involved in needs assessments, programme planning, service delivery, and evaluation. They may also participate in community-based research or advocacy efforts to improve access to services and resources. Finally, *user-centred design (UCD)* involves designing products, services, and experiences with the needs, preferences, and behaviours of users in mind. This approach places a strong emphasis on understanding the user's perspective and involves users in every stage of the design process, from ideation to testing. By involving users in the design process, user-centred design can lead to more usable and effective products and services.

4. Some Worked Examples

With these concepts in mind, in this section we will examine a number of case studies. We make the assumption that these case studies are broadly progressive and that they exemplify good models of improving outcomes in services for people with diagnosed mental health conditions (that is to say, they deliver good things). We can then examine them against the yardstick of co-production and the other models of practice outlined above.

4.1 SleepWell

Sleep is an area of concern both to and for people using mental health services, but it is rarely seen as a priority area.

Regular overnight nursing observations are designed to enhance care and reduce risk but may also increase sleep disturbance, and so have unintended negative effects on patient welfare. But to date, little research has focused on the effect of and need for regular overnight observations within psychiatry. Understandable concern about patient safety is one reason for frequent physical checks, despite no direct evidence that fixed timing checks reduce risk.

The SleepWell programme, introduced on psychiatric wards in Cumbria, Northumberland, Tyne and Wear NHS Foundation Trust in 2019, was designed as a pilot scheme in a large mental health trust after reviewing the current observation policy (Novak *et al.*, 2020). This programme included strategies such as reducing overnight noise and light, providing staff education about sleep and sleep disorders, and screening for sleep disorders such as sleep apnoea and restless legs syndrome. Additionally, a protected sleep period was introduced for patients who were considered safe. As the programme explicitly contradicted existing policy and practice, a pilot scheme was run.

Seven adult wards across the Trust were used for the pilot. To ensure a range of patients they included a 16-bed male and two 16-bed female adult acute in-patient units based on two separate sites, a 26-bed long-stay rehabilitation unit with shared house, a 16-bed mixed neurorehabilitation ward, a 12-bed in-patient dementia service, and an 18-bed psychiatric rehabilitation and recovery unit.

The pilot scheme was evaluated by assessing adverse events, including harmful behaviours, before and after the change in observation policy. Detailed feedback from patients, staff, and carers was also collected. Cognitive-behavioural therapy for insomnia (CBTi) was available on two of the seven wards that participated in the pilot. The use of hypnotic medication was also evaluated before and during the pilot period.

Post-pilot feedback from ward staff regarding the implementation of the SleepWell programme was overwhelmingly positive. Ward staff members observed that the ward environment became more peaceful and settled as a result of the intervention. They particularly noted that emphasising bed-time routines contributed to improved sleep among patients, a sentiment that was widely supported by staff.

However, prior to implementing the SleepWell programme, staff experienced initial anxiety regarding the shift away from frequent patient checks and risk assessment. This led to some disagreement among staff regarding which patients were suitable for the protected sleep period. Given that the evaluation primarily focused on safety and feasibility, it was not possible to conduct standardised sleep assessments. To address staff concerns and provide reassurance, a documented multidisciplinary team decision-making process was implemented, involving the night coordinators.

Patients who provided feedback on the intervention expressed positive views about being on protected sleep time. Some patients reported not noticing any significant differences and stated they had not been disturbed during the night. However, others described feeling safer without staff members looking into their rooms. Patients who had experienced readmissions also mentioned that the protected sleep time was an improvement compared to previous admissions.

Carers, too, had a positive perception of the intervention, with none of them requesting the reinstatement of more frequent observations. Neither patients nor carers expressed any concerns about the protected sleep time.

During the evaluation, all in-patients were asked about their experiences with the SleepWell programme. Comments from patients included statements such as 'better than last admission', 'I feel safer now', and 'I don't worry about people looking into my room at night'.

So, the programme was beneficial. But was it co-production? Neither the development, nor the implementation of the SleepWell programme involved the patients who participated in it. The programme was multidisciplinary in nature involving sleep specialists, ward staff, and the Trust estates department. The latter is, at time of writing, also working on environmental noise issues (soft closing doors and bins for example).

As a result, SleepWell would be better described as an example of evidence-based practice (EBP). The EBP process involves several key steps. First, topic experts identify a clinical question or problem that requires an evidence-based solution. Once the clinical question has been identified, a thorough search of the existing literature is conducted to identify relevant research studies. Following the evaluation of the literature, the evidence is applied to clinical practice. EBP has become an essential component of modern healthcare delivery, as it provides a systematic and rigorous approach to clinical decision-making. While there is no reason that patients cannot be involved in either the practice or the generation of evidence, this is not a necessary component of EBP.

In the case of SleepWell, it was the evidence that drove the case for change and a desire to test and develop the evidence base that led to the pilot programme.

4.2 Mental Health Foundation Self-Management Intervention, Wales 2009–2012

The Mental Health Foundation (MHF) developed a self-management intervention tailored to the needs of people with severe mental health diagnoses, using significant funding from the 2009 Big Lottery Fund's Mental Health Matters funding stream for Wales (Crepaz-Keay and Cyhlarova, 2012). The aim was to develop, deliver, and evaluate a testable intervention, which enabled people with a diagnosed psychiatric condition to manage their own mental health and support their peers to do the same. The key elements of the approach were goal setting and problem solving; everyone set and shared goals and the peer groups would work collectively to enable people to achieve their own goals and solve problems that may get in the way.

Development
In order to ensure that the intervention accorded with the needs of people who have used secondary mental health services, a development model was chosen that had a high degree of service user involvement. The initial development phase took place at a four-day residential workshop in Cwmbran, South Wales. This workshop was facilitated by experienced ex-service users who were research and development experts. The event brought together 24 people who had used secondary mental health services in Wales. Of these,

two had been involved with Bipolar UK's long established self-management course, two had other training experience, 12 belonged to self-help groups, and eight had no previous connection to self-help or training. The majority had no previous training or self-management experience. The group as a whole was typical of the target group we wanted to benefit from the intervention, in that they had lived with a diagnosed psychiatric condition and had received treatment for the condition from mental health services.

The workshop participants recognised the essential importance of peer support in self-management. There is evidence suggesting that peer support for people who experience mental ill health can have many benefits for their mental and physical health and well-being (Repper and Carter, 2011). The key conclusions from the development group were that self-management training needs to be goal-orientated (people chose their own),[3] and needs to be followed by peer support. The model that emerged from the workshop was a three-stage intervention in the following format:

1.   Two days of self-management training with a focus on goal setting and problem solving.
2.   Six half-day follow-up sessions, usually fortnightly.
3.   Ongoing peer support, at least monthly, for six months.

This would be delivered to a group of ten to fifteen people, and the whole series of sessions – from the two-day training to the last facilitated follow-up – would take about nine months to run. The inclusion of peer support as an additional component, alongside self-management training, was incorporated to try to increase the long-term effectiveness of the intervention.

Once this initial design was converted into a draft training manual and participant materials, all materials were reviewed by a group of service users from North Wales. The materials were then adjusted for a real-time pilot of the initial two-day training. This training was delivered in North Wales, by the facilitators of the workshop. The first pilot led to significant revisions, particularly on the volume of content; the schedule and materials were also adjusted

[3]   Some goals were directly related to people's diagnoses, but most weren't. The most common goals were: returning to education, improving relationships, losing weight/exercising more, giving up or reducing smoking, getting a job. There were many goals of differing levels of difficulty (simplest was 'paint kitchen door', most challenging was 'climb Everest'), but the important thing was that people set their own: they weren't chosen for them.

for a second pilot. The second pilot was run in South Wales and was facilitated by two people who participated in the first pilot. The development process took about 12 months from the recruitment of the initial team to the completion of the second and final pilot.

Delivery

Recruiting participants took a great deal of effort. To promote the courses, MHF held local launch events, often in collaboration with a local service user group. The events drew in a wide range of local people including mayors, community police, local companies, and clinicians. These events also succeeded in encouraging people to talk about mental ill health in public settings. A national campaign by Hafal (a leading Welsh mental health charity), to which MHF also contributed, significantly increased the profile of MHF's work and reached a greater number of people than would otherwise have been possible.

An average of 20 people were recruited for each course. Of these, typically a dozen would actually attend the first two-day training, and the final peer support group tended to include six to eight regular attendees. The dropout rate was lower where MHF worked with existing local groups, but there were no obvious indicators to suggest why some groups seemed more sustainable than others.

Between December 2009 and January 2012, 62 courses were delivered and 647 people trained across Wales. Of the total, 35 courses were the new courses developed by the MHF which reached 320 people. A further 27 courses were commissioned from Bipolar UK, an organisation run for and by people with a Bipolar diagnosis, in order to broaden the evidence base; these trained an additional 327 people. This also enabled potential beneficiaries to be reached from an early stage, and people to be offered a choice of courses.

The newly developed courses were entirely delivered by people who had previously been course participants (with the exception of the first pilot). This ensured that the facilitators had a good understanding of the materials and of the experience of learning self-management skills. It also enabled participants to identify closely with the facilitators, rather than perceive them as remote authority figures. It also offered encouragement for participants who wanted to go on to develop facilitation skills.

Peer support

In order to keep peer support groups going over time, the characteristics of a good peer support group needed to be established, and the potential blocks to sustainable groups identified. The consultation was conducted in two stages: a questionnaire, and two consultation days. A questionnaire was developed with the aim of gauging ideas about what would make people want to attend a peer support group, what makes it successful, long-lasting, and what the barriers are to playing a full role in the group. In total, 176 questionnaires were sent out; of these 146 went to self-management participants and 30 to other relevant organisations. 41 and 8 responses, respectively, were received. Building on the questionnaire responses, the two consultation days were carried out in South and North Wales (five and six participants, respectively). This process identified the following issues:

- One (or ideally more than one) person needs to take responsibility for keeping a group going. This person (or people) should come from the group, not from outside the group.
- The group needs to have a clear purpose: setting and reviewing goals was regarded as a good purpose.
- Groups need to have agreed ground rules.
- Groups need to have opportunities to share learning with other groups.

Once again, the question arises whether or to what extent this is a case of co-production. The answer is that the intervention exemplifies a mixed model, indeed mixed along several different dimensions.

The original intention was that the intervention would be co-produced with Welsh mental health services so that it would complement existing services and be easy to access for people while they were using them. But despite attempts MHF were unable to establish any co-production partnerships with mental health services. If co-production signals a partnership between service users and mental health professionals, then, the answer has to be 'no'.

As a result, this endeavour might best be characterised rather as service user-led, and illustrates the challenges associated with this model.

Nonetheless, in this case every step of the process was developed and delivered by service users. There were certainly barriers both to the service user leadership, and to professional acceptance of it. The latter is likely to have contributed to the failure to engage effectively with mental health services. The former was largely overcome by the fact that resource allocation was also service user-led once Lottery funding had been granted. Thus, although the service user-led nature of the intervention originated in failure to live up to expectations of co-production with health services, it arguably ended up exceeding even the 'gold standard' notion of co-production by putting service users in sole charge.

It may also be helpful, however, to think of the intervention in terms of user-centred design rather than co-production. The UCD process involves several stages: the research stage, to understand the perspectives, needs, and challenges of users; the ideation stage, to generate ideas for addressing user needs and challenges; the prototyping stage to test and refine the design before its finalisation.

Perhaps a key difference from co-production is that user-centred design, like any design process, involves a three-cornered relationship between designer, client, and end-user. Design becomes user-centred to the extent that different iterations of a design are responsive to end user needs. However, there is nothing intrinsic to this model which requires either designer or client themselves to be service users – indeed, typically they are not.

In this case, however, the intervention was initiated by the Mental Health Foundation (the client). The Mental Health Foundation is not service user-led, though strongly informed by attention to service user needs and interests. Moreover, the original idea came from a member of Foundation staff with existing psychiatric diagnoses and was then supported by a team of people, all of whom had used mental health services (bar one external consultant).

In addition, as already described, the development phase involved a four-day residential workshop facilitated by experienced service users who were research and development experts (the designers). The workshop brought together people who had used secondary mental health services in Wales, representing the target population of the intervention. This high degree of end user involvement ensured that the intervention's design and content were informed by the perspectives and experiences of those who would benefit from it. Consequently, while user-centred design may sometimes fall short of the equitable partnership ideals of co-production because of power differentials between client, designer, and end user (with end users at the bottom of that hierarchy), in this case, it did not.

There is one further complexity here. While co-production with mental health services did not take place, there was more success with community involvement. One key benefit of community involvement is that it can help to ensure that services are culturally appropriate and responsive to the unique needs and experiences of the community. By involving community members in the service provision process, we can gain a deeper understanding of the community's values, beliefs, and customs, and design services that are more

167

in line with their needs and preferences. Community involvement can also help to build trust and strengthen relationships between service providers and community members. By involving community members in decision-making processes, we can demonstrate a commitment to listening to and responding to the needs and priorities of the community. This can help to foster a sense of ownership and investment in the services, leading to greater participation and engagement over time.

In this case community involvement was valuable in a number of respects: it helped to understand the need for support in communities MHF were not familiar with, it increased awareness of and facilitated access to the services, it made the service feel like part of the community, and it provided us with access to expertise that supported the problem solving component of the intervention. This once again draws attention to the complexities in applying the concept of co-production: co-production with whom? Certainly there was a collaboration by two different categories of stakeholder, but the intervention doesn't fit the usual co-production profile because the partnership was not between service users and mental health professionals – which was attempted and failed – but between service users and community members.

4.3 East Lille

A particularly rich case study comes from Lille in Northern France, where the Eastern Lille Public Psychiatric Sector has seen a number of progressive developments in community psychiatry over the last 30+ years (Roelandt et al., 2014).[4] These developments were based in turn on Basaglia's work (Basaglia, 2010) in Gorizia and Trieste. Here is an (incomplete) list of the innovations in question:

1. Asylum closure, with service users' housing integrated into the town at large, including with host families
2. Open wards (though there is still involuntary detention)
3. Short waiting times for services
4. Transparency – patients have access to their own records
5. Wide range of therapies and rehabilitation interventions, including art therapies

---

[4] We set this out more schematically than the other case studies because, unlike the others, it has been published before.

6.   Involvement of ex-patients in staff training and allocation of housing
7.   User-run self-help groups
8.   Interventions to overcome a negative image of mental illness in the population of East Lille

Arguably these features all have the potential to positively affect patient welfare, and therefore represent positive models for service improvement. But to what extent do they fit the co-production concept?

In 7, service users themselves deliver the intervention. Thus, arguably, it isn't co-production. That is not because service users are not involved (obviously enough) but because it exceeds the aspiration of equalising the relationship between service user and mental health professional, by absenting the mental health professional from the scene. (Cp the previous case study.) It would thus be more accurately described as a service user-led service. Notice however that we only know (from the evidence of Roelandt *et al.*, 2014) that it is service user-led at the level of delivery. Informal conversations with professionals involved in leading services in East Lille suggests that the initial design was primarily led top-down, by professionals. 6 fits the co-production label well up to a point, in that service users are involved in doing something which they might have been excluded from (allocating housing), but with two qualifications. First, what is being delivered is not strictly speaking a mental health service, but a housing service. Secondly, it isn't clear to what extent service user involvement in housing allocation makes the allocation more sensitive to service user needs, as opposed simply to constituting one pathway to enabling service users to be meaningfully employed, and thus empowered. It thus could be seen as a means to social inclusion, or to equalising differences between clinical and non-clinical populations (i.e., something co-production is also good at), but without itself constituting co-production.

Something similar can be said, but with more certainty, about 4. Allowing patients access to their records is a way of addressing asymmetries between patient and mental health professional, and thus points once again in the direction of social inclusion. But it is not clear that in accessing a record, anything is 'produced', and so *a fortiori* not co-produced. On top of which, both the contents of the record and the transparency policy itself could, for all we know, have been produced top-down. 1 is also about equalising relationships, social inclusion, and stigma reduction, but the relationships in question are not between service users and mental health professionals but between service users and other non-clinicians, i.e., other inhabitants of East Lille. (Compare the community involvement in the previous case study.) Once again, it is not clear how living in a place constitutes 'producing' something, so living in an integrated or non-segregated way ought not to be classified as co-production even though its inclusive ambitions are shared by initiatives which should be so classified. And, at risk of being repetitive, we are not given any reason to suppose that the integrative housing *policy* was itself produced with service users as opposed to being arrived at top-down by enlightened mental health professionals, or by a coalition of various different professionals including East Lille local politicians and housing officials. Moreover, the role differentiation of service user/clinician is maintained, with the important exception that the 'clinical' role is broadened so as to include the host families as well as psychiatrists, psychiatric nurses, *etc*. This challenges conventional notions of who or what can deliver therapy, but not the asymmetric conception of therapy as somebody delivering something to someone, as against a 'doing with' or co-production model.

5 also bears some similarities to 4 and 1. Roelandt *et al*. (2014) stress that art was not only used as a therapy, but also designed as an activity service users could engage in together with other people, 'establishing equality between patients and non-patients'. So once again, there is an ambition to equalise relationships or even out hierarchies of knowledge and power. But as in 1, the relationship being equalised was between service users and non-clinical members of the population, not, as usually understood in discussions of co-production, between service users and clinicians or other mental health professionals. Indeed, in so far as art *was* used as a therapy, while the therapeutic method may have been innovative, the role differentiation between clinician and service user is preserved. Finally, the same is true of 8. Artists played a role in addressing negativity about mental illness among the population at large. Again the goals were social inclusion and the removal of stigma, but the relationship in focus was that between clinical and non-clinical populations as a whole, not between clinical populations and clinicians. And again, the drive towards doing so was organised 'by psychiatry teams and municipal authorities' (Roelandt *et al*., 2014, p. 11), with as far as we can tell no service user involvement at that particular point of intervention.

5. Conclusion

We have reviewed a number of progressive innovations in mental health services and indeed in services more broadly (e.g., housing) designed to benefit those with mental health difficulties. We have also argued that while some of these exemplify co-production, others do not, and indeed for various contrasting reasons. Some fail to fit the co-production model because they are more purely service user-led, i.e., service users do not create something *with* others ('co'), but on their own – indeed perhaps because co-production with professional services was not possible. Some fail to fit it for the opposite reason, i.e., the new service is designed top-down, either without service user involvement at all, by an enlightened multi-professional group excluding service users, or involving them in the manner of 'end user/consumer testing' – but with results modified for the better by the contingency that clients and designers were also service users (or included a number of service users) as described in UCD. So, is there anything these progressive innovations have in common with those innovations which *are* properly described as co-produced? Co-production is fundamentally about equalising relationships between service users and clinicians or other mental health professionals, since it is here that hierarchies of power and prestige in the absence of co-production may be most keenly felt. But some of our examples show that, for example with regard to social inclusion or the reduction of stigma, there are other relationships which it is good to equalise too, such as service user relationships with members of a local population who are neither service users nor mental health professionals; or, service user relationships with services other than mental health services. When that happens, the term 'co-production' is an uncertain fit. But other good features of progressive mental health services we have touched on show respect and humanity either in service design or service delivery, but where this doesn't involve equalising relationships of any sort. As Basaglia appears to have said, 'taking care of a person, not leaving him to his own devices under the cloak of some abstract notion of liberty, but at the same time avoiding controlling him and imposing on him preconceived therapeutic objectives' (Roelandt *et al.*, 2014, p. 16). The hypothesis that humanising isn't always equalising deserves further investigation.

References

Franco Basaglia *et al.*, *L'Istituzione Negata. Rapporto da un Ospedale Psichiatrico*, Baldini Castoldi Dalai (2010).

Børge Baklien and Rob Bongaardt, 'The Quest for Choice and the Need for Relational Care in Mental Health Work', *Med Health Care Philos*, 17 (2014), 625–32.

David Crepaz-Keay and Eva Cyhlarova, 'A New Self-Management Intervention for People with Severe Psychiatric Diagnoses', *The Journal of Mental Health Training, Education and Practice*, 7:2 (2012), 89–94.

Jayasree Kalathil and Nev Jones, 'Unsettling Disciplines: Madness, Identity, Research, Knowledge', *Philosophy, Psychiatry & Psychology*, 23:3–4 (2016), 183–8.

NHS Mental Health Taskforce, *The Five Year Forward View for Mental Health* (2016), accessed 7 July 2023: https://www.england.nhs.uk/wp-content/uploads/2016/02/Mental-Health-Taskforce-FYFV-final.pdf.

Catherine Needham, *Co-Production: An Emerging Evidence Base for Adult Social Care Transformation* (London: SCIE, 2009).

NHS, *Five Year Forward View* (2014), accessed 7 July 2023: https://www.england.nhs.uk/five-year-forward-view/.

NHS, *The NHS Long Term Plan* (2019), accessed 7 July 2023: https://www.longtermplan.nhs.uk/.

Chloe Novak, Emma Packer, Alastair Paterson, Ambrina Roshi, Rosie Locke, Patrick Keown, Stuart Watson, and Kirstie N. Anderson, 'Feasibility and Utility of Enhanced Sleep Management on In-Patient Psychiatry Wards', *BJPsych Bulletin*, 44:6 (2020), 255–60.

Julie Repper and Tim Carter, 'A Review of the Literature on Peer Support in Mental Health Services', *Journal of Mental Health*, 20:4 (2011), 392–411.

J.L. Roelandt, N. Daumerie, L. Defromont, A. Caria, P. Bastow, and J. Kishore, 'Community Mental Health Service: An Experience from the East Lille, France', *Journal of Mental Health and Human Behaviour*, 19 (2014), 10–18.

Jijian Voronka, 'The Politics of "People with Lived Experience"', *Philosophy, Psychiatry & Psychology*, 23:3–4 (2016), 189–201.

Simon Wessely, Steve Gilbert, Mark Hedley, and Julia Neuberger, *Modernising the Mental Health Act – Increasing Choice, Reducing Compulsion: Final Report of the Independent Review of the Mental Health Act 1983* (London, 2018).

Shared Decision-Making and Relational Moral Agency: On Seeing the Person Behind the 'Expert by Experience' in Mental Health Research

ANNA BERGQVIST

Abstract

The focus of this paper is the moral and scientific value of 'expertise by experience', that is, knowledge based on personal experience of ill mental health as a form of expertise in mental health research. In contrast to individualistic theories of personal autonomy and the first-person in bioethics, my account of shared decision-making is focussed on how a relational approach to the 'person' and 'patient values' can throw new light on our understanding of 'voice' in mental health research. The mistake, I argue, is to think that a commitment to listening to the patient voice in the process of perspective taking implies a threat to 'objectivity' in clinical practice and the very concept of evidence in the philosophy of science more generally. Instead, I use Helen Longino's account of epistemic validity in philosophy of science to argue that narrative experience and 'patient perspective' should be understood as an ongoing dynamic partnership working between the different stakeholders' knowledge perspectives. I also address the connection between *expertise by experience* and the psychiatric significance of the *personal self* for the entrenched topics of agency, self-hood, personal identity, and self-knowledge in psychiatric diagnosis. In contrast to identity politics, my model of shared decision-making preserves a critical distance between perspective-taking and value itself in self/other appraisal as the gold standard for good clinical practice.

1. Introduction

This article uses aspects of my (Bergqvist, 2020) narrative particularist framework to critically explore the role of lived experience (sometimes referred to a 'expertise by experience') in mental health research and other mechanisms for patient empowerment and agency centred on quality of life and shared decision-making. In contrast to individualistic theories of personal autonomy in bioethics,[1] my account is focussed on how a relational and co-creative

---

[1]   Social scientist Priscilla Alderson (1994) argues that while autonomy-driven approaches went some way to reinstate the importance of the person in medical science, medical ethics itself has developed into a new form of

doi:10.1017/S1358246123000243 © The Author(s), 2023. Published by Cambridge University Press on behalf of The Royal Institute of Philosophy

173

approach to subjectivity and patient values can throw new light on our understanding of 'voice' in mental health research. First, by looking at the scientific impact of patients as stakeholder experts, implicit in the received notion of 'expertise by experience' (often abbreviated 'EbE') in mental health research, rather than on individual vulnerability to mental ill-health and responsiveness to categorical diagnostic measures and treatment involving predictive biomarkers, I show how patient voice in terms of agency and shared decision-making reframes the philosophical question of subjectivity in 'lived experience' and the problem of scientific validation in relational terms.

Concepts like 'shared decision-making' and 'co-production' entered the scene alongside that of 'person-centred care' and demarcates a renewed interest in patient values in an attempt to democratize the practice of psychiatry in giving people 'voice' over their own care and, to some extent, resources for what Gerrit Glas (2019) calls 'self-management'. The theoretical and practical motivations for these concepts, alongside that of 'person-centred care' in health and social care more generally, were each concerned in different ways with restoring the patient to centre stage in healthcare. Importantly, however, in contrast to earlier autonomy-driven models of medical ethics such as Beauchamp and Childress (1989), the emphasis on the 'person' and the centrality of 'patient values' in these new person-centred concepts denotes a *particular individual person* in narrative terms (Bergqvist 2020, 2022). This difference is worth pause.

As noted by Fulford and Bergqvist (in press) earlier models of 'patient values' in terms of the principle of patient autonomy, scientific as well as ethical, the 'patient' was conceived as an abstract and generalized person standing in opposition to the equally abstract and generalized person of the 'clinician'. In the new person-centred models, by contrast, the patient is a particular *individual person* engaging with a particular individual clinician (or individual team members) in a particular healthcare interaction. Ben-Moshe argues that although the 'physician might be the expert when it comes to the patient's medical good, it is the patient who has intimate knowledge of his perception of the good' (2019, p. 4462). Nonetheless, the decision is shared and, in this sense, 'internal' to medicine because the proper treatment outcome can be (jointly) determined only through

---

increasingly professionalised medical science rather than towards offering mechanisms for empowering patients. (See Fulford and Bergqvist, in press.)

the discussion between the clinician and the patient. On this model, the outcome does not stand apart from the clinical process, but is rather constitutive of it. Similarly, the particularist critique of traditional moral theory (in medical ethics and medical epistemology alike) derives from the rejection of the claim that the normative content of ethics and medical discourse be specifiable *in vacuo* independently of concrete circumstances of assessment and choice. Particularists like Jonathan Dancy (2004) hold that responsible moral thought and judgement do not require a suitable supply of general principles that can serve as a premise for the conclusion in an inference, whether explicitly or implicitly and no matter how sensitively done. Instead, and this is the positive claim that I defend (but do not argue for here), practical moral knowledge is claimed to be a form of knowledge that results from the successful exercise of moral *discernment* in particular contexts of evaluative appraisal (Bergqvist 2018a, 2018b, 2019; see also Lindemann, 2014). This mirrors recent developments in medical epistemology.[2] In particular, the so-called 'biomedical model' implied by the evidence-based medical paradigm has made significant impact on thinking and policy regarding clinical reasoning, promoting the application of research-evidence from randomised controlled trials to clinical decision-making (Evidence-Based Medicine Working Group, 1992; Sackett *et al.*, 2000). These developments have been accompanied by a renewed interest in narrative in bioethics (Lindemann, 1997, 2001, 2014) and medicine (Charon 2006; Charon *et al.*, 2008), casuistry (Tonelli, 2014), and other attributes of a whole, integrated decision-maker.[3] Sackett (2000) himself makes it clear that clinicians must utilize other forms of medical knowledge, including clinical experience, in order to arrive at the best medical decision for a particular client. As moral particularism rules out some of the most popular answers given by traditional ethical theories, a good starting point for an investigation into the question of what an adequate justification

---

[2]   For excellent discussion of certain key new methods for research and clinical care that have reshaped the practices of medical knowledge over the last forty years, see Solomon (2015).

[3]   It is worth noting that proponents of Evidenced-Based Medicine and traditional bioethics of course recognize the need to 'integrate' specific features of cases into clinical reasoning. However, as emphasized in Tonelli (2014), much work remains to be done at the theoretical level on this issue, leaving the problem with practitioners who, despite the wealth of theory in the area, find they must work out for themselves what exactly it means to integrate these features across diverse cases.

of moral and clinical judgement can consist in is a confrontation with particularism, which forces us to widen the range of possible answers.

In what follows I will set to one side the complex question of cure in recovery-based models of shared decision-making to allow sharper focus on the interplay of *values* and *relational moral agency* in examining the implicit task of self-ownership in psychiatry.[4] The simple reason (which I develop in more detail below in section 2) for assenting to the relational claim about shared decision-making as a working partnership between the different individual stakeholders is that therapeutic success on associated models of recovery and person-centred management also involves complex existential issues surrounding self-ownership, personal identity, and responsibility in the recovery process, where the notion of self-ownership is also framed relationally as an ongoing mirroring process between self and others for the future (Jopling, 2000; Tekin, 2011; Bergqvist, 2018b).

On my view, what we need to avoid unhelpful dichotomies between the 'personal' perspective of lived experience as *expertise by experience* and 'objective' expert option is a better understanding of the idea of *point of view* in the dynamic 'working partnership' interplay between patient and clinician. I use this non-committal concept of 'value' and 'perspective' deliberately to avoid commitment to more loaded accounts of the relationship between the normative content of psychiatric discourse and practical moral agency, and the general notion of 'deliberating from a point of view' (Bergqvist, 2020, p. 157). To make this option visible, in section 2 below I discuss shared decision-making and draw on previous work (Bergqvist, 2020) of relational narrative structure in clinical judgement, where the concept of 'narrative' is to be understood as an interactive process of perspective-taking between patients and clinicians shaped by the context of their treatment setting. In section 3, I address the problem of asymmetry in stakeholder voice, power, and credibility between 'expertise by experience' and 'expertise by medical training' in exposing the

---

[4]   I will also not discuss at length the growing literature on knowledge imbalance and epistemic injustice in received models of shared decision-making and co-production in addressing the real barriers, contingent practical challenges, and intrinsic theoretical obstacles to genuine co-production that does exist in this space (discussed at length in Wilde and Spencer & Kidd's respective contributions to this volume). While there are pockets of good practice (see Harcourt & Crepaz-Keay's contribution to this volume), there is no general understanding and practice of co-production in research and knowledge exchange.

ways persons with lived experience of mental illness contribute as knowers based on their experience. I argue (section 3) that there is an irreducible normative aspect of knowledge in psychiatry and clinical practice, and further show how this prevents the slide from patient values and shared decision-making to both value relativism (as seen in Kingma and Banner's 2014 discussion of values-based practice) and value constructivism (as in Ben-Moshe, 2019) in understanding the moral and scientific importance of lived experience in mental health research. Section 4 discusses the conceptual relationship between *expertise by experience* and the psychiatric significance of the *personal self* for the entrenched topics of agency, self-hood, personal identity, and self-knowledge in psychiatric diagnosis in addressing the issue of (mis)recognition, romanticism and (self-) stigma. This discussion raises the explanatory desideratum for the penultimate section 5: what, if anything, does the idea of representing others and oneself *rightly* mean in shared decision-making? I identify the challenge of self/other appraisal with the discourse of giving uptake (Austin, 1975) as a dynamic and open-ended relational dialogical process of self/other appraisal in concept application. I end with some concluding remarks about what this tells us about the relationship between the idea of expertise by experience and the wider task of self-understanding (Tekin, 2019) and re-configuration of personal values in the recovery process.

2. Shared Decision-Making

The focus of my narrative philosophical approach to shared decision-making in mental health adopted here concerns the methodology of shared decision-making as the gold standard for good clinical practice in integrating the best evidence (what works best), professional experience, and stakeholder values – rather than treating the concepts of *expertise by experience* and *patient values* as something that must be reconciled with an 'objective' diagnostic approach and 'clinical expert opinion' in meeting the gold standard for health and social care. Shared decision-making of the kind that I am concerned with in this chapter is a procedural concept of decision-making in the service of patient empowerment and agency to facilitate recovery, *viz.* restoration of a quality of life from the point of view of the individual patient given their histories and situated ecological systems (Herring *et al.*, 2017). It means decision-making, based on evidence and values, that is shared between the individual clinician (or clinical team members) and the individual patient involved in the particular situation in question (Bergqvist, 2020; Bergqvist and Fulford, in press). Importantly, the notion of 'sharing' values here implies precisely not a consensus model of 'value agreement' between the individual patient and the individual clinician (or clinical team members); 'sharing values' here denotes rather the open-ended dialogical process of the different stakeholders coming together with the shared aim of *reaching a decision* given the contextual parameters of the local treatment situation and the wider healthcare system in question.

Shared decision-making of this kind may be challenging in both its evidence base and its values base. Evidence-based practice provides a process that supports clinical decision-making where the *evidence* in question is contested (because complex and/or conflicting), i.e., a process that typically relies on statistical and computational methods such as meta-analyses of high-quality research data. Values-based practice, in turn, relies on a range of more practical process elements that build on learnable clinical skills that supports clinical decision-making where the *values* in question are contested (again because complex and/or conflicting).[5] But the principle of relying on *process* rather than prescribing outcomes is the same (Bergqvist and Fulford, in press). The result is a dynamic process of shared decision-making on integrating evidence and values in what Fulford *et al.* call 'linking science with people' (Fulford, Peile, and Carroll, 2012, p. 1). I do not here have space to discuss Fulford's own model of values-based practice in detail, only note two salient parallels with its 'science driven' principle of values (see Fulford, Peile, and Carroll, 2015, chapter 12) and my narrative approach to expertise by experience in opening clinical decision-making to an ever-wider range of individual values in the very concept of evidence.

(i) Partnership building

Salient examples in psychiatry that centre on the individual historical person and their ecological context is found in associated models of recovery and person-centred management that is geared towards the restoration of well-being and re-engagement in major social,

---

[5]   Further information on values-based practice, including full text downloads of training materials, an extensive reading guide, and dedicated library resource is given on the website of the Collaborating Centre for Values-based Practice at St Catherine's College, Oxford: valuesbasedpractice.org.

vocational, and family roles (RCPCH, 2019; Maj *et al.*, 2020). This essentially relational concept expresses a working partnership between patient and clinician in a shared model of clinical decision-making. The relational concept of 'working partnership' between patient and clinician is also a central feature of what Annemarie Köhne (2020) refers to as the *relationalist turn* in psychiatry (a term used also in the recent enactivist works in the philosophy of psychiatry by Sanneke da Haan, 2020, and that of critical psychiatry). This movement in psychiatry seeks to move away from essentialist descriptive psychopathology and many of its diagnostic kinds and classification systems such as the *Diagnostic and Statistical Manual of Mental Disorders* (DSM) and the *International Classification of Diseases* (ICD) to instead view diagnostics and treatment as a dynamic dialectical process such that the diagnostician and patient 'co-create a patient's diagnosis, and the therapist and patient co-create the therapeutic relationship that mediates change' (Köhne, 2020, p. 136).

However, what is typically *not* addressed within relationalist psychiatry is the psychiatric significance of the *personal self* (Sadler, 2007) beyond that of identifying psychopathological categories and other 'problems of living' (Stein, 2021). As argued about psychopathology at length by Peter Zachar (2019) and in more recent critiques of critical psychiatry by Robert Chapman (2023) from what Sedgwick (1982) refers to a 'psycho politics', an important aspect of 'expertise by experience' transcends the psychiatric symptoms space of descriptive psychopathology. I return to this claim in section 4 below. As Peter Zachar (2020) expresses the point in a recent commentary on Köhne (2020), because psychopathology never exists on its own, in addition to transcending symptoms, relationality in clinical practice sometimes requires transcending psychopathology itself, in as much a 'psychopathology is a feature of persons who are embedded in communities, cultures and history' (Zachar, 2020, p. 143). As I have argued elsewhere (Bergqvist, 2020, 2022), because there is no such thing as a 'patient' *in vacuo* from the particular treatment context within which that concept operates, an essentially relational partnership model requires seeing the *person* behind general diagnostic categories.

Psychological differences between persons can be revealed through narrative structures in a way that matters for the provision of effective treatment and management. As Solomon (2015) emphasises, narrative reasoning is also motivated by distinctly first-personal concerns that are operative in the practitioner-client *relationship*. I hold that the dynamics of that interpersonal relationship are part and parcel of what it means to address the patient's needs to be seen *as* a person in empathetic care – without thereby reducing truth to an individual person's perspective to encourage positive transformation.[6] (I return to this below in section 3, and further defend this claim in Bergqvist, 2022.)

(ii) Assets focus

In Bergqvist (2018b, 2022), I argue that the notion of empowering narratives to encourage positive change is a central concept behind the emphasis on the critical role of empathy in explaining human development and psychoanalytic change within the self-psychology tradition but is also key to recovery-based models of the significance of person-centred *quality of life* in medicine more generally. This is defined in mental health as recovering a good quality of life as determined by the values of (by what matters or is important to) the individual concerned (Allott *et al.*, 2002; Fulford, 1989, 2004, 2012). The importance of strengths in this regard was reflected for example in the UK government programme on values-based mental health assessment. The *3 Keys* programme, as it was called (National Institute for Mental Health in England, NIMHE, and the Care Services Improvement Partnership, 2008), identified three shared 'keys' to good practice in mental health assessment: three things that were identified in a wide-ranging consultation as being important alike by health professionals of all kinds and by 'service users' thus understood as patients and carers (Fulford *et al.*, 2015a, 2015b). The third of these keys was defined in the subsequently published Good Practice Guidance, as 'a person-centred focus that builds on the *strengths, resiliencies and aspirations* of the individual service user as well as identifying his or her needs and challenges' (NIMHE, 2008, p. 6); and the guidance included a number of real-life case examples of best recovery practice reflecting this aspect of mental health care (Slade *et al.*, 2014).

While there are research development reports on what in the United Kingdom is known as Patient and Public Involvement (PPI) and Expertise by Experience (EbE)[7] in mental health research

---

[6]   Here I side with Goldie (2012) and Solomon (2015), who warn against confusing the notion of autographical narrative (clinical or otherwise) with its intentional object.

[7]   Other cognate terms to that of 'PPI' and 'EbE' (that are *not* equivalent in meaning) found in the literature surrounding shared decision-making include 'experience-based co-design' (EBCD), 'service-user engagement,

to support both principles of shared decision-making that I have called (i) 'working partnership building' and (ii) 'assets focus', what guides the design of shared decision-making, and indeed the inclusion of those with lived experience in mental health care design and treatment methodologies in a public mental health approach, is nevertheless dependent upon mediation of differing values. Mental ill health is commonly cited as being largely caused by social factors, and accordingly, individuals and differing social community groups prioritise different values and goals dependent upon their experience. Person-centred medicine purports to offer ways of competing values being accommodated, and a number of values-based practice guides exist, offering practical support for clinicians adopting a values-based approach. However, clinicians and those with lived-experience often disagree, which leads to debates around values and how best to proceed with preventative and recovery-focused interventions. For instance, how should public mental health accommodate the positive experience reported by many with the lived experience of a severe and enduring mental illness (SMI) of their symptoms? Philosophers have contributed to the debates surrounding the 'Mad Activism' movement (see, e.g., Rashed, 2019). Other important questions, discussed at length by Sofia Jeppsson's and Zsuszanna Chappell's contributions to this volume, concern the even harder question of what it is permissible to value as an 'expert by experience' based on one's one personal experience of mental health challenges and/or illness.

One option in understanding the process of shared decision-making in navigating such differences in mediating conflicting value perspectives internal to a positive procedure that would satisfactorily incorporate 'the patient voice' is to follow Ben-Moshe's (2019) constructivist account of the *ethos* of humanistic (mental) health and care. On this view, which I articulate in Bergqvist (2020), shared decision-making is achieved through an interactive dialogue where doctors are considered the clinical experts on how conflicting treatment outcomes will impact the patient, and the patient as having the knowledge of the degree to which they value those outcomes. As Ben-Moshe (2019, p. 4449) puts it, 'patients should be involved in the construction of medicine's morality not only because they have knowledge that is relevant to the internal morality of medicine – namely, their own values and preferences – but

---

'participatory research', 'action research', 'user-led research', 'survivor-led research' – to name but a few.

also because medicine is an inherently relational enterprise: in medicine the relationship between physician and patient is a constitutive component of the craft itself'. This, I maintain, is also the key normative element of the shared decision-making model that requires clinicians to make value judgements with the active participation of the patient in dialogue: the sources of normativity are internal to the dynamic process of interaction with patients, where the interaction between patients and clinicians is understood relationally as an open-ended process of perspective taking informed by the wider treatment context.

Where I depart from Ben-Moshe is in my standing commitment (not argued for here) to moral realism rather than moral constructivism in understanding the central internal normative requirement of shared decision-making as the gold standard for good clinical practice. My particularist narrative approach also works with a stronger moral realist notion of 'value' than the idiosyncratic perception and personal ranking of preferences (Ben-Moshe, 2019) and the noncommittal construal of the concept of value as 'what matters to you' that is given on Fulford's procedural values-based practice. I argue that it is a mistake to think that a commitment to moral realism implies a commitment to stance-independent views of 'objectivity' in clinical practice (as in Pellegrino, 2001a, 2001b) and philosophy of science more generally as the only option in understanding the idea of mind-independent value in good medical practice. Instead, we may follow Helen Longino (1990) and Arthur Fine's (1986) accounts of epistemic validity in philosophy of science and think of discernment in relational terms such that there is no 'outside' in shared decision-making.

3. Science as Social Knowledge and the Problem of Asymmetry in 'Expertise by Experience'[8]

In the previous section (§2), I suggested that the slide from patient values and shared decision-making to both value relativism and value constructivism seems tempting due to the implicit mistaken assumption that realist arguments about clinical understanding must be construed from a perspective outside clinical practice (and the 'working partnership' between different stakeholders there in play). Rather than thinking of narrative in this way, John McDowell

[8] This section relies on my previous arguments about narrative formulations and the problem of relevance found in Bergqvist (2020, pp. 156–8).

suggests a new test of narrative validity as determined from within an engaged scientific practice. He writes:

> Like any thinking, [narrative] thinking is under a standing obligation to reflect about and criticize the standards by which, at any time, it takes itself to be governed. [...] Now, it is a key point that for such reflective criticism, the appropriate image is Neurath's, in which a sailor overhauls his ship while still afloat. This does not mean such reflection cannot be radical. One can find oneself called on to jettison parts of one's inherited ways of thinking; and, though this is harder to place in Neurath's image, weaknesses that reflection discloses in inherited ways of thinking can dictate the formation of new concepts and conceptions. But the essential thing is that one can reflect only from the midst of the way of thinking one is reflecting about. (McDowell, 1994, p. 81)

Thus, on this view, while the test for validity in narrative formulation is in the end a matter of judgement, it is nonetheless a judgment made against general patterns of what makes rational sense from within an engaged practice – and all such concepts are continuously subject to critical scrutiny from the 'space of reasons' (McDowell, 1994). To see this, we may follow Fine's (1986) discussion of adopting a 'natural ontological attitude' in the domain of philosophy of science. Fine writes:

> The realist, as it were, tries to stand outside the arena watching the ongoing game [of science] and then tries to judge (from this external point of view) what the point is. It is, he says, about some area external to the game. The realist, I think, is fooling himself. For he cannot (really!) stand outside the arena, nor can he survey some area off the playing field and mark it out as what the game is about. (Fine, 1986, p. 131)

Despite Fine's rejection of traditional epistemological realism, he does not support a form of epistemological anti-realism. The claim is rather that the reasoning motivating both the traditional realist attempt to validate scientific reasoning and anti-realist efforts at undermining it fails, since it is impossible to take the sort of external perspective in science that these arguments seem to require. As emphasized by Nancy Cartwright (1999, 2009), the concern about external validation is not only a concern for narrative formulations and the medical humanities; *any* discipline where correctness is at issue requires background knowledge, presuppositions, and reliance on an acquired sense for what matters and when. As a result, on the assumption that the criterion of (value-neutral) empirical adequacy is the least defensible basis for assessing theories (if such a criterion is available at all), Longino (1990) further argues that a pluralism of stakeholder perspectives and diversity in 'expert voice' is *necessary* for scientific inquiry. Precisely because there is 'no outside' in scientific inquiry as a social enterprise, such diversity in knowledge-perspectives is necessary, Longino (1990) argues, to identify blind spots and problematic assumptions built into any scientific theory, methodology, or approach within a given knowledge domain. In Bergqvist (2020), I also note analogous methodological developments in prominent strains of social epistemology in philosophy of science, which seek to integrate descriptive modalities found in sociology and anthropology into the study of science more generally. Indeed, as Holman, Bernecker, and Garbayo (2018, p. 4359) note, a central reason why philosophers such as Goldman (1999), Solomon (2001), and Longino (1990) endorse the methodological reliance on detailed case studies (a focus on the particular) in philosophy is their acknowledgment 'that traditional approaches to philosophy of science were not well-grounded in the realities of scientific inquiry.'

Now, one such *specific* aspect of the *reality* of psychiatry as a specialist discipline of medicine is the social dimension of knowledge found in the *asymmetry* in stakeholder voice, power, and credibility between 'expertise by experience' and what we may think of as the contrastive concept of 'expertise by professional training' in exposing the ways persons with lived experience of mental illness contribute as knowers based on their experience. As argued at length by Mohammed Rashed (2019), the continuous debate over psychopathological classification within mad studies show that knowledge-creation within psychiatry as a discipline is an inherently value-value process: there is no neutral vantage point between psychopathology and the mental health survivor activist movement in determining whether someone classifies as 'mentally ill' or is better described as facing 'problems of living' (Stein, 2021) or, when a given psychopathological concept is deemed to apply, what should be done about it in managing the condition in question.

Moreover, Rashed (2019, p. 38) notes that, in the UK context of employment rights and reasonable adjustments in the workplace, resistance to a more equitable *horizontal* (rather than asymmetric) model of co-production has come from both sides applying the social model of disability to mad studies in articulating the controversial concepts of 'mental disability'/'impairment' and the less loaded concept of 'variation'. Rashed writes:

> Some psychiatric survivors/service users refuse to be associated
> with disability discourse as they do not consider themselves to
> have an impairment, nor do they want to be associated with the
> "pathologizing" implications of the term impairment [...].
> Conversely, others actively endorse the term disability as it
> creates a sense of community across the survivor/service-user/
> mad and disability movements [...]. Some are reluctant to use
> "disability" for fears of being accused that they are not disabled
> enough; that they do not have life-long impairments. (Rashed,
> 2019, pp. 37–8)

Let us take stock. Returning to Longino's (1990) argument about scientific validation as a social enterprise, on the assumption that the criterion of empirical adequacy is the least defensible basis for assessing theories (if that criterion is available at all), one may argue that the voice of 'expertise by experience' must be taken into account on the grounds that there is a *requirement* to seek out a plurality of other stakeholder voices in mental health research beyond that of the 'expert medical opinion'. While I am not in a position to defend this claim here, taking a leaf from Rashed's reading of the work of Axel Honneth (2007) on shame and (self-)stigma in the ethics of recognition – i.e., 'how can this person transition from drowning in a sense of shame [for *who he is*] to demanding that you accept him for who he is?' – a possible answer to our asymmetry dilemma is found 'in the discourse of civil rights' (Rashed, 2019, p. 102). Similarly, if indeed there is no neutral knowledge-perspective for drawing the line between what is a psychopathological 'mental disability' and what is not, we may also speculate that the debate over 'mental disability' in the discourse of survivor activism needs to be settled further downstream in addressing employment rights and reasonable adjustments in the workplace.

Now, according to intersubjectivity theorists like Chris Jaenicke (2008) and Donna Orange (2002), there are two parts to the implicit corollary that there is 'no outside' in understanding the value-laden nature of knowledge in psychiatry and psychotherapy. I will look at these briefly as both are relevant to best practice in mental health. The first claim is an epistemic 'no priority' claim about knowledge in intersubjective empathetic inquiry, whereby neither perspective of the parties involved in the therapeutic relationship is prioritized over the other. This is clearly relevant to shared decision-making and co-production as best practice in integrative and person-centred health care that is geared towards recovery and quality of life (Maj *et al.*, 2020) mentioned earlier (section 2). On this view in

Anna Bergqvist

psychotherapy, as I argue in Bergqvist (2018b), therapeutic inquiry does not assume that the clinician's perspective is more apt than the patient's or that we can directly know the perspective of the patient. As Stolorow expresses the point in psychoanalytic psychotherapy research, we can only 'approximate this reality [of the other] from within the particularized scope of the analyst's own perspective' (Stolorow, 1999, p. 385). The second claim is a claim about the meaning of individual concepts as a function of the wider interpersonal systems in which they operate (in psychoanalytic discourse and beyond). For psychotherapist Donna Orange (who defends a version of constructive internal realism), the core problem with failing to recognize the normativity of concepts in their contexts is that we may mistakenly come to believe that it is possible to describe, context free, 'what the patient is doing to me, or I to the patient, as if one or both of us could momentarily stand outside the system that we constitute together' in the psychoanalytic process (Orange, 2002, p. 698). Each of those perspectives may be more or less appropriate, depending on the task at hand and given the wider contextual parameters of the treatment situation (and wider health care systems).

I differ from Orange, Stolorow, and Jaenicke in my denial that the emphasis on perspective and point of view in shared decision-making commits us to constructivism rather than realism in understanding the nature of meaning and value itself. I maintain that we need to be careful not to confuse the general idea of upholding some notion of 'clinical expertise' (which some argue involves a prerequisite asymmetry between the clinician and the patient in the therapeutic relationship, see Jaenicke, 2008, p. 14) with a misguided idea of neutrality. What I mean by this is that we must also recognize the challenges that the necessity of relatedness places on individuals within the clinical commitment to the joint epistemic and political endeavour for positive change and recognition. However, understanding the general discourse of 'perspective' need not imply a special class of agent-relative values (as in Nagel, 1986). We can also think of *point of view* as an agent's standpoint on independent reality (evaluative or otherwise). This raises a number of meta-philosophical questions concerning the relation between point of view and the notion of non-perspectival value. If the notion of non-perspectival value is better understood in metaphysical realist terms, does it not follow that the concept of perspectival value is value that metaphysically depends on human perspectives and worldviews for its existence? No. We can talk of perspectival value in different ways. It might mean that value is fixed by our actual perspectives and worldviews, whatever those happen to be. This would lead to a highly subjectivist picture. But, as I have argued elsewhere (Bergqvist, 2018a, 2019), there is space for an alternative view according to which value would not exist but for creatures with perspectives and worldviews, but actual perspectives and worldviews can be mistaken. Such perspectival value is 'for us', and we can be better or worse at detecting it in realistic and continuous self-cultivation in concept application as a relational and historically situated endeavour (Bergqvist, 2019, p. 224).

To make this option visible in the present context about the significance of 'expertise by experience' in mental health, I again emphasise that my relational concept of narrative structure in experience is to be understood as a dynamic, interactive, and open-ended process of perspective-taking between different stakeholders shaped by their treatment setting and other contextual parameters and structures (such as background health care systems). It is this last claim, combined with Rashed's important (2019) work on identity (mis)recognition (and, more broadly, the discourse of civil rights), that illuminates the allusion to value-blindness in Longino's (1990) argument that the scientific assessment of theories *requires* a plurality of knowledge-perspectives to identify blind spots and problematic assumptions built into any scientific theory, methodology, or approach. For on this view, communicating across different perspectives found in intersubjective encounters can serve as a crucial corrective to being overly committed to '*the* voice' of the prevailing norms and ways of seeing the world – in clinical contexts and beyond (Bergqvist, 2022, p. 486). This raises the new question of what makes it *right* to say that use of a given concept in public discourse in the appropriate one on a given occasion.

4. The Problem of Romanticism and the Psychiatric Significance of the Personal Self

A corollary of Longino's (1990) interest in social conventions in science of relevance to our discussion of the moral and scientific value of 'experience by experience' in mental health research generally is the recognition that even the most open-minded theorists, when presenting themselves as studying specific issues in each scientific domain, are in fact always relying on background beliefs about the world. What still needs explaining is a way in which agents could, as Iris Murdoch once puts it, 'see different worlds' (1956/1998, p. 82) in shared decision-making as a mechanism for recognition.

Anna Bergqvist

As noted by Edward Harcourt (2016, p. 86), while ideals can support self-appraisal that is both realistic and ongoing, one concern with idealisation is that 'the romantic use' of fictional models mitigates against the continuous task of seeing things aright; another danger with romantic self-appraisal is that it obfuscates opportunities for self-cultivation in appraising the ideals in a healthy way. Here is the problem. Even if we grant that narrative understanding and self-experience are not easily separated in empathetic engagement and the search for interpersonal connection and intra-psychic integration, there remains the possibility of outright distortion and unintentional misrepresentation, self-deceit and, importantly, disavowal in relating, in a first-personal way, to aspects of one's life (Goldie, 2012; Harcourt, 2016; Schechtman, 2016; Bergqvist, 2018b). To borrow a helpful image from Richard Moran, part of the problem in creating opportunities for self-cultivation in concept application is that 'the fate of situatedness as such is not escapable' (Moran, 2012, p. 190). And yet, returning to the aforementioned challenge of (mis)recognition and responsibility (see section 4), we must at the same time acknowledge that individual thought and judgement is not thereby confined to commonly articulated concepts and familiar ideas in line with the default 'social conventions' of one's moral situation (Bergqvist, 2019, pp. 220–1). This concern, it seems to me, is also part and parcel of Lisa Tessman's (2005) and Havi Carel's (2017) pessimism about the power of self-examination to transform us on certain non-pluralistic virtue theoretical accounts of virtue and the idea of flourishing in illness. (For more about the general notion of moral transformation in illness, see e.g., the works of Brady 2018, 2021; Carel, 2018; McMullin, 2019; Tessman, 2005). In what follows I examine romanticism in connection with recognition and (self-)stigma in mental health in understanding the psychiatric significance of the personal self in psychiatric diagnosis (Sadler, 2007) and, with it, broader political discourse concerning the ethics of identity (mis)recognition in realistic self-appraisal.

Psychiatric diagnosis serves many functions in the struggle for recognition, including access to public mental health systems and legal compensation, but it is not necessarily well equipped for the task of self-understanding (Tekin, 2019) and re-configuration of personal values in the recovery process – and the likelihood of optimal outcome that is geared to the individual person's quality of life (Maj *et al.*, 2020). Patients who are diagnosed with a serious and enduring mental health condition often find it difficult to make sense of themselves in relation to their psychiatric diagnosis (Bergqvist,

2021). Specifically, they have problems with distinguishing their 'self', or 'who they are', from their mental disorder or diagnosis (Radden, 1996; Sadler, 2007; Dings & Glas, 2020; Carls-Diamante, 2022; Porter, 2022). Accordingly, several authors in this volume address the scientific value of *expertise by experience* in relation to the growing philosophical literature of self-diagnosis (see Sam Fellowes). Call this the *transformative* dimension of (mis)recognition in the complex journey from diagnosis to self-ownership in the doctor-patient relationship. Consider Gilardi and Stanghellini's (2021) dialogical reflection on the importance of relational narrative identity and dynamic therapeutic empathy at play between the person in psychiatric treatment of schizophrenia (which they argue is key for patient empowerment and recognition):

> Drugs don't cure. Meaningful relationships do. The recognition I got was instrumental in my own taking possession of my condition, and in delivering the same recognition for the people around me, starting from my mother and then everyone else. (Gilardi and Stanghellini, 2021, pp. 7–8)

Interestingly, as Rashed (2019, p. 102) notes, even on Honneth's (2007) critical theory discourse approach to the paradox of misrecognition alluded to earlier (section 3) – i.e., 'how can this person transition from drowning in a sense of shame [for the "schizophrenic" *who he is*] to demanding that you accept him for who he is?' – there is nonetheless an important normative implication that some empirical requirements for psychological health are also moral goods. Rashed writes:

> Implicit in Honneth's account is the idea that being loved, being respected, and being esteemed are desirable states. We can argue that any reasonable conception of psychological health must include an adequate realisation of these three states. If so, then recognition plays a key role in our psychological health as one key empirical condition. From there, it is only a short step to its converse: misrecognition can impair our psychological health (Rashed, 2019, p. 102).

On the working model of knowledge as a social enterprise, Rashed continues, one possible way forward in understanding such empirical requirements for psychological health – love, recognition, respect – as also moral goods is again found in social relations for Honneth. As Rashed puts it, given that recognition as a condition for psychological health is 'a desirable state for the individual' whereas misrecognition is 'a threat to its realization at the level of social relations', it is perhaps

Anna Bergqvist

not a surprise that 'Honneth (e.g., 1996) describes situations where social relations result in psychological harms of this kind as social pathologies that we ought, in some way, to socially and politically address' (Rashed, 2019, p. 102).

What my account adds to this idea is that, while such choices are revelatory or expressive of a distinctly first-personal psycho-political stance on the usefulness of the concept of mental illness, they do not constitute or *determine* self-hood and self-interpretation in a fixed way. Instead, on my use of the idea of narrative structure in self-understanding, the relevant sense of 'narrative' is instead treated as what I have in other work called a 'transcendental condition' for judgement (as expressive of one's agency and self-conception), as opposed to a feature of the object of evaluation itself (Bergqvist, 2020, p. 152).

5. Towards an Integrated Approach

A structurally similar worry about an overly atomistic conception of the self is found in contemporary discussions of perspectival realism in the psychological literature. Addressing the issues of reality and truth in empathetic enquiry, Donna Orange (2002) discusses a range of divisive and misleading dichotomies in differing schools of psychoanalytic thought.[9] Orange argues that each side of the perceived bifurcation is typically seen as more fundamentally real in each school of thought: where Freudians and Kleinians are described as prioritising the internal and the conflictual, self-psychologists emphasise developmental deficits and reject drive theory-generated conflict; interpersonalists, in turn, supposedly have a bias for the external here and now in the therapeutic process, treating other factors as secondary and defensive. Taking her cue from Hans-Georg Gadamer's (1991) hermeneutic ontology in her work on emotional understanding and, in particular, the empathetic process of attunement in psychoanalytic understanding, Orange argues that the target concepts of the relevant dichotomies are themselves part of wider intersubjective systems of meaning, systems outside which the very metaphor of the target concepts lack clear sense. I here take no stand on whether the analysis of specific schools of psychoanalytic theory is adequate *per se*. What matters for my present purposes in relation to the theme of relational self-cultivation in psychiatric ethics is the

---

[9] My discussion of this example draws on my previous argument on the importance of the idea of *uptake* in psychiatric ethics in Bergqvist (2022, pp. 487–9).

deeper claim about adopting the so called 'perspectivist attitude' (Orange, 2002). Orange writes:

> The question is not here-and-now versus then-and-then, nor is it conflict versus deficit. Rather, it is recognising with Gadamer that everything is past-loaded, that we converse and inquire within a conversation that is in part created by us, but within which we find ourselves. We are inside the conversation, which is itself always further embedded in larger cultural (political, racial, sexual, and so on) contexts. There is no outside. (Orange, 2002, pp. 698–9)

The central idea here is one of recognising the metaphorical quality of concepts in their contexts in understanding other points of view and, in particular, responsiveness and openness to the differences and vulnerabilities of others in securing understanding in a therapeutic conversation. Such pluralism in communication in meeting with other points of view in open-ended dialogue is one of humility and curiosity, rather than polarised conflict. By championing a philosophical approach to the co-production of research that is also reflexive and explorative, one key methodological strength is thereby a solution to psychiatry's 'othering' problem of how to integrate 'the lived experience' or 'service user voice' in shared decision-making and research design. For on this view, communicating across differences in the entrenched 'veiled' social world operative in pathologized interpersonal encounters in an explorative dialogue can serve as a crucial corrective to being overly committed to the prevailing norms and ways of seeing the world (see King, Fulford, and Bergqvist, 2020, p. 32). I have elsewhere argued (Bergqvist, 2018b) that this idea is helpfully understood in relation to Austin's (1975) notion of giving uptake as a form of ethical achievement, a professional virtue if you like. Nyquist Potter (2009) elucidates the applicability of Austin's idea of uptake in linguistic communication in mental health as the claim that there is a distinctive ethical dimension to communication in clinical practice that involves having the right sort of attentiveness to particulars, which explicitly moral general concepts such as 'respect' and 'dignity' fail to capture.[10] Nyquist Potter writes:

---

[10] As I read her, Potter Nyquist's argument about framing uptake in terms of virtue is neutral on the meta-ethical question as to whether the conventional norms of Austin's speech act theory could also be said to ground or constitute genuine moral facts. According to Terence Cuneo (2014), moral facts are among the prerequisites of our ability to perform illocutionary speech acts, such as asserting, promising, and commanding.

Anna Bergqvist

> All of us perceive, reason, and evaluate through conceptual schemes that are embedded in socially situated norms. So, for clinicians to fully embody the values and commitments of medical practice [such as values of respect, autonomy, dignity, benevolence, non-exploitation], they will need to extend their ethical framework. Learning to give uptake is an instance of ways that clinicians need to stretch themselves morally and, because uptake is a virtue, it is part of what is involved in living well. (Nyquist Potter, 2009, p. 144)

A central feature of giving uptake rightly, then, is the ability to communicate across differences in salient entrenched conceptual schemes that are operative. It is an open-ended communicative process which is described as 'ethical' because it also serves as 'a crucial corrective' to the default tendency of being overly committed to prevailing norms and ways of seeing the world (Nyquist Potter, 2009, p. 144) *from the communicator's position* – in ways that may require that we 'set aside preconceived ideas about value and meaning' in taking seriously the reasons that a person gives for her actions and beliefs (Nyquist Potter, 2009, p. 141).

The challenge that arises from the plurality of perspectives highlights an aspect of the moral difficulty of uptake in seeing the reality of others (and oneself) aright, something that I maintain is also key in re-appraising relationality as a tool in clinical contexts and, where necessary, empowerment for positive change. The mistake, I argue (Bergqvist, 2020), is to think that a commitment to moral realism in psychological self-appraisal implies a commitment to stance-independent views of 'objectivity' in the philosophy of science more generally as the only option in understanding the idea of mind-independent value in good medical practice. Instead, we may think of discernment in relational terms such that there is no 'outside' in the application of shared concepts in clinical practice. That the resulting account preserves a critical distance between perspective-taking and value in the model of shared decision-making as the gold standard for good clinical practice is, I claim, a key advantage of my account over the popular idea of self-hood or personhood as identical with or constituted by autobiographical narratives. And the reason is that one can also adopt a second-personal stance on one's own experience and address oneself, where the relationship

---

Consequently, if there are no moral facts we do not *speak*, in the sense that we do not perform ordinary illocutionary speech acts.

between the first- and the second-personal narrative perspective on experience and self-understanding is itself a dynamic and open-ended evaluative process. I end with some concluding remarks about what this tells us about the question of language in the paradox of (mis)recognition with which we started.

6. Concluding Remarks

In this paper, I have discussed the moral and scientific value of 'lived experience', that is, knowledge based on personal experience of ill mental health as a form of expertise in mental health research. In contrast to individualistic theories of personal autonomy and the first-person in bioethics, my account is focussed on how a relational approach to the 'person' and 'patient values' can throw new light on our understanding of 'voice' in mental health research. The mistake, I argued, is to think that a commitment to listening to the patient voice implies a threat to 'objectivity' in clinical practice and the very concept of evidence in the philosophy of science more generally. Instead, I followed Helen Longino (1990) and Arthur Fine's (1986) accounts of epistemic validity in philosophy of science and argued that narrative experience and 'patient perspective' should be understood in relational terms such that there is no 'outside' in shared decision-making.

What is missing in accounting for shared decision-making in understanding the moral and scientific importance of lived experience in mental health research as a social enterprise is a relational account of the person and the wider diagnostic treatment context in understanding the process of perspective taking. Such reorientation of focus makes available a distinctive conception of 'expertise by experience' as a form of knowledge based on lived (first-personal) experience of mental health challenges, in which claims to objective meaning in patient narratives are criticized not as false *per se*, but as failing to yield the insight into the problem it was the point of those claims to provide. The reason for this is that, on the new model, the voice of 'lived experience' is no longer understood in polarised contrast with the voice of 'clinical expert opinion' but as an ongoing dynamic partnership working between the different stakeholders.

Another dimension of the emphasis on patient narratives and lived experience in the philosophical literature (discussed in section 4) is the connection between *expertise by experience* and the psychiatric significance of the *personal self* for the entrenched topics of agency, self-hood, personal identity, and self-knowledge in psychiatric diagnosis. Here and elsewhere (Bergqvist, 2019), I have suggested that what marks out an 'owned' and, conversely, 'disowned' experience as such is the wider context of the subject possessing it seen as a *whole person* as characterised by a sense of oneself as an agent (Marcel, 2003). A variety of phenomenological and theoretical considerations strongly suggests that the psychiatric significance of the concept of selfhood is helpfully understood holistically by the five aspects of agency, identity, trajectory, history, and perspective that give us the sense of unity and control that generates the subjective sense of self (Neisser, 1988; Sadler, 2007). Although there are a few proposals in the psychological literature about therapeutic integration that resemble this claim (Freud, 1914; Radden, 1996; Tekin, 2011, 2019), few have made a general case in philosophy of psychiatry for thinking about *values* in understanding the psychiatric significance of the personal self in this way. My work is intended as a crucial step in that direction.

References

Pricilla Alderson, *Children's Consent to Surgery* (Buckingham: Open University Press, 1994).

Piers Allott, Linda Loganathan, and K.W.M. (Bill) Fulford, 'Discovering Hope for Recovery', *Canadian Journal of Community Mental Health*, Special Issue 'Innovation in Community Mental Health: International Perspectives', 21:2 (2002), 13–33.

J.L. Austin, *How to Do Things with Words* (Oxford: Oxford University Press, 1975).

Tom L. Beauchamp and James F. Childress, *Principles of Biomedical Ethics*, 3rd edition, (Oxford: Oxford University Press, 1989).

N. Ben-Moshe, 'The Internal Morality of Medicine: A Constructivist Approach', *Synthese*, Special Issue 'Medical Knowledge', Bennett Holman (ed.), 196:11 (2019), 4449–67.

Anna Bergqvist, 'Moral Perception, Thick Concepts and Perspectivalism', in Anna Bergqvist and Robert Cowan (eds.), *Evaluative Perception* (Oxford: Oxford University Press, 2018a), 258–81.

Anna Bergqvist, 'Moral Perception and Relational Self-Cultivation: Reassessing Attunement as a Virtue', in Sander Werkhoven and Matthew Dennis (eds.), *Ethics and Self-Cultivation: Historical and Contemporary Perspectives* (London: Routledge, 2018b), 197–221.

Anna Bergqvist, 'Companions in Love: Iris Murdoch on Attunement in the Condition of Moral Realism', in Christopher Cowie and Richard Rowland (eds.), *Companion in Guilts Arguments in Metaethics* (London: Routledge, 2019), 197–221.

Anna Bergqvist, 'Narrative Understanding, Value, and Diagnosis: A Particularist Account of Clinical Formulations and Shared Decision-making in Mental Health', *Philosophy, Psychiatry & Psychology*, 27:2 (2020), 149–67.

Anna Bergqvist, 'Schizophrenia as a Transformative Evaluative Concept: Perspectives on the Psychiatric Significance of the Personal Self in the Ethics of Recognition', *Philosophy, Psychiatry & Psychology*, 28:1 (2021), 23–6.

Anna Bergqvist, 'Psychiatric Ethics', in Silvia Caprioglio Panizza and Mark Hopwood (eds.), *The Murdochian Mind* (London: Routledge, 2022), 479–92.

Michael S. Brady, *Suffering and Virtue* (Oxford: Oxford University Press, 2018).

Michael S. Brady, 'Precis of Suffering and Virtue', *The Journal of Value Inquiry*, 55 (2021), 567–69.

Havi Carel, 'Virtue in Deficit: The 9-Year-Old Hero', *The Lancet*, 389:10074 (2017), 1094–5.

Havi Carel, *Illness: The Cry of the Flesh* (London: Routledge, 2018).

Sidney Carls-Diamante, 'Know Thyself: Bipolar Disorder and Self-Concept', *Philosophical Explorations*, 26:1 (2022), 110–26.

Nancy Cartwright, *The Dappled World: A Study of the Boundaries of Science* (Cambridge: Cambridge University Press, 1999).

Nancy Cartwright, 'Evidence-Based Policy: What's To Be Done About Relevance', *Philosophical Studies* 143:1 (2009), 127–36.

Robert Chapman, 'A Critique of Critical Psychiatry', *Philosophy, Psychiatry & Psychology*, 30:2 (2023), 103–19.

Rita Charon, *Narrative Medicine: Honouring the Stories of Illness* (Oxford: Oxford University Press, 2006).

Rita Charon and Peter Wyer for the NEBM Working Group, 'Narrative Evidence Based Medicine', *The Lancet*, 371: 9609 (2008), 296–7.

Terence Cuneo, *Speech and Morality* (Oxford: Oxford University Press, 2014).

Jonathan Dancy, *Ethics Without Principles* (Oxford: Oxford University Press, 2004).

Sanneke De Haan, 'The Need for Relational Authenticity Strategies in Psychiatry', *Philosophy, Psychiatry, & Psychology*, 27:4 (2020), 349–51.

Anna Bergqvist

Evidence-Based Medicine Working Group, 'Evidence-Based Medicine: A New Approach to Teaching the Practice of Medicine', *The Journal of the American Medical Association* (*JAMA*), 268:17 (1992), 2420–5.

Arthur Fine, 'The Natural Ontological Attitude', in Arthur Fine (ed.), *The Shaky Game* (Chicago: University of Chicago Press, 1986), 112–35.

Sigmund Freud, 'On Narcissism: An Introduction', in J. Strachey *et al.* (trans.), *The Standard Edition of the Complete Psychological Works of Sigmund Freud*, Volume XIV (London: Hogarth Press, 1914).

K.W.M. (Bill) Fulford, *Moral Theory and Medical Practice* (Cambridge: Cambridge University Press, 1989).

K.W.M. (Bill) Fulford, 'Ten Principles of Values-Based Medicine (VBM)', in Jennifer Radden (ed.), *The Philosophy of Psychiatry: A Companion* (New York: Oxford University Press, 2004), 205–34.

K.W.M. (Bill) Fulford and Anna Bergqvist, 'The Curatorial Turn in Aesthetics as a Resource for the Contested Values at the Heart of Person-Centred Clinical Care', in Helena Fox, Kathleen Galvin, Michael Musalek, Martin Poltrum and Yuriko Saito (eds.), *The Oxford Handbook of Mental Health and Contemporary Western Aesthetics* (Oxford: Oxford University Press, in press)

K.W.M. (Bill) Fulford, Ed Peile, and Heidi Carrol, *Essential Values-Based Practice: Clinical Stories Linking Science with People* (Cambridge: Cambridge University Press, 2012).

K.W.M. (Bill) Fulford, Lu Duhig, Julie Hankin, Joanna Hicks, and Justine Keeble, 'Values-Based Assessment in Mental Health: The 3 Keys to a Shared Approach between Service Users and Service Providers', in John Z. Sadler, Werdie van Staden, and K.W.M. Fulford (eds.), *The Oxford Handbook of Psychiatric Ethics* (Oxford: Oxford University Press, 2015a), 1069–90.

K.W.M. (Bill), Sarah Dewey and Malcolm King, 'Values-Based Involuntary Seclusion and Treatment: Value Pluralism and the UK's Mental Health Act 2007', in John Z. Sadler, Werdie van Staden, and K.W.M. Fulford (eds.), *The Oxford Handbook of Psychiatric Ethics*. Oxford: Oxford University Press, 2015b), 839–60.

Rory Dings and Gerrit Glas, 'Self-Management in Psychiatry as Reducing Self-Illness Ambiguity', *Philosophy, Psychiatry & Philosophy*, 27:4 (2020), 333–47.

Hans-Georg Gadamer, *Truth and Method*, 2nd edition, Joel Weinsheimer and Donald G. Marshall (trans.), (New York: Crossroads, 1991).

Lorenzo Gilardi and Giovanni Stanghellini, 'I am Schizophrenic. Believe It or Not! A Dialogue about the Importance of Recognition', *Philosophy, Psychiatry & Psychology* 28:1 (2021), 1–10.

Gerrit Glas, *Person-Centred Care in Psychiatry: Self-relational, Contextual and Normative Perspectives* (Oxford and New York: Routledge, 2019).

Peter Goldie, *The Mess Inside: Narrative, Emotion and the Mind* (Oxford: Oxford University Press, 2012).

Alvin Goldman, *Knowledge in a Social World* (New York: Oxford University Press, 1999).

Edward Harcourt, 'The Dangers of Fiction: Lord Jim and Moral Perfectionism', in Julian Dodd (ed.), *Art, Mind and Narrative: Themes from the Work of Peter Goldie* (Oxford: Oxford University Press, 2016), 80–8.

Jonathan Herring, K.W.M. (Bill) Fulford, Michel Dunn, and Ashok Handa, 'Elbow Room for Best Practice? Montgomery, Patients' Values, and Balanced Decision-Making in Person-Centred Clinical Care', *Medical Law Review* 25:4 (2017), 582–603.

Bennett Holman, Sven Bernecker, and Luciana Garbayo, 'Medical Knowledge in a Social World: Introduction to the Special Issue', *Synthese*, 196 (2019), 4351–61.

Axel Honneth, *The Struggle for Recognition: The Moral Grammar of Social Conflicts* (Cambridge, MA: MIT Press, 1996).

Axel Honneth, *Disrespect: The Normative Foundations of Critical Theory* (Cambridge: Polity Press, 2007).

Chris Jaenicke, *The Risk of Relatedness: Intersubjectivity Theory in Clinical Practice* (Rowman & Littlefield, 2008).

David A. Jopling, *Self-knowledge and the Self* (New York: Routledge, 2000).

Elselijn Kingma and Natalie Banner, 'Liberating Practice from Philosophy: A Critical Examination of Values-Based Practice and Its Underpinnings', in Michael Loughlin (ed.), *Debates in Values-Based Practice: Arguments for and Against* (Cambridge: Cambridge University Press, 2014), 37–49.

Annemarie Köhne, 'The Relationalist Turn in Understanding Mental Disorders: From Essentialism to Embracing Dynamic and Complex Relations', *Philosophy, Psychiatry & Psychology*, 27:1 (2020), 119–40.

Thomas Nagel, *The View From Nowhere* (Oxford: Oxford University Press, 1986).

Nancy Nyquist Potter, *Mapping the Edges and the In-Between: A Critical Analysis of Borderline Personality Disorder* (Oxford: Oxford University Press, 2009).

Hilde Lindemann, *Stories and Their Limits: Narrative Approaches to Bioethics* (London: Routledge, 1997).

Hilde Lindemann, *Damaged Identities, Narrative Repair* (Ithaca, NY: Cornell University Press, 2001).

Hilde Lindemann, *Holding and Letting Go: The Social Practice of Personal Identities* (Oxford: Oxford University Press, 2014).

Helen E. Longino, *Science as Social Knowledge: Values and Objectivity in Scientific Inquiry* (Princeton, NJ: Princeton University Press, 1990).

Mario Maj *et al.*, 'The Clinical Characterization of the Adult Patient with Depression Aimed at Personalization of Management', *Word Psychiatry*, 19:3 (2020), 267–93.

Anthony Marcel, 'The Sense of Agency: Awareness and Ownership of Action', in Johannes Roessler and Naomi Eilan (eds.), *Agency and Self-awareness: Issues in Philosophy and Psychology* (Oxford: Oxford University Press, 2003), 48–93.

John McDowell, *Mind and World* (Cambridge, MA: Harvard University Press, 1994).

Irene McMullin, *Existential Flourishing: A Phenomenology of the Virtues* (Cambridge: Cambridge University Press, 2019).

Richard Moran, 'Iris Murdoch and Existentialism', in Justin Broackes (ed.), *Iris Murdoch, Philosopher* (Oxford: Oxford University Press, 2012), 181–96.

Iris Murdoch, 'Vision and Choice in Morality', *Proceedings of the Aristotelian Society*, Supplementary Volume 30 *Dreams and Self-Knowledge* (1956). Reprinted in Iris Murdoch, *Existentialism and Mystics*, edited by Peter Conrad (Penguin Books, 1998).

Ulric Neisser, 'Five Kinds of Self-Knowledge', *Philosophical Psychology*, 1 (1988), 35–59.

National Institute for Mental Health in England (NIMHE) and the Care Services Improvement Partnership (2008), '3 Keys to a Shared Approach in Mental Health Assessment. London: Department of Health'. Available as a free full-text download from the Collaborating Center for Values-based Practice at: https://valuesbasedpractice.org/wp-content/uploads/2015/04/Three-Keys-to-a-Shared-Approach.pdf.

Donna M. Orange, 'There Is No Outside: Empathy and Authenticity in Psychoanalytic Process', *Psychoanalytic Psychology*. 19 (2002), 686–700.

Edmund Pellegrino, 'Philosophy of Medicine: Should It Be Teleologically or Socially Construed?', *Kennedy Institute Journal of Ethics*, 11: 2 (2001a), 169–80.

Edmund Pellegrino, 'The Internal Morality of Clinical Medicine: A Paradigm for the Ethics of the Helping and Healing Professions', *Journal of Medicine and Philosophy*, 26:6 (2001b), 559–79.

Elliot Porter, 'Bipolar Disorder and Self-determination: Predicating Self-Determination at Scope', *Philosophy, Psychiatry & Psychology*, 29:3 (2022), 133–45.

Jennifer Radden, *Divided Minds and Successive Selves: Ethical Issues in Disorders of Identity and Personality* (Oxford: Oxford University Press, 1996).

Mohammed Abouelleil Rashed, *Madness and the Demand for Recognition: A Philosophical Inquiry into Identity and Mental Health Activism* (Oxford: Oxford University Press, 2019).

Royal College of Paediatrics and Child Health (RCPCH), 'Child Health: A Manifesto from the Royal College of Paediatrics and Child Health' (2019).

David Sackett *et al.*, *Evidence-Based Medicine: How to Practice and Teach EBM* (Wiley, 2000).

John Z. Sadler, 'The Psychiatric Significance of the Personal Self', *Psychiatry*, 70:2 (2007), 113–29.

Peter Sedgwick, *Psycho Politics: Laing, Foucault, Goffman, Szasz, and the Future of Mass Psychiatry* (London: Pluto Press, 1982).

Marya Schechtman, 'A Mess Indeed: Empathetic Access, Narrative and Identity', in Julian Dodd (ed.), *Art, Mind and Narrative: Themes from the Work of Peter Goldie* (Oxford: Oxford University Press, 2016), 17–34.

Mike Slade, Michaela Amering, Marianne Farkas, Bridget Hamilton, Mary O'Hagan, Graham Panther, Rachel Perkins, Geoff Shepherd, Samson Tse, and Rob Whitley, 'Uses and Abuses of Recovery: Implementing Recovery-Oriented Practices in Mental Health Systems, *World Psychiatry*, 13 (2014), 2–20.

Miriam Solomon, *Social Empiricism* (Cambridge, MA: MIT Press, 2001).

Miriam Solomon, *Making Medical Knowledge* (Oxford: Oxford University Press, 2015).

Dan Stein, *Problems of Living: Perspectives from Philosophy, Psychiatry and Cognitive-Affective Science* (Elsevier Science, 2021).

Robert Stolorow, 'The Phenomenology of Trauma and the Absolutism of Everyday Life: A Personal Journey, *Psychoanalytic Psychology*, 16 (1999), 464–8.

Şerife Tekin, 'Self-Concepts Through the Diagnostic Looking-Glass: Narratives and Mental Disorder', *Philosophical Psychology*, 24:3 (2011), 357–80.

Serife Tekin, 'The Missing Self in Scientific Psychiatry', *Synthese*, 196:6 (2019), 2197–215.

Lisa Tessman, *Burdened Virtues: Virtue Ethics for Liberatory Struggles* (Oxford: Oxford University Press, 2005).

Mark R. Tonelli, 'Values-Based Medicine, Foundationalism and Causitry', in Michael Loughlin (ed.), *Debates in Values-Based Practice* (Cambridge: Cambridge University Press, 2014), 236–43.

Peter Zachar, 'Diagnostic Nomenclatures on the Mental Health Professions as Public Policy', *Journal of Humanistic Psychology*, 59 (2019), 438–45.

Peter Zachar, 'Psychopathology Beyond Psychiatric Symptomatology', *Philosophy, Psychiatry & Psychology* 27:1 (2020), 141–3.

Mad Pride and the Creation of Culture

MOHAMMED ABOUELLEIL RASHED

Abstract

Among the different approaches in mental health activism, there is an ongoing concern with the concepts and meanings that should be brought to bear upon mental health phenomena. Aspects of Mad Pride activism resist the medicalisation of madness, and seek to introduce new, non-pathologizing narratives of psychological, emotional, and experiential states. This essay proposes a view of Mad Pride activism as engaged in no less than the creation of a new culture of madness. The revisioning and revaluing of madness requires transformations in the basic concepts constitutive of current mental health narratives. This process is illustrated with the concept of self and its relation to passivity phenomena (thought insertion). The essay concludes with some of the challenges facing Mad Pride's ambition to enrich the cultural repertoire.

1. The End of Mental Illness?

In 2019 I wrote a short piece titled 'Mad Pride and the end of mental illness'.[1] The aim of the piece was not to argue that we were witnessing the end of mental health problems. The historical and cultural records, and everyday and clinical experience, show that psychological and emotional difficulties have always been part of being human and remain so. By 'the end of mental illness' I was asking whether it was time to end the dominance of medical and scientific language as a way of describing and understanding the wide range of experiences to which this language is currently applied. This is evident in categories like schizophrenia and bipolar disorder, in individual symptoms such as delusions and hallucinations, in the concepts of mental illness and mental disorder and, most broadly, in the idea that madness is a disorder of the mind. Dissatisfaction with this language has long been expressed by mental health activists, advocates, service-users, patients, and their allies. No better words express this dissatisfaction than those of Jacks McNamara, an artist and an activist who, many years earlier, was diagnosed with 'bipolar disorder':

---

[1]   Oxford University Press Blog, available online at: https://blog.oup.com/2019/06/mad-pride-end-mental-illness/.

doi:10.1017/S1358246123000188 © The Author(s), 2023. Published by Cambridge University Press on behalf of The Royal Institute of Philosophy
201

And the moments when I'd been soaring with eyes full of horizon and a heart branded like a contour map with the outlines of rocky sunrises and the fractal branching of so many threads of understanding [...] these seemed like the most important moments of my life. I didn't want to chalk them up to pathology, give them ugly labels like mania and delusion that seemed to invalidate them, make them less real. I didn't want to eradicate them all for the sake of 'stability' [...]. Yet as much as I resisted their words, they were all I could find, and over and over again these incredibly limited, awkward words seemed like the barest blueprints to my soul. (McNamara, 2004, p. 5)[2]

McNamara's powerful words go to the heart of the matter in two ways: *'these incredibly limited, awkward words seemed like the barest blueprints to my soul'*. There is a sparseness and negativity to the language of medicine when it is applied to certain kinds of experiences. It fails to express the richness, the intensity, and sometimes even the value of these experiences. *'Yet as much as I resisted their words, they were all I could find'*. The problem, though it centrally includes mental health concepts and practices, goes far beyond both to signal a cultural problem. The culture has become impoverished and is dominated by reductive concepts. The connection between madness and illness has been drawn too tight in the cultural contexts in which modern psychiatry developed. Mad Pride activists have been working to change this.

The aims of this essay are threefold: (1) to advance the view that Mad Pride activism, in aiming to revision and revalue madness, is engaged in the creation of culture; (2) to explore one area of cultural creation pertaining to understandings of the self and their relation to the psychiatric notion of passivity phenomena (such as thought insertion); (3) in those terms, to identify some challenges that face the cultural dimension of Mad Pride's project.

Before proceeding there are two points that I would like to state at the outset. First, there is no consensus in mental health activism on the question of diagnosis and medical language more broadly. Some people find value and meaning in their diagnosis and would not want to get rid of it. Additionally, diagnosis plays a crucial role in research and development of treatments, and some sort of classification of mental health phenomena is bound to be always with us. That is why I have referred to the *dominance* of medical language as

---

[2]   From *Navigating the Space Between Brilliance and Madness: A Reader and Roadmap of Bipolar Worlds*. Available online at: http://nycicarus.org/images/navigating_the_space.pdf.

the problem (and the corresponding lack of viable cultural alternatives), and not to the medical approach in itself. Indeed, something like a medical, or somatic, approach to mental and behavioural difference goes back to the Ancient Greeks, and physical theories of various degrees of sophistication exist all around the world today. But medical language has come to dominate, with alternatives being pushed aside, and that is the issue that we need to address. Second, I want to stress that the following exposition and arguments are not about glamourizing or romanticising madness, as if it is all about creativity, prophetic visions, and wisdom. Madness can be all of this, but often it is not. Often it is about fear, terror, paranoia, confusion, and challenges to everyday functioning and participation. Nevertheless, the question of how to understand all of this is precisely what is at stake. And the message now coming loud and clear is that for many people medical language is inadequate, and that the culture needs to change.

2. Some Definitions

Madness

Madness, in the sense employed in this essay, is at once a placeholder for a wide range of experiences, a ground for social identity, and a stance of resistance to the dominance of medical language in mental health. This quote by Maria Liegghio (2013, p. 122) captures these meanings:

> [...] madness refers to a range of experiences – thoughts, moods, behaviours – that are different from and challenge, resist, or do not conform to dominant, psychiatric constructions of 'normal' versus 'disordered' or 'ill' mental health. Rather than adopting dominant psy constructions of mental health as a negative condition to alter, control, or repair, I view madness as a social category among other categories like race, class, gender, sexuality, age, or ability that define our identities and experiences.

In terms of current psychiatric categories, madness subsumes – but is not limited to – 'schizophrenia', 'bipolar disorder', and the various 'psychoses' (see Gorman 2013, p. 269). As to the origin of activist uses of the term 'madness' and of constructions such as 'Mad identity', the starting point – as it often is with activism in general – are experiences of mistreatment and labelling by others. These experiences can generate group awareness further solidified by the identification of features that people share, if only loosely: 'once a reviled term that signalled the worst kinds of bigotry and abuse, madness has come to represent a critical alternative to "mental illness" or "disorder" as a way of naming and responding to emotional, spiritual, and neuro-diversity' (Menzies, LeFrancois, and Reaume 2013, p. 10).

Mad Pride

We can divide contemporary mental health activism into three phases: (1) civil rights activism (beginning in the 1970s); (2) consumer/survivor/ex-patient movements; (3) Mad Pride activism.[3] Today elements of all three phases exist. What is distinctive about Mad Pride is that it takes elements from the first two phases: from the civil rights movement it takes the passion and directness of grassroots activism; from survivor discourse it takes the focus on lived experience and the voice of survivors. Within Mad Pride there is not one but several related discourses or foci. Some activists emphasise the subversive aspects of madness and its relation to creativity; others emphasise the connection to spirits and spirituality. Some activists focus on community building and understand madness as grounds for culture and identity; others focus on developing social understandings of the distress and disability associated with mental distress. What unites these diverse perspectives are concerns with the meaning of madness, the language that should be brought to bear upon it, and the role of medical understandings in this process. In this sense, Mad Pride is concerned with culture and cultural change in a more direct and significant way than other phases of mental health activism.

Culture

The term 'culture' has several definitions, with the following three among the most common: (1) *Culture as an activity*: to cultivate the land or one's intellectual abilities – to become 'cultured'; to tend to the growth of organisms, be they farm animals or bacteria in a petri-dish. (2) *Culture as a noun*: the societal concept of culture, which denotes groups of people presumed to be united by shared beliefs,

---

[3]   For accounts and summaries of early activism consult Chamberlin (1990, 1988), Crossley (2006), Bluebird (2017), Curtis *et al.* (2000, pp. 23–8), and Rashed (2019, Ch.1). For accounts of Mad Pride and mad-positive activism consult Sen (2011), Triest (2012), Costa (2015), Clare (2011), Polvora (2011), and DeBie (2013). See Hoffman (2019) for some distinctions among different types of Mad Pride activism.

experiences, and practices (e.g., Egyptian culture, Jewish culture, Mad Pride culture). (3) *Culture as socially generated and acquired meanings and significances*: culture in this sense structures experience, behaviour, interpretation, and social interaction. It 'orients people in their ways of feeling, thinking, and being in the world' (Jenkins and Barrett, 2004, p. 5). For example, 'voices' can be explained in one community as communications from departed ancestors and in another as fragments of past trauma. These different explanations can be understood as differences in culture. It is the third definition of culture that I intend in this essay when I refer to the creation of culture. We could say that Mad Pride (in the sense of culture 2) is engaged in the creation of culture 3. In what follows, I occasionally use the term 'cultural worldview' to emphasise a community's broad postulates about the sort of beings that exist and our relation to them.

3. Unlikely Affinities: Mad Pride and the Dakhla Oasis

In 2009, when I began to learn about Mad Pride, I was engaged in ethnographic fieldwork in the Western Desert of Egypt (Rashed, 2012). I was based in the small town of Mūt in the Dakhla Oasis and ventured into the many surrounding villages. My central aim was to learn about spirit possession, sorcery, and Qur'anic healing as ways of understanding and managing psychological, social, and behavioural problems in the community. Part of what prompted my research in Egypt was my desire to investigate alternatives to mental health discourse and practice. Having just completed my psychiatric core training in London, I wanted to see what an alternative system would look like, and the Dakhla oasis offered the perfect opportunity: there were no psychiatric services, and even though there did exist some rudimentary physical explanations of mental health problems, the main explanations centred around spirits, faith, faithlessness, unseen forces, as well as troubled social relationships and their impact.

The oases of the Western desert are unusual places, locked in semi-isolation for centuries and only opening up slowly to the rest of the country over the course of the twentieth century. Yet, despite the vast social, cultural, and geographical distance separating the people of Dakhla from activists in the UK, the United States, and Canada (the typical centres of mental health activism), encountering Mad Pride while I was doing ethnographic fieldwork led me to a simple but important observation: Mad Pride activists were creating culture, and so what we were witnessing was the creation of culture in action. And what was being created had affinities with what was already the case in Dakhla. Not in the exact content, for that is bound to differ, but in activists' aspirations to widen the language of mental health away from an exclusive focus on the dysfunctional body or mind, and towards a broader concern with persons' relationships with the world around them and all that it contains or is imagined to contain. In this sense, Mad Pride is seeking to transform society's cultural understanding of what it is to be normal and the meaning of madness.

4. Battles for Re-Definition

The creation of culture in the deep sense intended here cannot be accomplished by using new words to refer to the same concepts. In order to have a genuinely different perspective on and valuation of a phenomenon, it is not always sufficient to call it something else: as long as the underlying framework is the same, a new term will carry through similar beliefs and values. This is evident in the evolution of mental health terms: mental disease, mental illness, mental dysfunction, mental disorder, mental health conditions, mental health problems, mental health issues, and now just mental health. I am not suggesting a chronological improvement here, but the final term, mental health, would seem to be the least stigmatising. Yet, not so long ago, I heard one person say to another in an attempt to disqualify a third: 'don't listen to him, he has mental health'. Much more is needed than changing words.

Responding to Mad Pride requires major transformations in the beliefs and values that inform popular and professional attitudes toward madness. Our ideas about 'mental health' are not floating on the surface of our conceptions of rationality, responsibility, self, personhood, and agency, but are constituted by them; for example, in order to explain why a group of people disvalue the experience of hearing voices (which they might describe as auditory hallucinations), our explanation has to invoke deeply held norms that touch on what it is to be a self and in control of one's mental life. As Jennifer Radden (2012, p. 3) argues:

> [...] much is implicated in a reconstruction of cultural ideas about mental health and illness, because the beliefs, metaphors, assumptions, and presuppositions affecting patterns of representation, communication, and interpretation about this kind of disorder are entwined with categories and concepts fundamental to our cultural norms and values: rationality, mind and character, self-control, competence, responsibility and personhood.

Revisioning and revaluing madness requires that we revision and revalue some of the basic underlying concepts. Now many social movements are trying to bring about a radical change in some of the concepts that people take as fundamental to who they are, such as gender categories, sexual orientation, race, ethnicity, and others. And as we see around us today, there is much tension in these 'battles for re-definition', something evident in current discussions about the meaning, the boundaries, and the stability of gender categories.

That there is tension is to be expected. Many people are invested in these concepts – they understand themselves through them and attempts to radically redefine them are bound to encounter some resistance. It is, therefore, also understandable that there will be resistance to Mad Pride, for if concepts like gender and sexual orientation are basic, then concepts like self, agency, and rationality are arguably even more fundamental to people's understanding of themselves and of the world around them. A philosophical account and support of Mad Pride would push against this resistance by examining whether some of the basic underlying concepts are defined in a way that perhaps unjustifiably excludes and pathologizes a range of experiences. By doing so, the promises and the challenges of Mad Pride's endeavours to create culture can be clarified.

5. The Self and its Mental States: Subjective Perspective

One of the basic concepts key to the process of the redefinition of madness is the concept of self. The concept of self has many definitions, and there is little agreement among philosophers and anthropologists as to what the self is. Melford Spiro (1993, p. 114) offered seven definitions, two of which are likely to be more widely acceptable: the self as an awareness of our separateness from others; the self as the centre of our sensations, emotions, perceptions, thoughts, and intentions (our mental states). Berrios and Markova (2003, p. 30) develop the latter point further by viewing the self as a core that can 'integrate, harmonize and tag all cognitive, emotional and volitional acts performed by each individual', and create 'a feeling of continuity with the past and future'.

While we might not agree with the exact phrasing of Berrios and Markova's view of the self, their definition is useful in that it implies two ways in which we can talk about the coherence of the self: the unity of self *at a time* where we integrate, and identify with, our present mental states; and the continuity of self *over time* where we identify with our past and future mental states

Mohammed Abouelleil Rashed

(see Radden, 1996, pp. 11–12). I shall focus on the former dimension of the self's coherence. At any given point in time, we expect to identify with, or to own, our mental states no matter how unsavoury we judge them to be. Imagine that you are going about your day, and an aggressive or indecent thought comes to your mind. To you at the time, it appears to be out of character and creates disharmony in your mental life. You try to think of something else, to brush it off, to push it away, and you might succeed. But throughout all of this, you continue to regard this thought as your own. You might even try to harmonise it with your other beliefs, and to use this occasion to develop a more rounded understanding of yourself. An analogy can clarify this predicament further and aid us in a distinction still to come.

Imagine a symphony orchestra all kitted up and ready to go. As the musicians begin the performance, one of the cellists plays the wrong score, or the right score but at a different tempo or key. Inevitably, the orchestra fails to produce harmonious music. The errant cellist is a disharmonious element, yet from the perspective of the orchestra, it is an element that should be there: it is a legitimate part of the orchestra and is accepted as such. Continuing the analogy, there is something else that could happen, and which would indicate a different sort of problem. Imagine that a person walks in with a whistle, finds a seat, and starts whistling randomly during the performance. The orchestra would still fail to produce harmonious music, but something more is going on: the whistle is not a legitimate part of the orchestra and should not be there at all. None of the musicians accept it as part of their ensemble. There is, then, a difference between the presence of a disharmonious element that nevertheless should be there (the cellist), and the presence of an element that should not be there (the whistle). The errant cellist undermines the harmony of the orchestra while the intruding whistle breaks down the unity of the orchestra.

If the orchestra is the self, then the musicians are the various mental states. The errant cellist is the out-of-character aggressive thought that popped into your mind in the example I gave earlier, i.e., the thought that created disharmony yet was accepted by you as part of your mental life. What about the whistle, what does it stand for? It seems to stand for a mental state that should not be there at all. What does that mean?

There are certain experiences that fit the predicament of the whistle. Psychiatrists and clinical psychologists refer to these by the general term 'passivity phenomena' (see Sims, 2003, pp. 164–71). What happens in such cases is that a person experiences a thought, an impulse to do something, or a feeling, but does not experience the familiarity that people ordinarily have in relation to their thoughts, impulses, or feelings. What is going on is more than having an unsavoury thought; there is a lack of identification with the thought and it doesn't feel like the person's own. In clinical language, this particular experience is described as 'thought insertion', and the following description illustrates the certainty with which such thoughts are experienced as alien:

> I wasn't confused and I wasn't disillusioned by anything. I feel I was receiving something. I could feel it. You sense things when you know something. I do believe it is possible to communicate telepathically. At one stage I was with people and they would give us a sign to say I was. I was definitely receiving thoughts. It wasn't my own thoughts made up in my own mind. You can tell the difference. I know my own mind, I know my own self. It's hard to express. Just that you can communicate to people with your mind, without using your mouth. I was recepting [sic] people's thought patterns. It's not as if it's my own thoughts being made up in my own mind.[4]

The orchestra analogy helped us distinguish two ways in which the unity of the self can be put into question: disharmony and lack of identification. The former is evident in the experience of random or inapposite thoughts that are still one's own, and the latter is evident in the experience of alien and inserted thoughts.

Throughout the preceding analysis we were observing from the point of view of the self as it attends to its mental states. We can now adopt an observer perspective and look at the self from the outside, as it were, and assess the way in which it attends to its mental states.

6. The Self and its Mental States: Observer Perspective

The experience of a disharmonious mental state is relatively common and readily comprehensible. On the other hand, the experience of an absolute lack of identification with a mental state, such as with thought insertion, is relatively uncommon and, for outside observers, resists everyday empathic understanding. If you are having the latter experience, you would typically seek some explanation as to who had placed the thought in your mind; what other person, being, or force

---

[4] This report is cited in the *Oxford Handbook of Philosophy and Psychiatry* online clinical-case resource. Available at: http://fdslive.oup.com/www.oup.com/booksites/uk/booksites/content/9780199579563/clinical/fulford_cases_section1.pdf.

can be credited as its author? Through such an explanation, thought insertion becomes, for you, a potential source of knowledge and an enrichment of the self. From an observer perspective, there is something concerning about the way in which the self is unable to experience itself as the author of its own mental states. From that perspective, passivity phenomena, such as thought insertion, constitute a breakdown in the unity of self and a threat to self-knowledge. For this reason, so the argument goes, they are rightly considered within the domain of psychopathology or, at least, are undesirable experiences. If that is the case, then in the limited domain of so-called passivity phenomena, there is an obstacle to the revisioning and revaluing of madness that Mad Pride is calling for.

If we pare down this line of argument to its essentials, we will find that the disagreement between the subjective and observer perspectives concerns the right explanation for the self's lack of identification with its mental states. From the subject's perspective, this lack is taken at face value, and the absence of familiarity with a particular thought is explained by citing an external agent as the author of that thought. From an observer perspective, this explanation won't do. In place of it, various theories are invoked, ranging from neuropsychological and cognitive models to psychodynamic and phenomenological interpretations. All such theories begin by rejecting the subject's explanation, and then reason as follows: given that external authorship of mental states is not possible, how else do we explain the self's lack of identification with its mental states? The fundamental point of disagreement between the subjective and observer perspectives, therefore, concerns the possibility of external authorship of mental states.

A glance at the anthropological literature, on spirit possession for instance, would reveal that there are conventions of the self grounded in particular cultural worldviews that affirm the possibility of external authorship of mental states. Let us not concern ourselves for now with the validity of these conventions, but only register their existence. In contrast to these views, the convention of the self implicit in the observer perspective outlined in this section does not permit external authorship of mental states. As a convention, it insists on maintaining clear boundaries between the self and other agents, who can only influence my mental life indirectly through conversation and shared activities. Horacio Fabrega (1989, p. 53) describes such a convention as follows:

> [The ideal self is] autonomous, separate, sharply bounded and wilful. It originates or is the source of its own activity, and outside influences cannot control it. Properties of the self

include thoughts (as well as actions and feelings), which are like language statements that are a part of the mind, and the self owns and controls them. They are secret and private things no one except the self can know about.

According to this convention, the boundaries of the self are not permeable in the way presupposed in thought insertion and passivity phenomena more generally. Furthermore, according to the cultural worldview that animates this convention, there are no forces or beings in the world that have the assumed power of placing thoughts in people's minds or controlling their actions. If we can describe this cultural worldview in one word, we can say that it is disenchanted. I borrow this term from Charles Taylor's *A Secular Age* (2007, pp. 29–31), where he describes a disenchanted world as one where:

> [...] the only locus of thoughts, feelings, spiritual élan is what we call minds; the only minds in the cosmos are those of humans [...] and minds are bounded, so that these thoughts, feelings, etc., are situated "within them" [...]. Meanings are "in the mind," in the sense that things only have the meaning they do in that they awaken a certain response in us, and this has to do with our nature as creatures who are thus capable of such responses.

A disenchanted worldview is categorically opposed to the subjective perspective on passivity phenomena, and lack of identification with one's mental states is seen as a psychological aberration. What about conventions of the self that allow for external authorship of mental states – how would they view passivity phenomena?

7. The Dakhla Oasis II

During fieldwork in the Dakhla Oasis of Egypt, I met a young man who recounted to me his involvement with a *jinni* (a 'spirit') – I refer to him as Mahdi (see Rashed, 2012):

> I have a woman cohabiting with me for several years, ten years. When she first appeared, I was not able to stay at home; I would run away and walk the town all night. I am *mekhawy* [attached/in a relationship with a *jinni*]. In the beginning when she used to appear, I would be terrified, but she beautified herself along the years. In the beginning I wanted to go to a Sheikh to get rid of her, but she began to help me, she cares about me. For example, she would tell me the personality of the person in front of me, and if a person would hurt me I would just leave

and find some excuse. I show people nothing but a surface, but I know a lot and I understand people.

She only appears at night when everyone is asleep. I go to my bedroom and she spends the night with me. We copulated several times. To the extent that her love for me makes her complicate the engagements I enter. To the extent that I would be at the coffee-house and she would tell me "go check on this woman you love, see her true nature." Or, she would put thoughts in my mind that my fiancé is not to be trusted. I would go and find that it was true, that she was standing with a man talking. And this happened several times, and she was always right. She can read my thoughts and know what is worrying me [...] she [the *jinni*] gets very jealous.

[How often does she talk to you?] Most of the time, but it increases when there is a problem. She tells me the personality of the person in front of me and advises me. Could you know who to trust and who not to trust? You can't know yourself, but she tells me. I could ask for anything, thousands of pounds, cars, but I don't want to let her control me. But I am so used to her now. When she goes away for a few days, I miss her.

As we can see from this fairly long quote, Mahdi's experiences with the *jinni* have elements of a complicated and dramatic human relationship: love, jealousy, care, insecurity, loss, and control. From the perspective of descriptive psychopathology (and its underlying disenchanted cultural worldview), his experiences recall several symptoms: auditory hallucinations (second-person and command hallucinations), thought insertion, volitional passivity, and passivity of impulse. From the perspective of his own community in the Dakhla Oasis, a rich picture emerges, certainly richer than what is possible through the vocabulary of disenchantment.

For many people in the Dakhla Oasis, mood changes, unwanted thoughts, and unsanctioned compulsions and desires, can be brought about through the effects of non-human agents intent on drawing us into their world in a variety of ways. These agents are referred to as *jinn*, and there is a cultural script that describes their nature, powers, and avenues of interaction with humans. One possibility for interaction was noted by Mahdi when he described himself as *mekhawy*. This word is derived from the Arabic root for brother, and refers to a state of closeness, and possibly intimate involvement, between a human being and a spirit. The spirit can affect the person's moods, perceptions, and directly influence thought and action. In Mahdi's case it was regarded by him as a source of knowledge, providing him with useful information about people, who to trust, who to trade with, and who to avoid. At times, it did so by placing thoughts directly into his mind. At no time did Mahdi or others in his social circle regard his experiences as a breakdown of self; it was an enrichment of self through the relationship with the spirit and the information it can give. Of course, this relationship was sometimes a source of distress for Mahdi, but that was not because he understood himself to have a psychological difficulty – rather, it was in the nature of relationships to sometimes be difficult.

We can see that, in contrast to the disenchanted cultural worldview, conventions of the self that allow for external authorship of mental states have a radically different view of passivity phenomena – no longer a breakdown in the unity of the self but a possible enrichment of the self.[5] Could such a convention play a role in the revisioning and revaluing of madness that Mad Pride are calling for?

8. Mad Pride and the Cultural Repertoire

And so, we are back to Mad Pride and to the key theme of this essay: the creation of culture. We can now more precisely understand the creation of culture (in the case of the concept of self) as the attempt to generate and popularise conventions of the self, its environment, and its possibilities through which things like passivity phenomena could be seen as potentially enriching experiences, and not as psychopathology. But achieving this is far from easy. To the modern sensibilities of many people, stories about outlandish beings, ethereal forces, and porous selves are no longer part of the cultural imagination. They stretch the boundaries of intelligibility or, otherwise, are considered endearing though obsolete notions. There are many ways of telling this familiar story, with at least two from within philosophy.

---

[5]   Note that it is *descriptively* true that diverse cultural worldviews and conventions of the self allow for opposing takes on the possibility and value of external authorship of mental states. But descriptive truth is merely an account of what is and does not by itself dictate that we employ it as a sufficient basis for judgements about psychological difficulties. Accordingly, we could ask: is it the case that judging the presence of a psychological difficulty (e.g., a breakdown in the unity of the self) should be determined relative to local conventions of the self? I address this question under an analysis and discussion of the concept of cultural congruence (Rashed, 2013).

Mohammed Abouelleil Rashed

Philosophers can reasonably ask whether spirits (and similar beings) can exist and if they can really account for the phenomena they supposedly cause. Spirits raise ontological and epistemological questions, i.e., questions concerning the nature of the world in which these beings could exist and whether it is possible to gain knowledge of them. In the manner they are culturally represented, spirits have a paradoxical nature. On one hand, they are ethereal beings that exist outside the causal realm available to our senses; on the other hand, they are able to exert effects in the physical world (through possession and influence), an ability that casts doubt on their ethereal nature. On the former view, the very possibility of spirits becomes questionable on epistemological grounds, for how else would we know about them if not through our senses? On the latter view, spirits become superfluous interpretations, for what we are clearly talking about are causal mechanisms of this world. This paradoxical representation of spirits is only possible given a substance dualist interactionist ontology, or Cartesian dualism. Spirit possession requires that there are two distinct substances in the universe (material/physical and immaterial/spiritual), and that two-way causal interactions between these substances are possible. Interactionist dualism is not a popular view in philosophy and has received several, potentially fatal, objections. For example, the physicalist doctrine that any state that has physical effects must itself be physical (or supervenes on the physical) excludes the possibility of immaterial substances exerting effects in the world as presupposed by interactionist dualism.

In addition to these difficulties, there are other issues to do with broader developments of a philosophical-anthropological nature. Taylor (1982, 2007) writes of a distinctive epistemological stance that accompanied the rise of modern science. This stance involved a separation between understanding and attunement – between, on the one hand, registering the world ascetically and, on the other, feeling at home in it. Until this stance took hold, there was an assumed mutuality between understanding and attunement: the order of things of which individuals would have to be a part constrained the process of evaluating evidence and challenging theories (a seventeenth century refutation of Galileo's discoveries held that, contra the observations of the Astronomer, there had to be seven planets exactly since the different domains of being were all aligned to this number). With the scientific revolution, the idea that the world has a meaningful order and is an object of attunement 'was seen as a projection, a comforting illusion which stood in the way of scientific knowledge' (Taylor, 1982, pp. 96–7). Breaking the connection between understanding and attunement involved the rejection of the idea that the world has a meaningful order imposed on us from above. This in turn required relocation of meaning from the beings and forces that imposed it on us to the interiority of the mind and to human interaction (Taylor, 2007, pp. 29–31). This relocation is the process referred to earlier as disenchantment.

It is clear that there are obstacles to full engagement with at least one kind of narrative that could play a role in the revisioning and revaluing of madness. Transformations in modes of engagement with the world and lingering charges of incoherence prevent certain ideas from meaningful incorporation in the cultural repertoire. If Stephen Lukes (2008, p. 14) is correct in asserting that 'there is no route back from modernity', then revisioning and revaluing madness cannot be achieved by rehabilitating spirits and sprit influence. At the same time, we must acknowledge that we need to move beyond the restrictions of the disenchanted cultural worldview, restrictions that have impoverished our cultural repertoire: the rarefied language of medicine and psychiatry is often inadequate for expressing our psychological, emotional, and experiential complexity. The challenge facing Mad Pride activists is to generate and popularise narratives of madness that can address these inadequacies while having the potential for large-scale cultural acceptance. It is a challenge that activists have already taken on: from the narrative of 'healing voices' that restores meaning to 'auditory hallucinations',[6] to accounts of spiritual transformation – in Carl Jung's (1970) sense of *metanoia* – that move beyond spirit influence and embrace ecological perspectives (e.g., Fletcher, 2018), to the Icarus Project's powerful notion of 'dangerous gifts',[7] we are witnessing the creation of culture in action.

References

G. Berrios and S. Markova, 'The Self and Psychiatry: A Conceptual History', in T. Kircher and A. David (eds.), *The Self in Neuroscience and Psychiatry* (Cambridge: Cambridge University Press, 2003).

[6] From the documentary *Healing Voices*, directed by P.J. Moynihan (2016). See also Eleanor Longden's TED Talk: *The Voices in My Head* (2013), available online at: https://www.ted.com/talks/eleanor_longden_the_voices_in_my_head/up-next.

[7] See *Crooked Beauty* (2010), the first movie in the *Mad Dance Mental Health Film Trilogy,* directed by Ken Paul Rosenthal. Also, see DuBrul (2014).

G. Bluebird, 'History of the Consumer/Survivor Movement', available online at: https://power2u.org/wp-content/uploads/2017/01/History-of-the-Consumer-Survivor-Movement-by-Gayle-Bluebird.pdf, (2017).

J. Chamberlin, *On Our Own: Patient Controlled Alternatives to the Mental Health System* (London: MIND, 1988).

J. Chamberlin, 'The Ex-Patients' Movement: Where We've Been and Where We're Going', *The Journal of Mind and Behavior*, 11:3 (1990), 323–36.

Clare, 'Mad Culture, Mad Community, Mad Life', *Asylum: The Magazine for Democratic Psychiatry*, 18:1 (2011), 15–7.

L. Costa, 'Mad Pride in our Mad Culture', *Consumer/Survivor Information Resource Centre Bulletin*, No. 535 (2015), available online at: http://www.csinfo.ca/bulletin/Bulletin_535.pdf.

N. Crossley, *Contesting Psychiatry: Social Movements in Mental Health* (London: Routledge, 2006).

T. Curtis, R. Dellar, E. Leslie, and B. Watson (eds.), *Mad Pride: A Celebration of Mad Culture* (Truro: Chipmunkapublishing, 2000).

A. deBie, 'And What is Mad Pride? Opening Speech of the First Mad Pride Hamilton Event on July 27, 2013', *This Insane Life*, 1 (2013), 7–8.

S. DuBrul, 'The Icarus Project: A Counter Narrative for Psychic Diversity', *Journal of Medical Humanities*, 35 (2014), 257–71.

H. Fabrega, 'On the Significance of an Anthropological Approach to Schizophrenia', *Psychiatry*, 52 (1989), 45–64.

E. Fletcher, 'Uncivilizing "Mental Illness": Contextualizing Diverse Mental States and Posthuman Emotional Ecologies within The Icarus Project', *Journal of Medical Humanities*, 39:1 (2018), 29–43.

R. Gorman, 'Thinking Through Race, Class, and Mad Identity Politics', in B. Lefrancois, R. Menzies, and G. Reaume (eds.), *Mad Matters: A Critical Reader in Canadian Mad Studies* (Toronto: Canadian Scholars' Press, 2013), 269–80.

G. Hoffman, 'Public Mental Health without the Health? Challenges and Contributions from the Mad Pride and Neurodiversity Paradigms', in K. Cratsley and J. Radden (eds.), *Developments in Neuroethics and Bioethics Volume 2: Mental Health as Public Health: Interdisciplinary Perspectives on the Ethics of Prevention* (London, United Kingdom: Elsevier, 2019), 289–326.

J. Jenkins and R. Barrett, 'Introduction', in J. Jenkins and R. Barrett (eds.), *Schizophrenia, Culture and Subjectivity* (Cambridge: Cambridge University Press, 2004), 1–28.

C. Jung, *Civilization in Transition: The Collected works of C.G. Jung, Volume 10* (London: Routledge and Kegan Paul, 1970).

M. Liegghio, 'A Denial of Being: Psychiatrisation as Epistemic Violence', in B. Lefrancois, R. Menzies, and G. Reaume (eds.), *Mad Matters: A Critical Reader in Canadian Mad Studies* (Toronto: Canadian Scholars' Press, 2013), 122–9.

S. Lukes, *Moral Relativism* (London: Profile Books, 2008).

R. Menzies, B. LeFrancois, and G. Reaume, 'Introducing Mad Studies', in B. Lefrancois, R. Menzies, and G. Reaume (eds.), *Mad Matters: A Critical Reader in Canadian Mad Studies* (Toronto: Canadian Scholars' Press, 2013), 1–22.

Polvora, 'Diagnosis "Human"', *Icarus Project Zine*, April (2011), 4–5, available online at: http://www.theicarusproject.net/article/community-zines.

J. Radden, *Divided Minds and Successive Selves: Ethical Issues in Disorders of Identity and Personality* (Cambridge, MA: MIT Press, 1996).

J. Radden, 'Recognition Rights, Mental Health Consumers and Reconstructive Cultural Semantics', *Philosophy, Ethics and Humanities in Medicine*, 7:6 (2012), 1–8.

M.A. Rashed, *Subjectivity, Society, and the Experts: Discourses of Madness* (PhD Thesis, University College London, 2012).

M.A. Rashed, 'Culture, Salience, and Psychiatric Diagnosis: Exploring the Concept of Cultural Congruence and its Practical Application', *Philosophy, Ethics and Humanities in Medicine*, 8:5 (2013), 1–12.

M.A. Rashed, *Madness and the Demand for Recognition: A Philosophical Inquiry into Identity and Mental Health Activism* (Oxford: Oxford University Press, 2019).

D. Sen, 'What is Mad Culture?', *Asylum: The Magazine for Democratic Psychiatry*, 18:1 (2011), 5.

A. Sims, *Symptoms in the Mind* (Philadelphia: Elsevier, 2003).

M. Spiro, 'Is the Western Conception of the Self "Peculiar" within the context of the World Cultures?', *Ethos*, 21:2 (1993), 107–53.

C. Taylor, 'Rationality', in M. Hollis and S. Lukes (eds.), *Rationality and Relativism* (Cambridge, MA: MIT Press, 1982), 87–105.

C. Taylor, *A Secular Age* (Cambridge, MA: Belknap Press, 2007).

A. Triest, 'Mad? There's a Movement for That', *Shameless Magazine*, 21 (2012), 20–1.

Values-Based Practice: A Theory-Practice Dynamic for Navigating Values and Difference in Health Care

ASHOK HANDA AND BILL (K.W.M.) FULFORD

Abstract

This chapter introduces values-based practice as a resource for working with individually diverse values in health and social care, and describes its origins in an ongoing development through the resources of philosophy. The chapter is in two main sections. Section I, Values-Based Practice, builds on two brief interactive exercises to introduce and explain the key features of values-based practice. As a relatively recent addition to the range of resources for working with values in health and social care, values-based practice is distinctive in focussing on the diversity of values comprising individual lived experience. Like evidence-based practice, values-based practice is a process-driven rather than an outcome-driven methodology. That is to say, rather than offering prescribed answers, both approaches offer processes that support decision-makers in coming to answers for themselves based on the particular circumstances presented by the situation in question. Although entirely complementary, the processes involved are of course different. Where evidence-based practice relies on meta-analyses of the results of high-quality clinical trials to inform a consensual model of decision-making, values-based practice builds on learnable clinical skills and other process elements to inform a *dissensual* model of decision-making rather than seeking to overcome value-conflicts in reaching consensus. Working within a premise of mutual respect for differences of values, and guided by three key principles linking values and evidence, values-based practice, as described in the chapter, supports dissensual decision-making, balanced according to the circumstances presented by the decision in question, within frameworks of locally-set frameworks of shared values. Section II, The Theory-Practice Dynamic, then outlines the theory-practice dynamic on which values-based practice is based. The origins of values-based practice in mid-twentieth century ordinary language philosophy of the Oxford School are outlined. As the chapter illustrates, although a limited area of analytic philosophy, many aspects of values-based practice are informed by ordinary language philosophy, ranging from its premise, through the training exercises and other process elements described in Section I, to its role in hybrid empirical studies supporting its model of service delivery. The development of values-based practice, furthermore, as section II goes on to describe, is ongoing, with key initiatives drawing not only on both analytic and Continental traditions of European philosophy, but also on non-European philosophies such as those of Africa and the Caribbean.

doi:10.1017/S1358246123000279 © The Author(s), 2023. Published by Cambridge University Press on behalf of The Royal Institute of Philosophy

Ashok Handa and Bill (K.W.M.) Fulford

Introduction

Dancing with Angels[1]

Natalie (not her real name) was accompanied by angels. They used to sing to her and she to them. Natalie would often dance with her angels and though she caused no problems she was regularly taken to hospital and prescribed antipsychotic medication. Natalie refused to take medication because she believed that it killed her angels. In her mid-twenties she was detained on an involuntary basis and put on depot medication without her consent. Natalie subsequently took her own life. She left a note saying she couldn't face living without her angels.

Natalie's tragic story captures much that is important about values-based practice in health and social care. Below in this chapter we describe values-based practice in detail. But Natalie's story anticipates a number of key points about values and values-based practice that we should bear in mind throughout:

- Values as what matters to the individual person: health-related values include *anything that matters or is important to* those directly involved in a given situation; Natalie's voices mattered more to her than anything else in her life.
- Values beyond moral judgement: health-related values thus *include but are wider than ethical and legal values*; those concerned with Natalie's care genuinely thought they were doing 'right' by her and they used their powers of involuntary (i.e., compulsory) treatment entirely within the legal rules; yet, it was the failure to take seriously what mattered to Natalie that led in this story to tragedy.
- Health-related values *include centrally (but are not limited to) those of the service user concerned*; this is why the story makes a point of noting that Natalie's dancing with her angels caused no problems for other people. Had her voices been, for example, urging her to harm someone, the balance of values would have been less unequivocal.
- Health-related values require *a process for balanced decision-making* where values conflict: Natalie's story is very individual to her and (beyond the importance of the individual uniqueness of values) implies no general rule about voice hearing; as just

---

[1] Based on real events but with identifying details altered – from Crepaz-Keay and Fulford (2021).

noted, had her angels told her to harm other people, her story would have been a different story requiring different decision-making.

- A process-based model of balanced decision-making is *provided by values-based practice*: it starts from a recognition of the diversity of individual values as they impact on health care (some people who hear voices want to get rid of them; Natalie's voices mattered so much to her that she couldn't live without them); and rather than seeking a rule defining pre-set 'right' outcomes, values-based practice relies on clinical skills and other process elements (described below) for balanced decision-making in the situation in question.
- As a decision-support tool, values-based practice is a *partner to evidence-based practice*: there is good evidence that a recovery-oriented person-centred approach to supporting Natalie with her voices would have had a positive outcome for everyone.

So described, values and values-based practice *raise a whole series of long-standing philosophical issues,* not least in the long-running 'is-ought'debate about the relationship between facts and values (or descriptive and evaluative meanings). This is why values-based practice remains a product of an ongoing theory-practice dynamic. Practical implementation is not contingent on the underlying theoretical issues being resolved. But engaging with these issues both enhances philosophical work in relevant areas while at the same time ensuring that values-based practice continues to develop as a research-led discipline rather than collapsing into pragmatically-driven received simplifications.

In this chapter, we will first describe values-based practice as it is used in contemporary health and social care, and then indicate a number of future developments arising from the continued operation of the theory-practice dynamic on which it is based.

Section I: Values-Based Practice

As a practical discipline, values-based practice is best understood by 'doing not saying', that is to say, being a skills-based approach it is most effectively learned through practical engagement with the issues rather than from merely reading about them. Hence, we will introduce it here with two of the interactive exercises we have developed for medical students and other healthcare workers as part of their training for front-line clinical and social care. We will describe these exercises and their usual outcomes so there is no need to do

Ashok Handa and Bill (K.W.M.) Fulford

them for yourself. But they take only a few moments each, and you may find doing them for real illuminating.

Exercise 1: The Three Words Exercise[2]

Although based on the philosophical principles outlined below, the 'three words' exercise works as an exercise in word association.

> The exercise is simply to 'write down *three words* (or very short phrases) that *mean 'values' to you.*
>
> If you try this for yourself, take a few moments to actually write down your own 'three words' before reading on – in training exercises we find writing your answers down rather than just doing the exercise 'in your head' makes a big difference to learning (remember, this is about 'doing not saying'!).

Figure 1 (over page) shows the answers given in one of our training exercises – how did your three words compare with these? What strikes you about Figure 1?

There are two key learning points to take from this exercise:

1) The diversity of values – this is reflected in the variety of triplets people come up with. There are repeat words, certainly ('principles', for example, and 'best interests') but even running this exercise with up to 200 students we have never yet had two respondents come up with exactly the same three words.

If you are not surprised by this perhaps you should be. After all, 'values' is not an unfamiliar word. In a sense we all know what it means. But when it comes to a challenge of this sort, it appears we all mean something slightly different by this term! On the other hand, once we identify 'values' as the non-technical and pre-reflective notion to simply mean 'what matters to you', the diversity of individual values should perhaps not come as a surprise.

In the next exercise we will see how the diversity of meanings we attach to the word 'values' is reflected in the diversity of the personal values that drive our choices in health and social care.

2) Values and 'what matters to you' – if we look again at Figure 1, we notice something else – yes, everyone's triplet is different; but

---

[2] This exercise was devised originally by Kim Woodbridge, a nurse trainer at the Sainsbury Centre for Mental Health, who worked with Bill Fulford to develop the first training manual for values-based practice (see Woodbridge and Fulford, 2004).

Preferences Needs Best interests	How we treat people Attitudes Principles
Respect Personal to me Difference ... diversity	Non-violence Compassion Dialogue
Beliefs Right/wrong to me What I am	Responsibility Accountability Best interests
Belief Principles Things held dear	What I believe What makes me tick What I won't compromise
Subjective merits Meanings Person-centred care	'Objective' core Confidentiality Honesty

Figure 1. A sample of the triplets of words given by participants in a training session in values-based practice.

there is nothing in the triplets of words people come up with that seems simply nothing to do with values.

So, we can think of the results of this exercise as picking out different aspects of what – despite the everyday familiarity of the word 'values' – is a complex multifaceted notion. We will return to this point in the second half of the chapter when we look at the theory underpinning values-based practice. For now, one way of drawing together these different meanings, is to say that for clinical purposes, 'values' include ...

- anything that matters or is important to those concerned in the situation in question.

This (admittedly tautological) definition may perhaps be lacking philosophically in clarity and depth as much as in content. But it works well in clinical contexts to emphasise the breadth and diversity of relevant issues. It also provides a helpful nominal link between values-based practice and the growing international 'what matters to you?' movement, which as its name suggests, promotes the importance of finding out 'what matters to you?'.[3] The next exercise shows why this is significant, why it is that (as in values-based practice) clinical decision-making should be based on asking not only 'what is the matter *with* you?' but also 'what matters *to* you?'.

Exercise 2: A Forced Choice Exercise

Where the three words exercise is an exercise in word association, the 'forced choice' exercise requires an effort of the imagination.

Imagine you have developed early symptoms of a potentially fatal disease.

There are two possible evidence-based treatments available, both of which offer advantages but neither of which is perfect:

- TREATMENT A – gives you a guaranteed period of remission but no cure
- TREATMENT B – gives you a 50:50 chance of 'kill or cure'

It's your decision – what is the *minimum* period of remission you would want from Treatment A to choose that treatment rather than choosing the 50:50 'kill or cure' option offered by Treatment B?

Write down, 1) your minimum period, and then, 2) your reasons for choosing the period that you did.

Figure 2 illustrates the wide range of minimum figures people come up with when they do this exercise. This is nothing to do with differences in the evidence-base of the decision: everyone had *the same*

---

[3] See https://wmty.world. Many organisations have their own websites dedicated to WMTY – see for example, The Institute for Healthcare Improvement website at: https://www.ihi.org/Topics/WhatMatters/Pages/default.aspx.

Choosing treatment A over B ...

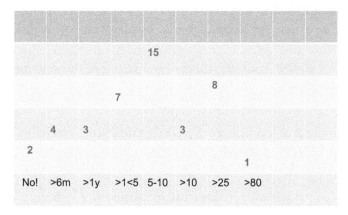

Figure 2. A typical range of responses in the forced choice exercise.

evidence base (an artificially constrained evidence base at that). Nor has it to do with diversity in the target group: the range of responses in Figure 1 happens to be from a group of medical students, roughly 50:50 men and women, though otherwise with similar backgrounds and ages; but we find a similar range is the norm with whatever group the exercise is used.

The second part of the exercise then shows us that we get this wide range because, despite their apparent similarities, individuals bring very different personal values to the choices they make. This is the message of the 'what matters to you?' movement – different things matter or are important to different people. In this exercise, one person may choose perhaps 20 years because he or she has a young family and wants enough time to see them safely grown up; another may choose only a year because that person is finishing a project that he or she feels passionate about and that will take a year to complete; and so on.

Again, if you did this exercise for real, revisit your minimum figure and the reasons behind it – what mattered or was important to you in this imaginary situation?

Learning Points from the Forced Choice Exercise

The key learning point from the forced choice exercise is the link between diversity of individual values and clinical decision-making. We can sum this up as:

- *same evidence + different values = different decisions*

This in turn carries other important learning points:

- *The importance of shared decision-making based on evidence and values*

As clinicians we are familiar with the importance of the evidence-base for decision-making. The forced choice exercise reminds us that it is also important to take the values-base of decision making into account.

In the context of a training exercise this may seem obvious. That it is however far from obvious in practice is shown by the need for a whole international movement (noted above) pushing the importance of asking 'what matters to you?'. The need for such a movement, furthermore, continues despite growing emphasis on the importance in clinical care of shared decision-making – that is, decision-making that is shared between clinicians (as experts on the evidence) and patients (as experts on what matters to them) within contemporary models of patient-centred care. In the United Kingdom, for example, professional guidance for doctors has made shared decision-making of this kind the basis of consent to treatment for at least the last two decades (see General Medical Council, 2008). This guidance was reinforced by a decision of the UK Supreme Court in 2015 (the *Montgomery* ruling, Montgomery v Lanarkshire Health Board, 2015; see also, Herring *et al.*, 2017), and it has been further reinforced by evidence-based guidelines from NICE, the UK's National Institute for Health and Care Excellence[4] (NICE, 2021).

So shared decision-making, it would seem, is harder than it appears. Once again, the forced choice exercise helps to explain why this should be so. We here draw attention to three salient considerations.

- *It is hard for patients*

One reason shared decision-making is difficult is that it is hard for patients. If you did the forced choice exercise for real you probably found it more challenging than exercise 1 (the 'three words' exercise). This is partly because the situation it asks you to imagine is not a pleasant one: though of course it is not unrealistic – it may indeed be a situation similar to one with which you have personal experience.

---

[4] NICE is responsible for providing evidence-based guidelines for the interventions that can and cannot be provided within the UK's National Health Service.

But either way, the challenge most people find is to answer it *for your-self*. It is easy enough to say what 'most people' would choose as a minimum period; or what the 'rational choice' would be; but answering the question in the form of your own personal decision, taken for yourself as you are currently placed (at your own age and in your own situation), is, most people find, surprisingly challenging.

This is in itself an important learning point from the exercise – that answering the forced choice question (and its cognates) even in the relatively safe environment of a training session is surprisingly hard. How much harder therefore must it be for someone faced with this or an equivalent choice in circumstances of personal exist-ential threat in choosing one's personal treatment outcome.

- *It is also hard for clinicians*

Understanding what matters to a given patient is also hard for clini-cians. This is because as clinicians we are trained to understand 'what is the matter *with* you' and (wrongly) extrapolate this to understand-ing 'what matters *to* you'. This is well illustrated by the experience of Zoe Barber, one of the pathfinders for training in values-based prac-tice in Oxford, of her first experience as a participant in the forced choice exercise. Mindful of her impending marriage and wish to start a family, Zoe chose twenty years as her minimum period; but was shocked when she found her partner, Tom, chose eighteen months. When he explained his reasoning (this was the time he needed to finish his PhD), she understood, but as she wrote later, it was a 'light bulb moment – If I could so misjudge the values of the man I share my life with, just how wrong might I be in assuming that I know what is important to the patient I met perhaps only five minutes ago!' (in Handa *et al.*, 2016, pp. 20–7).

- *Shared decision-making and recovery in person-centred mental health*

Shared decision-making is especially important in person-centred mental health care as the basis of recovery. 'Recovery' in this context means recovering a good quality of life as defined by the values of – by what matters or is important to – the person concerned (Slade *et al.*, 2014; Hughes *et al.*, 2018). This is challenging in several ways. First, as Natalie's story at the start of this chapter illustrates, recovery, so defined, may but in other cases it may not coincide with traditional professional concerns such as symptom control. It is challenging, second, because the operative values in a number of mental health con-ditions may present particular difficulties of understanding (we return to the philosophical resources supporting understanding in the second half of the chapter). It is challenging, third, because in mental health, what matters to the patient may be in conflict with what matters to everyone else (which is where the resources of values-based practice for balanced decision-making that we describe immediately below, come into play). But for all these challenges, without an understanding of what matters to the individual concerned, recovery in mental health cannot even get started.

The Process Elements of Values-Based Practice

We do not have space here to describe the process elements of values-based practice in detail (but see for example, Fulford, Peile and Carroll, 2015, and other Resources on the website for the Collaborating Centre for Values-based Practice in Oxford at: valuesbasedpractice.org).

The process of values-based practice is shown in the form of a summary flow diagram in Figure 3 and brief definitions of its constituent process elements are given in Figure 4. As these indicate, values-based practice is premised on mutual respect for differences of values. This does not mean that in values-based practice 'anything goes'; on the contrary, any form of racism or other discriminatory values are by definition excluded by the requirement for mutuality (we return to the philosophical origins of this premise in the second half of the chapter).

Premise of Mutual Respect for Differences of Values		
Key Process Elements • **4 clinical skills** • **2 Aspects of clinical service model** • **3 Principles linking values and evidence** • **Model of partnership in decision-making based on dissensus**	**Together these** **support** ➡	**Balanced decisions made** **within Frameworks of** **Shared values**

Figure 3. A Flow Diagram of Values-based Practice.

Key Process Elements	Brief definitions
Premise of mutual respect	Mutual respect for differences of values
Learnable Clinical Skills	
Skills – awareness	Awareness of values and of differences of values
Skills – knowledge	Knowledge retrieval and its limitations
Skills – reasoning	Used to explore the values in play rather than to provide answers
Skills – communication	Especially for eliciting values and conflict resolution
Clinical Service Model	
Patient-*values*-centred care	Care centred on the actual rather than assumed values of the patient
***Extended* Multi-disciplinary Team**	MDT role extended to include a range of value perspectives (as well as of knowledge and skills) for interagency working
Relationship between Evidence and Values	
Two feet principle	All decisions are based on the two feet of values and evidence
Squeaky wheel principle	We notice values when they cause difficulties (like the squeaky wheel) but (like the wheel that doesn't squeak) they are always there and operative
Science-driven principle	Advances in medical science drive the need for VBP (as well as EBP) because they open up choices and with choices go values
Model of Decision-making	
Partnership	Decisions in VBP (although informed by clinical guidelines and other sources) are made by those directly concerned working together in partnership
Frameworks of shared values	Values shared by those in a given decision making context and within which balanced decisions can be made on individual cases
Balanced dissensual decision-making	Decisions in which the values in question remain in play to be balanced sometimes one way and sometimes in other ways according to the circumstances of a given case

Figure 4. Brief Definitions of the Process Elements of Values-Based Practice.

Ashok Handa and Bill (K.W.M.) Fulford

Within the premise of mutual respect, values-based practice then builds on four key areas of learnable clinical skills (awareness, knowledge, reasoning, and communication) within a particular model of service delivery (one that is person-centred and multidisciplinary) and guided by three key principles linking evidence and values (namely, the Two Feet principle, the Squeaky Wheel principle, and the Science-Driven principle). Together, these support balanced decision-making on questions of values through a particular model of partnership (dissensual partnership) operating within (locally set) frameworks of shared values.

You will see how the above two exercises provide an introduction to values-based practice. In any actual training session, a focus on individual lived experience (as a service user or service provider) is of course essential. But with this caveat, the three words exercise sets the scene for training by making participants aware of the diversity of values. Hopefully, participants come to recognise for themselves that there is more to 'what matters to you?' than can be captured in ethical and legal guidelines. The forced choice exercise then builds on this, acting as a focus for discussion of almost any aspect of values-based practice. This is a guided discussion aimed at understanding the practical importance of shared decision-making based on values ('what matters to you?') as well as evidence (of what works in dealing with 'what's the matter with you').

Section II: The Theory-Practice Dynamic

The importance of ensuring that values-based practice remains driven by an ongoing dynamic between theory and practice received early endorsement from what at first glance might appear an unlikely source, namely a Senior Advisory Board of experienced clinicians, managers, and politicians, who generously took on the task of guiding the VBP Centre in Oxford through its early days of developing its impact within the UK health service.[5]

The background to this endorsement is worth brief reprise. Values-based practice was developed originally as a practical discipline mainly within mental health. As described further below, it was based originally on theoretical principles derived primarily from mid-twentieth century ordinary language analytic philosophy; but the philosophy as such had largely fallen out of view as the discipline started to take root in practice. For example, although the

[5] For details of our Founder Advisory Board, see https://valuesbasedpractice.org/who-are-we/advisory-board/.

230

underlying philosophy had been instrumental in the development of a number of training exercises (see above), explicitly philosophical material was entirely absent from the first practical training manual for values-based practice (Woodbridge and Fulford, 2004).

It was perhaps understandable, therefore, that when we set up The Collaborating Centre in Oxford[6] with the aim of extending values-based practice from mental health to other areas of health care, our focus at the time should have been on practice rather than theory. At the first meeting of our Advisory Board, correspondingly, we described how rather than developing the theory of values-based practice, we had identified three key areas of practice on which we would focus – training, regulation, and teamwork. Yes, good thinking, our Advisory Board commented, drawing on their considerable experience; but not, they continued, if this is at the expense of theory. There should instead be an ongoing partnership between theory and practice underpinning the work of the Centre as a whole. Theory, the Board explained, was vitally important if values-based practice was to avoid the fate of so many other initially promising initiatives, in becoming 'dumbed down' under the bureaucratic and other inevitable pressures of day-to-day clinical and managerial concerns. Remember, they said, the American humourist, J.L. Mencken's aphorism, variously cited along the lines of, 'For every complex problem, there is always at least one solution that is clear, plausible – and wrong!' (Mencken, 1920).

This made sense in our circumstances. Through an exchange in the early days of the Centre with (the now late) David Sackett, we were aware of his disappointment that his originally rich model of evidence-based practice, developed in his role as the Founder Director of Oxford's Centre for Evidence-based Medicine, had been, precisely as our Advisory Board warned, dumbed down. Sackett's original model of Evidence Based Medicine had three elements: it combined evidence of various kinds (appropriate to the question of concern) with clinical experience, and, yes, patients' individual values (Sackett *et al.*, 2000, p. 1) – a far cry then from much of today's evidence-based medicine in which evidence, and indeed evidence of only one kind (prototypically from randomised controlled trials), is considered relevant.[7]

[6] Its full title is The Collaborating Centre for Values-based Practice in Health and Social Care, St Catherine's College, Oxford, see https://valuesbasedpractice.org.
[7] The relevance hierarchy is upended for values-based practice in which lived experience comes out at the apex (see Fulford, 2020).

Ashok Handa and Bill (K.W.M.) Fulford

Thus forewarned, the work of the Centre for Values-based Practice has been pursued explicitly within an ongoing dynamic between theory (primarily but not only philosophical theory) and practice. The dynamic, we should add, is indeed 'ongoing': there is much of theory that remains untouched let alone explored. But by way of illustration, we will outline two areas showing the power of the theory-practice dynamic to which our Advisory Board pointed us – first, the origins of values-based practice in ordinary language philosophy; second, its ongoing development by way of a now growing range of other philosophies, both European and non-European in inspiration.

Origins in Ordinary Language Philosophy

The poster child of mid-century ordinary language philosophy of the 'Oxford school' was J.L. (John Langshaw) Austin, at the time White's Professor of Moral Philosophy and a Fellow of Corpus Christi College. In developing his philosophy, Austin built on the observation that we are in general better at using everyday concepts (including many of the concepts with which philosophers struggle) than we are at defining them. Something similar had been pointed out several centuries previously by the early Neo-Platonist philosopher and Bishop of Hippo, St Augustine, in his *Confessions* (Book 11, Chapter 14, No. 17): 'What then is time?', Augustine wrote, 'Provided that no one asks me, I know. If I want to explain it to an enquirer, I do not know' (Chadwick, 1992). Why not, therefore, Austin and others argued, explore the way concepts are actually used in ordinary (i.e. non-reflective) contexts rather than (as philosophers have traditionally done) getting out of our depth with trying to define them.

Ordinary language philosophy, so defined, has been subject to much criticism, some for what it is, some for what it is not (see for example various essays in the collection by K.T. Fann, 1969). Rather than exploring its pros and cons in general we will focus here on four aspects of the resources it brings to the development of values-based practice.

1) Focusing where practice 'is at'

As a method, ordinary language philosophy is highly compatible with the challenges of practice in that it focuses on where the conceptual problems of practice are 'at', i.e., in ordinary everyday usage. Much of clinical care (at least in acute hospital medicine) can

232

proceed up to a point effectively with little regard to conceptual problems; there are after all in such contexts sufficient empirical problems with which to engage. But where conceptual issues arise in health care (notably, as we describe further below, in mental health care), they arise as problems in everyday practice and are framed in the language of practice.

The language of practice, moreover, as Austin himself pointed out, is particularly well displayed, again consistently with clinical experience, through case studies. Towards the end of one of Austin's most explicitly methodological papers, *A Plea for Excuses*, having worked from legal case reports, he directs philosophers to the (as he believes) richer resources of case material in (what he calls) 'abnormal psychology': 'There is', he says, anticipating by some forty years the development of values-based practice in mental health (described below), 'gold in them thar hills' (Austin, 1956/7, p. 24).

2a) A more complete view: the three words training exercise
Austin had a very modest view of his proposals for ordinary language philosophy. Indeed, he repeatedly caveated its potential. One such caveat was the extent of its outputs: it gave us, at most, and only with concepts of the kind for which it was suited, a 'more complete view' of their meanings. When we try to define a complex concept, so Austin argued, we tend to focus on one or other aspect of its meaning; exploring ordinary usage, on the other hand, expands our view to encompass a more complete view of its meaning. Exploring ordinary usage thus gives us what another philosopher working in this tradition, Gilbert Ryle, called the 'logical geography' (Ryle, 1949, 1963 edition, p. 10).

The Austin/Ryle 'more complete view' is directly reflected in the three words training exercise for values-based practice described above. Merely asking participants to 'define' what they mean by 'values' would leave them at best bemused. As a word association exercise, by contrast, participants see for themselves the diverse aspects of the meaning of this complex concept: that it is broader than ethics, highly individual, and so on (though not inchoate); and through guided discussion they come to embrace a shared summary of these meanings for practical use as 'anything that matters or is important to the individual concerned'.

2b) A more complete view: the fact/value distinction in health care
The Austin/Ryle 'more complete view' also has substantive implications for our understanding of the concepts (disease, illness, *etc.*)

defining health care. Indeed, the guiding model of values-based practice – as a partner to evidence-based practice supporting clinical decision-making in all areas of healthcare – is itself an aspect of this more complete view.

Again, we will not have space to develop this aspect of the theory underpinning values-based practice in detail (but see the More about Values-based Practice at: values-basedpractice.org). The model starts from an observation of another of Austin's pupils, and a successor as White's Professor, R.M. Hare, that we can sum up as 'diverse values become visible values' (Hare, 1952, p. 123 *et seq.*; Hare, 1963; this idea is incorporated in the process elements of values-based practice as the Squeaky Wheel Principle, see Figure 4). Combining this with the work of the American philosopher Hilary Putnam on facts and values being distinct but not dichotomous (Putnam, 2002)[8] suggests that health concepts are always hybrid, i.e. part-fact/part-value (Fulford, 1989). We see this, notably, in the overtly value-laden concepts of mental disorder (discussed further below); but health concepts may appear to be value free where (as in the context of life-threatening acute hospital care) the operative values (such as, in this case, relief of pain and saving life) are widely shared.

It is this hybrid model, in essence, by which values-based practice has been guided throughout: from its original theoretical formulation and development in mental health, through its wider partnership with evidence-based medicine, to contemporary applications such as the shared decision-making based on evidence and values that (as described above) is at the heart of today's person-centred clinical care.

3) A collaborative approach

Integral to Austin's modest conception of ordinary language philosophy is his idea that philosophers should model themselves on empirical scientists by collaborating in teams rather than (as they have traditionally done) working alone as 'sole traders'. Austin's inspiration for this idea was his experience as an intelligence officer in the Second World War: he had been impressed by the way teams could solve complex problems by tackling them piecemeal.

---

[8]   Read as arguing that the distinction between fact and value (or description and evaluation) is necessary to ordinary usage even though it cannot be traced all the way back to individual examples of pure forms of either.

In the development of values-based practice we combined Austin's ideas on team work with the quasi-empirical nature of ordinary language philosophy (he calls it at one point, philosophical 'fieldwork', Austin, 1979, p. 25), to employ a hybrid philosophical/social science methodology to explore differences of implicit values within multi-disciplinary teams (Colombo *et al.*, 2003; and Fulford and Colombo, 2004). The key result from this work – that the range of implicit values exhibited by team members matched the range of implicit values exhibited by patients – became the basis for the 'extended' multidisciplinary team of values-based Practice (see Figure 4).

4) A starting point – sometimes the first word, never the last
Ordinary language philosophy comes with a further important caveat, again, repeatedly emphasised by Austin, namely that he was not proposing anything in the way of a philosophical sinecure. One of Austin's pupils, and later biographical editor, Sir Geoffrey Warnock, reports Austin as opening a seminar on ordinary language philosophy with 'I want to say something today about one way of possibly getting started with some kinds of philosophical problem' (Warnock, 1989, p. 6). Elsewhere Austin himself writes in similar vein to the effect that ordinary language philosophy may sometimes be 'the first word (but) never the last' (cited by Warnock, 1989, p. xx).

This caveat, so often ignored by the critics of ordinary language philosophy, has many important consequences for values-based practice, not the least of which is its recent flowering into other areas of philosophy. Ordinary language philosophy has proven highly effective in getting values-based practice started. In Austin's terms it has been a fruitful 'first word'; but as Austin himself anticipated, and as we illustrate in the next section, it is far from being the 'last word'.

Ongoing Development and Other Philosophies

As several times noted, values-based practice was developed first in mental health. This might seem surprising given the widely perceived 'second-class' status of mental health among health disciplines. It reflects, however, another of Austin's insights, namely that the most productive areas for ordinary language philosophy are often just those areas where the concepts of interest appear to break down or in other ways cause difficulties. This is not unlike the medical example of diabetes (where the pancreas stops working properly) leading to the eventual discovery of insulin. Austin used the metaphor of a 'blinding veil of ease and obviousness' to capture the idea that the full meanings of complex concepts may be hidden from us by the facility with which we use them in unproblematic contexts (Austin, 1956/57, p. 23).

Following Austin's lead, the conceptual challenges presented by mental health are thus opportunities for breaking through the 'blinding veil' to a more complete view of the meanings of the health concepts as a whole. This is indeed what we find. If the conceptual insights summarised above are correct, the overtly value-laden concepts of mental disorder are not an indication, somehow, of deficiencies in the mental health disciplines, but a sign rather that the health concepts as a whole are (in part and albeit often covertly) evaluative in nature.

This is of course an arguable claim (though the argument, as recent commentators have pointed out, has moved on from *whether* the health concepts are in part evaluative in nature to *where* the line between fact and value should be drawn, see Stein *et al.*, forthcoming, 2023). But even if it is correct, we should anticipate (again, following Austin, point 4 above) that this will not be the last word on the subject. This indeed has been our experience in developing values-based practice. We noted above the results of combining ordinary language philosophy with methods derived from the social sciences. We will focus in the rest of this section on the results of extending the theoretical base of values-based practice to other areas of philosophy in the context, first of mental health, then of health care as a whole.

Philosophy, Values-Based Practice and Mental Health

As noted above, values-based practice, reflecting the overtly value-laden nature of concepts of mental health, was developed first for use in this area of health care. And it is the challenges presented by the values operative in mental health that continue to drive the development of values-based practice in mental health.

To be clear, there is much in mental health (as of course there is in bodily health) that is susceptible to values-based interventions based only on its original formulation in ordinary language philosophy. The outcome of Natalie's story at the start of this chapter, of 'Dancing with Angels', was a tragedy precisely because it could have been avoided if her self-evident values had been listened to. Indeed, the very concept of 'recovery' in mental health is values-driven in that, as noted above, recovery means recovering a good quality of life as defined by the values of (by what is important to) the person concerned. Which makes it all the more important to recognise that the operative values may be considerably more obscure than in Natalie's story. How, for example, should we understand people with anorexia who make clear, just as explicitly as Natalie made her values clear, that they value fasting and weight loss even more than their own death? Or how should we understand people with addictive disorders who both wish and do not wish to continue their addictive behaviour?

Developments in phenomenologically-enriched values-based practice are proving effective in areas such as these, where the operative values are obscure to ordinary empathic understanding. Thus, the Italian philosopher and psychiatrist, Giovanni Stanghellini, has developed a range of insights based on Jean Paul Sartre's three-way phenomenology of the body, into the pre-conscious (or pre-reflective) life world of people with anorexia (Stanghellini, 2017). Combining this with empirical methods he has developed both therapeutic (Stanghellini, 2019) and research interventions (Stanghellini *et al.*, 2012). Similar phenomenologically-inspired work on addictive disorders, drawing in this instance on dialectical methods and extending to policy-level interventions, has been developed by the Brazilian phenomenologist and psychiatrist, Guilherme Messas (Messas, 2021; Messas and Fulford, 2021a and 2021b).

In this and other areas, then, we have seen a coming together in values-based practice of two traditionally separate strands of European philosophy, respectively analytic philosophy and phenomenology. Analytic philosophy has much to offer still, it should be said. Take, for example, Anna Bergqvist's work on the relationality of values in psychiatric ethics and shared decision-making (described below). And in a contrasting area, the mathematician and philosopher, Philipp Koralus, has developed a computable model of rationality based on semiotic logic (his 'erotetic theory' of rationality, see Koralus and Mascarenhas, 2013) with potentially important implications for understanding and intervening in severe mental disorders such as schizophrenia (Parrott and Koralus, 2015).

A further and quite different area of development has drawn on philosophies that are non-European in origin. Such philosophies have found important applications for example in relation to the much-contested area of race relations in mental health. Leading the field in this has been the activist and expert-by-experience, Colin King, drawing notably on the work of the French Caribbean philosopher and psychiatrist, Franz Fanon (King *et al.*, 2021; Fulford, King, and Bergqvist, 2023). King's work identifies the origins of racial bias in psychiatry in unacknowledged values of whiteness operating through judgements of rationality implicit in psychiatric diagnostic categories. This has implications for a remedial approach based on values-based principles of co-production across lines of colour.[9] This work is important in its own right and in addition has wider implications for reducing the notorious vulnerability of psychiatry to abusive uses for political (rather than legitimately medical) ends.

Philosophy, Values-Based Practice, and Health Care

Given Austin's mental health first message, we should not be surprised to find theoretical developments in the rest of healthcare following the lead set by mental health, drawing that is to say on both European and non-European philosophical sources. The driver though in the context of bodily health is not (in general) empathically obscure values but the need to expand the horizons of values-based practice from individual to social values.

The need for such an expansion was pointed out originally by the Indian analytic moral philosopher Shridhar Venkatapuram (2014). Pointing to the findings of the epidemiologist Sir Michael Marmot, with whom he had been working, Venkatapuram argued that in focussing on individual values, values-based practice was misaligned with current evidence suggesting that the main drivers of pathology in most areas of bodily health were not individual and biological but social and political.

Our response to this has been, in part, an open access collection of case studies in social values and health care edited by the Bulgarian psychiatrist and philosopher Drozdstoj Stojanov (Stojanov *et al.*, 2021). This includes case studies from the South African philosopher and psychiatrist Werdie van Staden on what he has called Batho Pele, a distinct form of values-based practice based on African philosophical concepts that, uniquely, transcend the individual/social divide: van Staden's contributions to Stoyanov's volume illustrate the impact of Batho Pele in both clinical (Van Staden, 2021) and policy (Ujewe and Van Staden, 2021) contexts.

A second philosophical response to Venkatapuram's challenge has been work by the the analytic philosopher Anna Bergqvist (who is Theory Lead for the Collaborating Centre), based on Iris Murdoch's work on the relationality of values in psychiatric ethics (Bergqvist, 2022), moral philosophy (Bergqvist, 2018a, 2018b), and

[9]   See https://valuesbasedpractice.org/co-production-in-mental-health-as-a-path-to-race-equality/.

shared decision-making (Bergqvist, 2020). According to this work, we should understand values in general, whether expressed individually or socially, as arising not as it were 'within one's head', but discursively in the interactions between people. The analytic philosophy driving this conclusion has wide-ranging implications for all areas of health care. In Bergqvist's own work, it has been guiding her development of closer collaboration between experts-by-experience and experts-by-training in multiple areas ranging from the shared clinical decision-making, outlined above, through to policy based on new models of public mental health.[10]

Conclusions

In this chapter we have introduced by way of two interactive exercises the key features of values-based practice and then outlined the importance of philosophy both in its origins and its ongoing development.

A couple of caveats – one practical, the other philosophical – are necessary. The practical caveat is that values-based practice is only one tool in an increasingly rich toolbox of resources available to health and social care for working with values. Besides ethics and medical law, other tools in the values toolbox include decision analysis (the basis of online and other clinical decision aids) and health economics. Values-based practice as we have described adds to the toolbox a resource for working particularly with individual values (whether or not relationally derived) in the context of shared clinical decision-making. Values-based practice, so understood, is in this respect, again as we have indicated, a partner to evidence-based practice in supporting shared clinical decision-making. In its partnership with evidence-based practice, however, values-based practice is most effectively deployed alongside other tools in the values toolbox.

Our philosophical caveat is that the theory-practice dynamic described in the second half of the chapter should be understood as a two-way dynamic, with philosophy benefitting as much from its exposure to practice, as practice benefits from its exposure to philosophy. Both sides of the dynamic are important. So important has been the contribution of philosophy to practice that there is a sense in which values-based practice could be regarded as a philosophy-into-practice offshoot of the wider resurgence of interdisciplinary

---

[10] See https://valuesbasedpractice.org/what-do-we-do/networks/values-based-practice-in-public-mental-health-network/.

Ashok Handa and Bill (K.W.M.) Fulford

work between philosophy and psychiatry that emerged in the 1990s (Fulford *et al.*, 2003). There are of course many relevant areas of philosophy that have still to pick up the opportunities offered by values-based practice (the philosophy of science, for example, and political philosophy). But from the start there have been clear examples of the benefits the other way, of interdisciplinary work in philosophy and psychiatry being of as much benefit to philosophy as to practice.[11]

The opening story in this chapter, of the tragic outcome of Natalie being denied her dancing with angels, was intended to root the chapter in the realities of day-to-day clinical care. As a story from mental health, the 'mental health second' stereotype still so widely prevalent in health care, may make the story appear less relevant to other 'more scientific' areas. This is perhaps why, it may be thought, so much of the recent practical development of values-based practice noted in the first half of the chapter has been in areas of bodily medicine such as surgery. But Austin's observation guiding the philosophical development of values-based practice shows the opposite to be the case. Recall that in ordinary language philosophy, Austin argued, we have most to learn from where things go wrong. This then suggests a quite different – a 'mental health *first*' – bottom line from Natalie's story: that mental health in leading the development of philosophically-informed values-based practice, far from being in second place, is showing the way forward for person-centred health care as a whole.

References

John Austin, 'A Plea for Excuses', *Proceedings of the Aristotelian Society*, 57 (1956/7), 1–30. Reprinted in A.R. White (ed.), *The Philosophy of Action* (Oxford: Oxford University Press, 1968).

John Austin, *Philosophical Papers*, 3rd edition, (Oxford: Oxford University Press, 1979).

Anna Bergqvist, 'Moral Perception and Relational Self-Cultivation: Reassessing Attunement as a Virtue', in S. Werkhoven and M. Dennis (eds.), *Ethics and Self-Cultivation: Historical and Contemporary Perspectives* (London: Routledge, 2018a), 197–221.

Anna Bergqvist, 'Moral Perception, Thick Concepts and Perspectivalism', in Anna Bergqvist and R. Cowan (eds.),

---

[11] For an early example, see Hoerl (2001).

Evaluative Perception (Oxford: Oxford University Press, 2018b), 258–81.

Anna Bergqvist, 'Narrative Understanding, Value and Diagnosis: A Particularist Account of Clinical Formulations and Shared Decision-Making in Mental Health', *Philosophy, Psychology & Psychiatry*, 27:2 (2020), 149–67.

Anna Bergqvist, 'Psychiatric Ethics', in Silvia Caprioglio Panizza and Mark Hopwood (eds.), *The Murdochian Mind* (London: Routledge, 2022), 479–92.

Henry Chadwick (trans.), *St Augustine Confessions* (Oxford: Oxford University Press, 1992).

Anthiny Colombo, Gillian Bendelow, Kenneth Fulford, and Simon Williams, 'Evaluating the Influence of Implicit Models of Mental Disorder on Processes of Shared Decision Making within Community-Based Multidisciplinary Teams', *Social Science & Medicine*, 56 (2003), 1557–70.

David Crepaz-Keay and Kenneth Fulford, 'Voices, Values and Values-Based Practice: Engaging with What Matters in Voice Hearing', in I. Parker, J. Schnackenberg, and Mark Hopfenbeck (eds.), *The Practical Handbook of Hearing Voices: Therapeutic and Creative Approaches* (Monmouth, UK: PCCS Books, 2021), 113–22.

K.T. Fann (ed.), *Symposium on J.L. Austin* (London: Routledge and Kegan Paul, 1969).

Kenneth Fulford, *Moral Theory and Medical Practice* (Cambridge: Cambridge University Press, 1989, reprinted 1995 and 1999).

Kenneth Fulford, 'Editorial', *JNDS (Journal of the Nuffield Department of Surgical Sciences)*, 1:4 (2020), available at: https://journal.nds.ox.ac.uk/index.php/JNDS/article/view/125.

Kenneth Fulford, Katherine Morris, John Sadler, and Giovanni Stanghellini (eds.), *Nature and Narrative: An Introduction to the New Philosophy of Psychiatry* (Oxford: Oxford University Press, 2003).

Kenneth Fulford and Anthony Colombo, 'Six Models of Mental Disorder: A Study Combining Linguistic-Analytic and Empirical Methods', *Philosophy, Psychiatry & Psychology*, 11:2 (2004), 129–44.

K.W.M (Bill) Fulford, Ed Peile, and Heidi Carrol, *Essential Values-Based Practice: Clinical Stories Linking Science with People* (Cambridge: Cambridge University Press, 2012).

Kenneth Fulford, Colin King, and Anna Bergqvist, 'The Inter-Personal Lived World of Values and Race Equality in Mental Health', *PSN (Psychiatrie. Sciences Humaines and Neuroscience)*, 21:1 (2023), 31–46.

General Medical Council, *Consent: Patients and Doctors Making Decisions Together* (London: The Genral Medical Council, 2008).[12]

Ashok Handa, Lucy Fulford-Smith, Zoe Barber, Thomas Dobbs, Kenneth Fulford, and Edward Peile, 'The Importance of Seeing Things from Someone Else's Point of View', *BMJ Careers online journal* (2016), available at: http://careers.bmj.com/careers/advice/The_importance_of_seeing_things_from_someone_else's_point_of_view.

Richard Hare, *The Language of Morals* (Oxford: Oxford University Press, 1952).

Richard Hare, 'Descriptivism', *Proceedings of the British Academy*, 49 (1963), 115–34. Reprinted in R.M. Hare, *Essays on the Moral Concepts* (London: Macmillan, 1972).

Jonathan Herring, Kenneth Fulford, Michael Dunn, and Ashok Handa, 'Elbow Room for Best Practice? Montgomery, Patients' values, and Balanced Decision-Making in Person-Centred Care', *Medical Law Review*, 25:4 (2017), 582–603.

Christoph Hoerl, 'Understanding, Explaining, and Intersubjectivity in Schizophrenia', *Philosophy, Psychiatry & Psychology*, 8:2 (2017), 83–8.

Julian Hughes, David Crepaz-Keay, Charlotte Emmett, and Kenneth Fulford, 'The Montgomery Ruling, Individual Values and Shared Decision-Making in Psychiatry', *British Journal of Psychiatry Advances*, 24 (2018), 93–100.

Colin King, Simon Clarke, Steven Gillard, and Kenneth Fulford, 'Beyond the Color Bar: Sharing Narratives in Order to Promote a Clearer Understanding of Mental Health Issues across Cultural and Racial Boundaries', in Drozdstoj Stoyanov, Giovanni Stanghellini, Werdie Van Staden, Michael Wong, and Kenneth Fulford (eds.), *International Perspectives in Values-Based Mental Health Practice: Case Studies and Commentaries* (Berlin: Springer Nature, 2021), 403–9.

Philipp Koralus and Salvador Mascarenhas, 'The Erotetic Theory of Reasoning: Bridges between Formal Semantics and the Psychology of Deductive Inference', *Philosophical Perspectives*, 27:1 (2013), 312–65.

H.L. Mencken, *Prejudices: Second Series* (Whitefish, Montana: Kessinger Publishing, 1920, reprinted 2006).

Guilherme Messas, *The Existential Structure of Substance Disorders: A Psychopathological Study* (Berlin: Springer Nature, 2021).

---

[12] For an update published 9 November 2020, see https://www.gmc-uk.org/ethical-guidance/ethical-guidance-for-doctors/consent.

Guilherme Messas and Kenneth Fulford, 'Three Dialectics of Disorder: Refocusing Phenomenology For 21st Century Psychiatry', *Lancet Psychiatry*, 8:10 (2021a), 855–7.

Guilherme Messas and Kenneth Fulford, 'A Values-Based Phenomenology for Substance Use Disorder: A New Approach for Clinical Decision-Making', *Estudos de Psicologia (Campinas)*, 38 (2021b), 1–11.

Montgomery v Lanarkshire Health Board (judgement delivered 11 March 11 2015): https://www.supremecourt.uk/cases/uksc-2013-0136.html.

NICE, *Shared Decision Making NICE Guideline* (London: National Institute for Health and care Excellence, 2021).

Matthew Parrott and Philipp Koralus, 'The Erotetic Theory of Delusional Thinking', *Journal of Cognitive Neuropsychiatry*, 20:5 (2015), 398–415.

Hilary Putnam, *The Collapse of the Fact/Value Dichotomy and other Essays* (Cambridge, MA, and London, England: Harvard University Press, 2002).

Gilbert Ryle, *The Concept of Mind* (London and New York: Penguin Books, 1963).[13]

David Sackett, S.E. Straus, Scott Richardson, William Rosenberg, and R.B. Haynes, *Evidence-Based Medicine: How to Practice and Teach EBM*, 2nd edition, (Edinburgh and London: Churchill Livingstone, 2000).

Michael Slade, Michaela Amering, M. Farkas, B. Hamilton, M. O'Hagan, G. Panther, Rachel Perkins, G. Shepherd, S. Tse, and R. Whitley, 'Uses and Abuses of Recovery: Implementing Recovery-Oriented Practices in mental Health Systems', *World Psychiatry*, 13 (2014), 12–20.

Giovanni Stanghellini, *Lost in Dialogue: Anthropology, Psychopathology, and Care* (Oxford and New York: Oxford University Press, 2017).

Giovanni Stanghellini, 'The PHD Method for Psychotherapy: Integrating Phenomenology, Hermeneutics, and Psychodynamics', *Psychopathology*, 52:2 (2019), 75–84.

Giovanni Stanghellini, G. Castellini, P. Brogna, C. Faravelli, and V. Ricca, 'Identity and Eating Disorders (IDEA): A Questionnaire Evaluating Identity and Embodiment in Eating Disorder Patients', *Psychopathology*, 45:3 (2012), 147–58.

Dan J. Stein, Kris Nielsen, Anna Hartford, Anne-Marie Gagné-Julien, Shane Glackin, Karl Friston, Mario Maj, Peter Zachar

---

[13] Original date of publication, 1949.

and Awais Aftab, 'Philosophy of Psychiatry: Theoretical Advances and Clinical Implications', *World Psychiatry* (forthcoming, 2023).

Drozdstoj Stoyanov, Giovanni Stanghellini, Werdie Van Staden, Michael Wong, and Kenneth Fulford (eds.), *International Perspectives in Values-Based Mental Health Practice: Case Studies and Commentaries* (Berlin: Springer Nature, 2021).

Sanuel Ujewe and Werdie Van Staden, 'Policy-Making Indabas to Prevent "Not Listening": An Added Recommendation from the Life Esidimeni Tragedy', in Drozdstoj Stoyanov, Giovanni Stanghellini, Werdie Van Staden, Michael Wong, and Kenneth Fulford, (eds.), *International Perspectives in Values-Based Mental Health Practice: Case Studies and Commentaries* (Berlin: Springer Nature, 2021), 257–62.

Werdie Van Staden, '"Thinking Too Much": A Clash of Legitimate Values in Clinical Practice Calls for an Indaba Guided by African Values-Based Practice', in Drozdstoj Stoyanov, Giovanni Stanghellini, Werdie Van Staden, Michael Wong, and Kenneth Fulford (eds), *International Perspectives in Values-Based Mental Health Practice: Case Studies and Commentaries* (Berlin: Springer Nature, 2021), 179–87.

Sridhar Venkatapuram, 'Values-Based Practice and Global Health', in M. Loughlin (ed.), *Debates in Values-Based Practice: Arguments For and Against* (Cambridge: Cambridge University Press, 2014), 131–41.

Geoffrey Warnock, *J.L. Austin* (London: Routledge, 1989).

Kim Woodbridge and Kenneth Fulford, *Whose Values? A Workbook for Values-Based Practice in Mental Health Care* (London: Sainsbury Centre for Mental Health, 2004).[14]

---

[14] Portuguese translation: Arthur Maciel, 2012. Also available as a free download at: https://valuesbasedpractice.org/more-about-vbp/full-text-downloads/ (and scroll down to Whose Values: A Workbook).

Index of Names